THE

LAUGHALACHIAN

TRAIL

A Green Zealot's Uncensored Celebration of Thru-hiker Humor

TOM WAITE

BookLocker.com, Inc.
2010

Acknowledgments

There are so many people I could thank, but why pretend to be grateful when I did it all myself? All kidding aside, I'm truly grateful to the many kind souls – trail angels, saints, friends, and halfway decent mortals – who helped me on my A.T. yo-yo, a southbound thru-hike (Maine to Georgia) and northbound thru-bike (Georgia to Maine).

Thanks to all the town angels, including Navigator, Ole Man, Double Zero, Stratton Sue, Andover David, Arla+Chris+Josh, Rob Bird, The Mayor, Vickey, Pat, Elmer, Bob Peoples, Leigh & Josh, Lori MJ, VW72, RJS, Bubbles, and Derwood. Thanks to my trailfriends, including Jukebox, Chin Music, Sad Hands, Gonad, High Strung, Lil Quantum, Lost Cause, Jelly Belly, Beagle, Zamboni, Sir Woodchuck, *Wren*, Urban Walker, Poison Sumac, Cargo Pockets, Wet Money, 12 String, and Privy Reader. Thanks to the kind folks at my writing spots, including the Frontier and Little Dog cafés in Brunswick, ME, and especially the Queen Bean Café ("Where you belong!") in Modesto, CA. Thanks to my sista, Luru the Guru, for everything. (You know not what you've done – in a good way.) Thanks to Jelly Belly for lending me her comedic ear and editorial eagle eye and encouraging this walk down memory lane. Thanks to LGC and KG for feedback on portions of the manuscript. Thanks to others too numerous to name.

A portion of the proceeds – I know, that's a laugh and a half – will be donated to charity, namely the Huntington's Disease Society of America, Appalachian Trail Conservancy, and Green Press Initiative.

Dedication

To the thru-hiker Class of 2009
and the whole parade of wacky bipeds I met along the way,
for being so thoroughly amusing.

In Loving Memory
of
Nick Hughes

Contents

Preface xi

CHAPTER 1: Desperately Seeking Thru-love 1

    A MIRACULOUS MATCH MADE IN A.T. HEAVEN 1

    A MATCH NEARLY MADE IN MAINE 10

CHAPTER 2: Gonad the Barbarian 15

CHAPTER 3: A.T. in the News 25

CHAPTER 4: Brief Encounters with Middle-aged Advice
Machines 31

CHAPTER 5: Cultivating that Hiker-sexy Look 43

    THRU-BEARDS AND DOPPELGANGERS 43

    SIGNIFICANT SHRINKAGE... 48

CHAPTER 6: Fuel for the Hiker Furnace 54

CHAPTER 7: All Things Scatological 64

CHAPTER 8: United States of Appalachia 73

    MAINE: THE WAY THE WHOLE TRAIL SHOULD BE.............. 73

    NEW HAMSHIRE: LIVE FREE OR HIKE.............................. 75

    VERMONT: BEN COHEN FOR PRESIDENT 80

    MASSACHUSETTS: HOW WOULD HENRY HIKE?.................. 84

    CONNECTICUT: THE COUNTERFEIT NUTMEG STATE......... 101

NEW YORK: I'M WALKIN' HERE 106

NEW JERSEY: WE DON'T EXPECT TOO MUCH 112

PENNSYLVANIA: WHERE HIKING BOOTS GO TO DIE 117

MARYLAND: COME CAMP AT CAMP DAVID 121

WEST VIRGINIA: ALMOST 0.1% OF THE TRAIL 125

VIRGINIA: WE'RE FOR SWITCHBACK LOVERS 129

TENNESSEE: WE DON'T NEED NO STINKING PRIVIES 131

NORTH CAROLINA: COME GET LICKED BY PONIES 136

GEORGIA: ON YOUR MIND 141

CHAPTER 9: Trail Towns as Hiker Havens 145

CHAPTER 10: Hitch-hiker's Guide to the Trailaxy 156

CHAPTER 11: Our National Social Trail 167

CHAPTER 12: Delusions of Awesomeness 181

EVERYONE'S A ROCK STAR 181

WE RULE, YOU DROOL 195

TRAIL-CRED MATTERS 199

PACK WEIGHTY MATTERS 202

IT'S NOT EASY BEING GREEN 212

CHAPTER 13: Laughing Matters 220

LIFE'LL KILL YA 220

MEDICINAL HUMOR 225

HUMOR DEFICIT DISORDER 228

GENTLE TIPS FOR MINDFUL HIKING 235

CHAPTER 14: Traveling at the Speed of Bike 241

Glossary 249

Notes and Recommended Resources 269

Preface

I'm easily amused. I admit it. But I swear several thousand undeniably funny things happened during my recent yo-yo, a southbound thru-hike on the Appalachian Trail and return northbound thru-bike alongside the trail. I could easily recount 21,790 funny observations – 10 for each trail mile – many of the laugh-out-loud, Gatorade-out-the-nostrils variety. For me, the smiles-to-miles ratio exceeded 10, by a wide margin. What can I say, I got great smileage.

Over the years I'd asked dozens of former A.T. thru-hikers about their experience. They routinely complained about foot pain and rain in Maine. They talked about raging hunger. They bemoaned their bouts with diarrhea and Lyme disease. And they usually alluded to camaraderie. But why didn't any of them ever tell me how amusing the experience was? That chronic sin of omission is what I try to atone for here.

But what's a guy like me – ordinarily, a serious academic ecologist – doing frittering away the prime of his career? Why would I choose to write a book about humorous encounters with fellow hikers and other wacky apes I met along the way? Why not a serious diatribe showing we would need six planet Earths if everyone behaved like a typical thru-hiker? Why not a book about the impending loss of boreal ecosystems on mountaintops in Maine and New Hampshire due to global warming? Why not just keep writing inscrutable scientific journal articles? What was I thinking? Well, a funny thing happened on my way to Georgia. I discovered that these apes – all of them tame and upright, some of them as hairy as the GEICO caveman, some as skinny as bicycle rickshaw drivers in Mumbai, all of them toxically smelly – are hilarious. And it's not just their stench or emaciated serial-killer look that makes them so damn funny. It's also their witty repartee, delusions of awesomeness, voluntary celibacy, bromantic relationships, dietary excesses, and so much more. So, try as I might, I just couldn't resist the temptation to share a smattering of amusing anecdotes from my A.T. adventure, while procrastinating on more earnest projects.

I began my adventure by pedaling to Millinocket, Maine, the trail town near the northern terminus of the A.T. I then mailed my bike to Georgia. I'm addicted to self-powered modes of travel, so my fate was sealed. In keeping with my insufferably overzealous ultra-green lifestyle, I walked the A.T. all the way to Georgia – every white blaze – to pick up my bike.

I heard a breath-taking tragicomic tale in Millinocket the evening before starting the thru-hike. And the humor poured in daily. A few weeks later I heard the best story ever about a couple's meeting on the trail. At that moment, I resolved to back-burner other projects and put together this collection of vignettes capturing one of the most surprising aspects of the trail experience: the superabundant humor. Evidence of this special brand of humor can be found scattered in blogs and journals and other books, but I thought a book devoted strictly to A.T. humor was long overdue. If you don't agree, I'll give you 100 pages to change your mind.

What sort of humor am I talking about? Is it erudite, nuanced, or cryptic? Sometimes. Is it elusive like *New Yorker* cartoons? Rarely. Is it laden with double entendre? Occasionally. Is it a bunch of lame puns? Oh yeah. Is it about natural body functions? Yeah, 'fraid so. But it's so much more. Not to get all hyperbolic, but in its finest form thru-hiker humor strikes me as an emergent byproduct of exquisitely synergistic individual creative bursts uniquely triggered by the trail experience. Seriously.

Thru-hikers arrive on the trail with a shared sense of freedom, adventure, and openness to possibility. This creates ideal conditions for the spontaneous formation of improvisational comedy troupes. These unpaid cast members assume co-starring roles in an experiential play that lasts several months. Along the way, many of them prove to be standout surrealist comedians. Sometimes they're like a present-day band of Merry Pranksters or cast members in a Monte Python skit. This book celebrates their special brand of humor, in all of its forms – even scatological.

My recipe is an 80:20 mixture of straightforward reportage and quirky spin. I'm a storyteller at heart, but I see my task here partly as one of documenting an underappreciated phenomenon, reminiscent of how a musicologist might attempt to preserve old-timey Appalachian music. My stories, all inspired by real events, are fictionalized only minimally. Naturally, I couldn't resist the urge to embellish some of them ever so slightly for your comedic betterment. But none of the stories is apocryphal. In most cases I've altered identifying details such as trailnames, to protect the guilty and the shy. I've encrypted most trailnames, substituting an anagram, antonym, or play-on-words corruption. (That way, you'll know who you are.) So, while the stories all contain a big kernel of truth, the characters are all fictional. Wink, nudge.

A few words about my target audience: I've written this book as a gift for fellow Earthlings, hikers and non-hikers alike. If you'd enjoy a vicarious trail experience, this book's for you. If you care about ecological sustainability, this book's for you. If you'd like to believe humor can improve your health even while living with a terminal disease, this book's for you. And if you could really just use a good laugh, this book's for you. For this last group of prospective readers, I offer these gentle instructions. Stand in front of a mirror. Dangle your arms. Try a little grin, now a barely audible giggle. Go ahead, jiggle while you giggle. Think about a funny word, like underpants, persnickety, or pinochle. Now try a chortle, guffaw, or belly-laugh. If that doesn't help, read on. Maybe you're just rusty. But take heart. If laughter really is the best medicine, my grandiose pledge is: this book will add years to your life. You'll thank me later, when your cartilage, ligaments, and tendons are shot and you can't hike a lick.

Disclosure: This book is not for readers with prim sensibilities. Although most of it is wholesome, some of it is crude, rude, and socially unacceptable. To help you winnow stories accordingly, I've included a rating system throughout. Each chapter is denoted as B for benign, R for risqué, or U for unsavory.

A few words about style: My goal was to use the vernacular of the trail, to write the way hikers speak. This means the book is replete with jargon. But fear not, I've included a glossary for readers who don't speak fluent trailese.

Finally, I've rated the comedic value of each chapter, using emoticons. One smiley face connotes something like, "This is so lame I probably shouldn't have included it." Two smiley faces connotes, "This is about as amusing as seeing a trailfriend fall facedown into a pile of moose droppings." And three smiley faces connotes, "Be careful not to hurt yourself having a laughasm."

CHAPTER 1

Desperately Seeking Thru-love☺☺☺[R]

A MIRACULOUS MATCH MADE IN A.T. HEAVEN

Gliding solo along the trail in late afternoon, the footing is smooth and soft. It's been another perfect day in late July, in Vermont. As thru-hikers like to say, I'm living the dream, loving the trail. I'm meditating to the clickety-click of my trekking poles, but then I begin hearing cars. That breaks the reverie. It's well before hiker midnight when I arrive at US route 4, near the Killington ski area eyesore. I cross the road, anxious to get away from the din. But rather than continue south on the trail into the forest and away from the madness, I impulsively do an about-face and begin hitch-hiking. My spur-of-the-moment destination is the Inn at Long Trail, where plates of hot food and pints of Guinness await. (Rumor has it the Guinness is expertly poured with clover leaf in foam.) No luck hitching. The cars roar by. The drivers seemingly don't want to lose momentum as they charge up and over the little pass. So, I trudge the nine-tenths of a mile up the hill, cursing the pukers in their motorcars and doing my best to ignore the searing pain in my feet. (Road-walking after a 20-something-mile day usually hurts.) But just minutes later, I arrive and I'm glad to be there.

The owner is bartending. He acknowledges my thru-hiker status and pours me a Guinness without even asking. He then begins his presumably daily venting ritual. He tells me the A.T. used to pass right through the grounds of the inn. What infuriates him is that the decision to move the trail was made by representatives of several well-meaning organizations — while they were dining on *his* food, while luxuriating in *his* inn. He's holding onto the bitterness and sharing it nightly with his captive audience.

A half hour goes by. I'm sitting at the bar chatting with a couple of ballcap boys on my right and just getting started on my second dinner, when the guy sitting to my left says, "OK, that confirms our suspicion. Back-to-back dinners in one sitting: you must be a thru-hiker?"

"Yeah," I say, "my trailname's Ledge. Are you two hikers?"

"Well, we don't do much hiking these days," he says, "but we did *meet* on the A.T., 14 years ago."

"That's so cool. How'd you meet? Tell me, tell me."

"Well, it's a minor miracle," he says. "It all started in 1983 – my dream of meeting someone on the trail – when I did a southbound thru-hike."

He goes on to explain that he spent all day everyday of his hike longing for the miracle, hoping and praying that *she* would suddenly appear. She'd be no mere ephemeral antidote to his loneliness. She'd be implausibly athletic, kind, hilarious, brilliant, tall, lovely, exuberant, and she would ooze virtue from every pore. (The woman sitting to his left rolls her eyes.) There would be an instant spark, an electric conversation, an undeniable connection. They'd fall for each other, accelerating at 9.8 meters per second per second, as if in a vacuum. It would be classic injudicious love at first sight and they would immediately get down to the business of spending every possible blissful moment together. Forever.

But as a SOBO in 1983, when there were precious few thru-hikers, he didn't meet a single thru-hiking woman who was going his way. Not one. He was one of just a handful of SOBOs to complete a thru-hike that year and none of them had complimentary genitalia. He barely met any SOBOs at all, never mind a woman, never mind his dream partner-for-life. The NOBOs he met, ever so briefly, were going the wrong way, of course. It didn't help that he was a shy guy. How could he make a connection with anyone? And the mini-throngs of unattainable NOBOs petered out by the time he reached Massachusetts. So he trudged along, wallowing in loneliness and feeling foolish that he had ever dreamed of meeting the love of his life on the trail.

After pouting all the way to Springer, he returned to his anti-Thoreauvian quiet-life-of-desperation working at a soul-sucking, mind-numbing sales job in Asheville, NC. Nine lonely years slip by. He doesn't go hiking even once in that entire time. Suddenly, he gets the urge to go hiking. He digs out his old gear – the external frame pack, seven-pound tent, and so on – and heads to the Whites for a week-long section hike on the A.T.

Late on day three, he arrives at the Ethan Pond Lean-to. He's in for the night. He's there alone for about an hour. And then it happens! This criterion woman – athletic, tall, open, spontaneous, earthy, smiley, kind, sweet, crunchy, verbal, hilarious and oh so clever – appears out of nowhere. The long-imagined electric conversation begins. Within minutes, he's over-the-top in lust. She makes his knees wobbly. He's having trouble breathing.

He's sure she's the one.

But he's beating himself up on the inside because he knows he's going to blow it. He has no "game." He has no idea what to say, how to let her know he's "feeling her." Besides, he's a genuinely decent person and knows it's a faux pas to hit on someone on the trail. But he's disgusted with himself even during the conversation because all he knows is her trailname and that she's going in the opposite direction first thing in the morning.

He may never see her again. He has to do something, but he just can't figure out what. He wants to say, "You're on my mind," or "I can't stop thinking about you." But he knows this would sound absurd. He just met her an hour ago. How could he say something like that? He wants to push the pause button. Suddenly, she announces she's going off to find a tent platform. Damn. She says goodnight and goodbye and happy trails and that it was great to meet him. He's miserable. He's blown it. He's lost his one chance at permanent bliss.

He's so upset that he tosses and turns all night long, never falling asleep for a moment. Finally, at first light, he springs into action. He's desperate. He knows he has to do something, but what? He takes a business card from his Ziploc®-bag wallet and writes a note on the back and then races off to find her tent. He goes from one tent platform to another. They're all empty!

She's gone! She's an early hiker.

Now he's really miserable. He's desperate, but he knows he shouldn't chase after her. She's probably long gone anyway. It might take him days to catch her and then he would only ruin everything by freaking her out. So he sticks to his original plan and sets out in the opposite direction. A few days later he finishes up his section hike.

He returns to his outside life, to his miserable job. But he can't shake her – her laugh, her smile, her essence. He can't sleep. He can't focus at work. He can't think of anything else. So, he racks his brain trying to remember details from their conversation he could use to track her down. He remembers she owned a tiny red car, a Ford Fiesta. And he remembers that she also lives in North Carolina and that she was about to start a new job, teaching

English at a community college. So, he gets out his phone book and starts calling every community college in North Carolina asking for someone, a new faculty member in English, who fits her description.

Nothing. Denied. He strikes out.

He waits a couple weeks and tries again. After several dozen calls, he hits the jackpot. He finds a campus where someone fitting her description recently joined the English faculty. He drives straight to the campus to search for the tiny red car. He searches every parking lot on campus, trolling up and down, up and down. Nothing. Distraught, he spends another sleepless night. But at first light he goes back to the campus to resume his search. He patrols a few parking lots and then, suddenly, BINGO – a tiny red car. Is it a Ford Fiesta? He closes in. Yes, it's a Fiesta.

Now what? He digs out a business card and writes a note on the back. It says,

> Hi, I'm the guy from the Ethan Pond Lean-to on the A.T. I sure hope I get to see you again someday.

He leaves the card under her windshield wiper and drives home, hoping for a miracle.

She leaves her office a few hours later and, sure enough, finds the business card. She reads the hand-written note – and freaks out. This guy's tracked her down. He's **stalking** her! What the bleep! Is he in the back seat? Is he watching her from nearby?

But then she turns over the card to read the front. She almost vomits and faints. The front of the card has his full name, complete with middle initial. It also gives his phone number, e-mail address, and business affiliation ... the usual stuff. *But what really freaks her out is his home address – it's the same as hers:* 69 Tulip Poplar Lane, Asheville, NC.

What's wrong with this guy? He's so obsessed and deranged that he's had business cards made up listing his home address as the same as hers – as if he's already moved in?! He's obviously criminally insane, probably a serial killer – or worse. She starts having a panic attack, but somehow manages to gather herself.

She drives straight to the local police station. She meets with a detective who has some experience with stalking cases. He's mildly reassuring. He tells her, "Stalkers don't usually get all weird and menacing until they've been rejected by their target. And you haven't rejected this guy. So, maybe, just maybe, the fact that he has your home address on his business card is nothing more than an innocent coincidence."

"But that would be one helluva coincidence," she says.

"Yes, but we see these sorts of things all the time in police work. In fact, seemingly impossible coincidences like this sometimes lead to false accusations and even convictions. To guard against this in my work, I sometimes need to remind myself that with six billion of us humans roaming around, coincidences – even really eerie ones like this – are actually inevitable."

"I see what you mean," she says, "but this is the only eerie coincidence I care about right now. So, unless you can convince me this is an innocent coincidence, I want a restraining order against this guy."

"OK, let's see if we can solve this case," he says. "This address, is it a single residence? An apartment building? What?"

"It's an apartment building, with about 20 units."

"Do you happen to remember the apartment manager's phone number?"

"No, sorry" she says.

"No problem. I can just do a quick reverse look-up." A few seconds later, he phones the manager and voila! The case is solved. "It turns out your stalker has lived at that address for the past seven years."

"Unbelievable," she says, "I've only lived there for three years. Wow, maybe this is fate."

"Or maybe he's been *stalking* you for awhile," he says. "Maybe he followed you from the apartment to the Appalachian Trail in New Hampshire, and hiked in the opposite direction to make it look like a chance meeting."

"Damn, I hadn't even thought of that possibility. How do we figure that out?"

"Well, you could just ask him," he says. "Or I could talk to him myself."

She thinks for a minute and says, "No, I'd like to handle it myself. The address thing seems like just a big coincidence after all, so I doubt he followed me. Besides, he seemed like a really sane and decent guy when I met him on the trail."

She decides to give it some time. She doesn't want to fall for this guy, especially after he stalked her, just because of the fate thing. She waits 10 days. Finally, late on Sunday morning she calls his number. He answers. She identifies herself. He seems thrilled to hear from her, and not too overeager or creepy. She launches into the speech she's been rehearsing for days. She reads from her script.

"Against my better judgment, I'm calling you for three reasons. First, you should know that the way you tracked me down is called stalking. I've been terrified and furious ever since. What you did was borderline illegal. This brings me to the second reason I've called. You should know that I've been to the police and they now know that you have definite stalker tendencies. But the good news is: you have a spotless record. Pristine. Never so much as a parking ticket. That's impressive, especially for a wannabe stalker. Anyway, the third reason I'm calling is to let you know why I was so scared. There's a colossal coincidence that you don't seem to know anything about."

"What's that?" he asks.

"Where do you think I live?" she asks.

"Somewhere in North Carolina."

"Yes, that's right," she says.

"OK, you're not going to believe this. Brace yourself. I hope you're sitting down. Don't faint. Don't panic. But the final reason I've called is to let you know that I'm going out for a walk and a newspaper. If you give me five minutes to get ready and then come down to apartment 2C, you can go with me."

"What the Hell! What are you talking about?! Is this a joke?! Are *you* stalking *me* now? Do you know someone who lives in apartment 2C?" He's incredulous, needless to say.

"*That's* the coincidence: *I* live in apartment 2C!"

It takes her a minute or two to convince him she's not playing a vindictive practical joke on him. And then he springs into action, thunders down the hallway and stairwell, and knocks, knocks, knocks upon her door.

∞

At this point, with me applauding, he looks over at me and says in the smoothest wink-nudge way he can muster, "Yeah, it was only about a month later that I knew we were a couple."

She rolls her eyes at me and says facetiously, "All of the men in his family operate that fast."

Then, after a pregnant pause, he says, "Yeah, one year to the day after I put the business card under her windshield wiper, I proposed marriage and she said, 'OK'"

At this point, I say, "Wow, incredible, that's the best story I've heard in months, probably years. That could be the best story I've *ever* heard!" I look at her and say, "OK, now *you* tell it!"

And she does. Her version is short and sweet, and differs from his in one key way: she emphasizes the stalking aspect. (In my retelling, I blended their versions.)

I then make a feeble attempt to reciprocate. I tell them an unsavory story I heard just a couple of days ago. It's about another couple who met on the trail. Long story short, this guy starts a southbound thru-hike with his girlfriend. They meet a solitary woman on Day 1 on Katahdin. He falls for her. They form a threesome, initially just hiking together but later sharing a two-person tent through the 100-mile wilderness. In Monson, the original girlfriend goes MIA. A year later, the scoundrel and his replacement girlfriend are still together. The end.

We all agree this is a vastly inferior story, which of course is why I told it.

It's now well past hiker midnight and I'm ready for a deep slumber. They insist on paying for my dinner – yet another act of trail magic. I insist on paying for theirs. It's a stalemate.

∞

Fast forward eight months. I've finished my thru-hike from Maine to Georgia, and then pedaled all the way back from one book-end hostel (The Hiker Hostel) in Dahlonega, Georgia to its northern counterpart (The Appalachian Trail Lodge) in Millinocket, Maine. I'm now in California getting ready to do a thru-hike on the Pacific Crest Trail. After the PCT, I plan to pedal cross-country back to Maine. This leg of my trek will take me through their town, by pure coincidence (wink, nudge). I'll cyberstalk them. I'll find a

Kinkos®, where I'll make fake business cards. And, finally, I'll pedal to their house and festoon their windshield wipers and plaster their bay windows and stuff their mailbox with *my* card.

On the front of the card, I'll include my full name, trailname, phone number, e-mail address. And to recreate the fully macabre effect, on the back I'll write:

Hi, I'm the guy from the Long Trail Inn. I sure hope I get to see you again someday!

And then I'll sprint away, with my cell phone vibrating in a pannier.

A MATCH NEARLY MADE IN MAINE

It's the first of June, 2009. I'm in Millinocket, 19 miles from Katahdin Stream Campground in Baxter State Park, where tomorrow I'll begin my southbound thru-hike. It's early evening and I've just had black-bean burritos at the Appalachian Trail Café, followed by a couple of strings of candlepin bowling with NaviGator, Santi, Jukebox, and Sessile. We wander back to the Appalachian Trail Lodge, co-run by Ole Man and NaviGator. The others settle in for the night, but I'm a night owl and I'm always keen to commune with the locals, so I wander over to a pub.

It's a rough crowd. The universally surly men glower at me as if to say, "We don't wear shorts around here, son." After a few awkward minutes, one of the local women takes pity on me. She starts chatting me up. I feel instantly rescued from all that close scrutiny. She asks me about my hike. She says she wouldn't walk a mile on the A.T., but she's glad to use the trail to access her favorite trout streams, as she did today.

Then she launches into her *big* A.T. story. Growing up in this end-of-the-trail town she's met lots of hikers over the years, but she's hardly ever warmed up to them. They're privileged, over-educated, trust-fund babies "from away." As she puts it, they're mostly "stuck up out-of-state college boys hiking the trail on mommy and daddy's credit card, and they think they're God's gift."

"But there was this one guy," she says. "Like you, he came in here the night before starting his hike. I dunno why, but we really hit it off. We talked for hours. He was a sweetheart. My friends kept hitting on him, but he just wanted to hang out with me. We shot pool and did a crossword puzzle together. It felt like we were on a date.

"But it was all pointless," she says, "'cause he was hiking all the way to Georgia and I'd never see him again. Just in case, I gave him my phone number and said something wicked corny like, 'If you're ever in this part of the world again, maybe you'll give me a call?'

"I still remember his exact words. He said, 'Be careful what you wish for,' as he put my number in his cell phone. I walked him over to the hostel and we talked about bad timing and what a shame it was that he was leaving so soon. We hugged and said goodbye. I walked home, thinking I'd never see him again.

"A year goes by and suddenly I get a text message – from him!

"I still have it on my phone," she says while scrolling through her inbox. "Here it is. He texted, 'U said i shud call if ever bac in Maine. B in M'nocket in 1 hour. U free? Meet @ café?'

"I couldn't believe it. Here's what I texted back," she says as she shows me her phone: 'What a surprise! I am down. Sounds gr8. C u soon. I will b there.'

"Then we started flirtexting. I've saved all of our messages. Here's what he texted: 'Been thinkin bout u 4 past year. Hope u r not seein anyone?'

"'Just u! lol.' I texted back.

"But then I got nervous and joked, 'My boyfrnd got hit by train last nite, so I am free.'

"He texted right back, 'Gud timing then. But u will need 2 spend some time buryin him.'

"And I texted, 'Of course, but I am free this eve if u wanna fall in luv & get hitched. I kno a preacher and I got 9 beers. LOL.'

"And look, check out his next text: 'LMAO. I kno that song, btw. OK, gr8. Better drive now. C u soon!'

"My last text said, 'OK, b safe & don't miss me 2 much. Ttyl.'

"I was thrilled. I paced around my apartment. I talked to my cat. I took a shower and paced some more. I counted the minutes. Then I drove to the café. I was 20 minutes early. I waited and waited and waited. He was late. I didn't think too much about it until he was an hour late. Then I started worrying. I thought maybe I'd scared him off by joking about a fake dead boyfriend and about getting married tonight. Or maybe he chickened out for some other reason. Maybe he's married and his conscience started getting the better of him the closer he got to town. Maybe he wasn't really coming to see me in the first place. Maybe he was just passing through, or coming to start another thru-hike. Maybe I came on too strong. Or maybe he just had car trouble and didn't have any bars on his cell phone.

"I texted him: 'U OK?'

"I waited a few minutes and then called and left a voice-mail message.

"I waited another hour or so and then finally decided to jump in my truck and go look for him. Maybe it was just a simple miscommunication. I assumed he meant the Appalachian Trail Cafe, but maybe not. Maybe he was waiting for me at one of the diners in East Millinocket or Medway. So, I'm driving along, watching for out-of-state license plates and suddenly I see flashing lights up ahead.

"I pull over to see what's going on. There's been an accident. I hop out and walk toward the wreck. I see the tow-truck driver. He's my cousin. And I recognize the EMT guy. He's an old friend. He tells me some out-of-stater hit a moose.

"I ask my EMT friend whether he's going to be OK. And he tells me some eyewitnesses said it was a big bull and he just kinda dusted himself off and loped into the woods. Apparently, he wasn't limpin' or bleedin' or nothin'.

"So, I say, 'Not the moose! Is the *driver* going to be OK?'

"And my friend says, 'Naw, he's DOA, dead on arrival. Body parts everywhere.'"

∞

At this point, I interject and say something vaguely consoling like, "Wow, that's the saddest story I've ever heard. That's like finding your match, but then he gets hit by a meteorite on your wedding day."

"I know," she says, "I probably jinxed him by joking about a fake dead boyfriend and telling him to drive safely."

"But why was the EMT guy so callous?" I ask. "No offense, I know he's a friend of yours, but doesn't he have any human emotions at all? Is he always so jaded?"

"I dunno," she says, "he was probably just relieved the dead guy wasn't a native, you know, a local. It's gotta be awful workin' that job in a little end-of-the-road town like this. Whenever he gets called out there's a good chance he's going to find another dead friend or relative when he gets there.

"Anyway," she says, "it's been a couple of years and I'm getting over it. I can joke about it now. And I'm glad it worked out for the moose. We usually eat those road-killed moose, but it would've been weird to eat the moose that killed my future husband."

CHAPTER 2

Gonad the Barbarian☺☺☺[U]

six bowls in the morn
THC all thru the day
who *was* that woman?

Several hikers were so over-the-top hilarious that they deserve their own chapter. But one particular southbounder trumped all others combined in pure entertainment value. Using an anagram of his initial and subsequent trailnames, I'll call him "Gonad," short for "Gonad the Barbarian." As you'll soon see, he would be proud of this new pseudonym. He's not bashful or self-conscious or humorless. He's young, wicked good-looking (his opinion), smiley, graceful, athletic, magnetic, impulsive, flamboyant, manic, irreverent, nonconformist, charismatic, and highly desirable (his opinion). And he lets his gonads do most of his thinking (everyone's opinion).

Gonad spewed a steady stream of witty repartee along the trail. He also issued forth a colorful, unfiltered stream-of-consciousness commentary meant to scandalize, titillate, and amuse. It worked. Over and over, I got so annoyed with his politically incorrect antics that I vowed to shun him for the rest of my hike. But then he would blurt out something so inane and outrageous that I would get sucked back into his vortex.

Without further ado, here's a little sampler of Gonadisms, in chronological order. This first little ditty I overheard during an impromptu reunion of nine SOBOs gathered smack dab on the trail in Maine. Gonad was bragging to the whole group about his sexual prowess, claiming he was a truly phenomenal lover despite one very serious shortcoming: *"You homies have no idea how freakin' tiny my penis is!"*

That was just Gonad's opening, attention-grabbing salvo. He then launched into an impassioned speech on the topic, arguing vehemently that we couldn't begin to imagine the truly infinitesimal nature of his thingamabob or the magical feats he could perform with it.

∞

A few days later, I descend Old Blue Mountain (mile 244 from Katahdin). The trail's steep and primitive, with no steps or hand holds and nary a switchback. (It's perfect.) I crash and burn several times. But I make it down, no big deal. I'm almost to South Arm Road and Black Brook when I spot a hand-written note duct-taped to a tree. In large pen-gripped-in-fist printing, it says,

HELP!!! I LOST MY WALLET!!! IF U FOUND IT, I'LL BE WAITING AT THE POST OFFICE IN ANDOVER FOR 3 DAYS. THEN I'LL BE OFF THE TRAIL!!!

THANKs,
GONAD, SOBO '09

Poor guy, I think. What a lousy way for an attempted thru-hike to end. A broken long bone? That would be a valid reason. A death in the family? Sure. But a lost wallet? That doesn't seem legit. But maybe someone will find it, I think. If he left it at a lean-to or dropped it right on the trail, there's a pretty good chance he'll get it back.

Minutes later, I cross South Arm Road and then rock-hop across Black Brook. There, scattered through the balsam fir thicket, is a gaggle of 11 SOBOs busily staking their claim to tent sites. They greet me with hugs and high fives and fist bumps. Someone asks, "Ledge, did you see Gonad's note?" And then someone tells me Prep School has his wallet. I seek out Prep School and tell him I'd be glad to hitch into Andover to return Gonad's wallet. He hands it over.

I rock-hop back across Black Brook to South Arm Road. I'm still trying to figure out which way to hitch, when the first car stops – more great luck hitching in Maine! A few minutes later, while chatting up my volunteer chauffeur, I happen to notice a lone tent pitched in the middle of a long-neglected, weed-infested baseball field complete with decrepit backstop on the outskirts of the village.

"That's gotta be my friend's tent," I say to my driver, "but he's supposedly waiting at the post office, so I don't wanna get out here."

"No problem," she says, "the post office is just up the road."

There's no sign of Gonad at the post office, but I hop out anyway. I find another note, this one duct-taped to the front door of the post office. I take down the note and start walking back toward the ball field, hoping to find Gonad along the way at the only logical place, *the* general store. He's not there. I spend a few minutes refilling my food bag with power bars, trail mix, honey roasted cashews, and such. Then I walk back to the ball field. As I approach the tent, I yell "Gonad, you there?" No answer. I get closer and yell again. No reply. No movement. No backpack. He's not here. Damn. But as I get right up to the tent and yell one last time, Gonad suddenly comes to life.

"Yo, who's there?" he yells from inside the tent.

"It's Ledge," I say.

"Hey, Ledge, did you hear? I lost my fuckin' wallet, man. I'm off the trail, unless somebody finds it. I'm screwed. My hike's over."

"That's terrible," I say. "I don't know anything about your wallet. I just happened to see your tent, so I stopped to say 'hi' on my way back to the trail. Sorry 'bout your wallet. Wish I had it. I can't make your wallet magically reappear, but how 'bout if I give you a twenty dollar bill so you can get something to eat?"

"Word, yeah. That's cool, Ledge. A twenty would be awesome. I have like 47 cents."

I reach through an opening in the mosquito netting of his tent. But when he reaches to take the bill, he realizes he's been punked. I've placed in his hand not a twenty dollar bill but instead his wallet, complete with weed stash.

He screams and bolts upright, nearly destroying his tent. He tackles me right off my feet, pins me like a Newfoundland lab about to lick my face, and thanks me profusely, "Dude, Ledge, you're the man! You're the man! You're so the man! Too bad you don't smoke weed, Ledge, or I would get you so fuckin' high. I would totally smoke out with you, dude."

"Yeah, too bad it triggers my asthma," I say. "Self-medicating with THC the way you do before breakfast would put me off the trail with bronchitis by noon and I'd have pneumonia by sundown."

"That blows donkey, dude. I don't know how you do it, living your life like a monk all weed-free and car-free and meat-free. You're badass, Ledge. Anyway, man, you totally saved my hike! I was so done. My mom was gonna come get me tomorrow. I'm serious, you totally fuckin' saved my hike. You rock, Ledge! I will totally pay you back, homes."

∞

Early on, I started noticing elements of Gonad's modus operandi. For instance, upon arriving in each trail town in Maine, Gonad would approach the first likely candidate and ask, "Hey, homes, you a local? Know where I can get weed?" This tactic always worked.

Later, in Vermont, I observed a key aspect of Gonad's daily routine. Each morning he would roust his hiking partner, High Strung, using a little sing-songy ditty like: "Yo, High Strung, wakey wakey, let's get bakey. Get up get up get up. It's four o'clock."

Still hours till first light, they'd smoke a couple of bowls and then start walking. The super-early start counterbalanced by just the right dosage of THC led to consistent 20-mile days – and chronic smiling.

∞

I hadn't seen Gonad in weeks, but suddenly there he was in the barn at the free hiker hostel in Bennington, VT. It was a zero day for him and he was spending it competing against other SOBO lads in a decathlon-like, feats-of-strength competition. He was writhing in mid-air struggling to win the pull-up event as I arrived. My arrival prompted a time-out.

After bear-hugging me, he says, "Ledge, dude, it's so great to see you! You're the man! You totally fuckin' saved my hike. You rock, dude. I still can't believe you brought me my wallet. And you like muled my weed, without even fuckin' knowing it was in my wallet. Dude, you could've gotten busted for possession. That would've been like fuckin' hilarious. Anyway, I'm really glad you're here because I have something to tell you. I should've thought of this when I first got to know you in Maine. I don't know why it took me so long. It's like so fuckin' obvious now. I've been

19

talking to other SOBOs and they agree. **Dude, Ledge,** *you totally gotta do my mom!*"

Overwhelmed by a 70:30 mixture of prudishness and flattery, I'm stunned and momentarily speechless.

"And if you and my mom hook up, you and I will be, like, stepbrothers or something," Gonad says.

"Wrong," I say, "I'd be your step*father*, your *evil* stepfather. And I'd let you rot in jail when you screw up."

"Oh, dad, why you gotta do me like that?"

∞

The next morning four of us SOBOs – Gonad, High Strung, Lost Cause, and yours truly – start wandering through Bennington, searching for one of those genuine aerodynamic diners with the glimmering stainless steel exterior. This one's supposed to be spectacular, with dozens of breakfast options, huge portions, and a perpetual line of patrons extending out the front door. We're all craving a feast, after fasting overnight while sleeping together in the rumpus room, on the barn floor.

We're strolling along two-by-two. Lost Cause and I are walking in front of the lads. He's telling me how he got his trailname. In the other world, he's a professional canoe guide in a national wildlife refuge, where he once got lost for several days. Following the helicopter rescue, his brush-with-death story was featured in several local media outlets – and his business boomed. It seems people would rather be guided by someone infamous rather than someone competent. It also seems his moniker is well-deserved. He's known for getting lost almost daily on the trail, where to get lost you'd really have to try to get lost. Or you could do as Lost Cause does and just wander off in an arbitrary direction looking for water. The obvious alternative approach, of course, is to listen for the nearby stream and simply walk in that direction. Oh well.

Lost Cause is a beloved trail character. He's a poet and likes to speak in metaphors and non-sequiturs. If he's had a good day on the trail, he'll say, "it was a steak-dinner-and-a-whore kinda day." So, Lost Cause is keeping me entertained as we stroll to brunch. He's entertaining, yes, but he can't hold a candle to Gonad, not even one of those tiny birthday-cake candles.

It's a lovely start to our zero in Bennington. But suddenly something seems off. There's a void in the conversation. It's Gonad. His incessant yammering has stopped. I turn back to see what's up. High Strung's still right on our heels, but he's alone. I give him a quizzical look. He clarifies by pointing down the street ahead of us.

I spot Gonad. In keeping with his in-the-moment style, in *this* moment he's affixed himself to the back of a tractor-trailer rig. In his mind, he's just hopped another freight train. He's smiling that beautiful smile at the three of us. We smile back.

∞

Mile 482.7 from Katahdin (1696.4 from Springer). Walking solo, I arrive at Lower Cold River Road and can't quite resist the temptation to hitch to the W.E. Pierce Store, only a mile away, in the miniature village of Cuttingsville, Vermont. No luck hitching, so I walk the 5280 feet. I'm glad I did. This is no ordinary general store. This is a *Vermont* general store. It's a community cooperative, run by the Preservation Trust of Vermont. It has all the quintessential general store stuff, the decades' old inventory and those nasty pickled eggs in the massive jar on the counter.

But it also has a full deli and, incongruously, a wine nook and many copies of today's *New York Times*. So, I get myself ensconced in the wine nook with a colossal sandwich and a mammoth cappuccino and a pristine copy of the *Times*. (Springer isn't getting any closer, but it isn't getting any farther away either, I rationalize.) I'm all settled and ready to fritter away a good chunk of the afternoon, when suddenly a woman in head-to-toe equestrian garb approaches and says, "Hey, you want a ride back up to the trailhead?"

"Of course, yes, thanks," I say as I scramble to gather my stuff and follow her to her truck.

She thinks it's hilarious that I'm heading back to the trail with a cappuccino and the *Times*. She tells me she routinely gives thru-hikers rides to and from the trailhead. And then she mentions that she met a particularly fascinating SOBO just the other day. She starts telling me about him, like how he's gone so ultra-light in recent weeks that he no longer carries a sleeping bag. He just wraps himself up at night in a sheet of Tyvek®, like a pupa in its cocoon.

"I know Gonad," I interject. "He keeps all the light sleepers awake at night."

"Because he snores?" she asks.

"No, because his plastic cocoon makes a racket when he shivers," I say.

She's astonished that I know Gonad, that he and I are trailfriends. She's surprised to learn how socially interconnected we are on the trail.

And then I ask the 64,000 dollar question, "Did he ask you for anything?"

"Yeah," she says, "he asked for two things: sex and weed."

"In that order?" I ask.

"No, he asked for weed first. I was slightly offended."

"Don't be," I say, "even though he treats *every* woman like an object, he *always* asks for weed first."

∞

A few days later, I catch up with Gonad. Sure enough, he's strutting around with a new micro-volume super-ultra-light pack. And he's apparently lost his trekking poles. When I mention his polelessness, he explains that he hasn't lost them. He's intentionally gotten rid of them. I probe for his rationale and he explains, "You can't smoke weed and handle trekking poles at the same time." Apparently, it was simply too inefficient to stop hiking every time he wanted to smoke. The poles, it seems, were messing up his hike, by hurting his mileage *and* his THC levels.

∞

Gonad's perpetual efforts to engage in mock reproductive acts with perfect strangers failed — through Maine, New Hampshire, Vermont, Massachusetts, and most of Connecticut. Lines like, "Hey, wanna be my baby mamma?" and "I fuck like a mountain man" had nothing but the expected anti-aphrodisiacal effect. They were an instantaneous turn-off. They induced lots of nasty retorts and presumably never induced ovulation. But then, suddenly, while milling about on a sidewalk in snooty Kent, Connecticut, all that Gonadal persistence finally paid off.

A car pulled over as if to offer him a ride back to the trailhead, but the driver made an offer of a different kind. She yelled out the window to Gonad, who was hanging with several thru-hikers, "Yo, cowboy, you a thru-hiker?"

"Yeah, girrrrrrl, you know it," said Gonad.

"Whaddup?" she asked.

"Just chillin' with my homies."

"You wanna do it?" she asked.

"Giddy up, thought you'd never ask," said Gonad, while his incredulous trailfriends looked on, mouths wide open.

"You got any condoms?" she asked.

"Naw."

"Go get some at that convenience store," she instructed.

Gonad obeyed. His trailfriends stared in disbelief as he bounded across the street, ran into the store, and then hustled back. He got into the car, miniature intromittent organ and all, and then climbed back out – prematurely, in less time than it would take to utter the Serenity Prayer and eat one of those teensy fun-size Snickers® bars.

His trailfriends honored him with a smattering of halfhearted applause, followed by a flurry of deep bows.

The woman drove away, but just a block down the street she ran into a utility pole. In more ways than one, it seems, she was operating under the influence.

Gonad walked down to the scene of the crash, presumably concerned about the well-being of his first copulatory partner in months. But just as a police cruiser arrived with lights flashing and siren blaring, Gonad reached into the back seat of his partner's car and retrieved something. The used condom? Nope. In his post-coital daze, he'd forgotten something: not his wallet-and-weed this time but his cell phone.

CHAPTER 3

A.T. in the News☺☺☺[U]

While we're on the topic of reckless sexcapades along the Appalachian Trail, I might as well tell the Mark Sanford story. (Raise your hand if you know this one.) It was along this part of the trail, in Connecticut, when I finally decided to expose myself to the full sordid tale. Until then, I'd just heard dribs and drabs. I'd overheard fellow hikers chatting about some scandal involving the Governor of South Carolina. Who cares, I thought. Something about an affair. Yawn City. Something about a mistress. Boring, snoring. A subterfuge. Whatever. A trip to Argentina. Not interested. This sounded like yet another example of parasites posing as journalists, exploiting someone else's private foibles and capitalizing on society's addiction to titillation.

But when I got into a trail-town motel and pressed the "on" button on the remote control, I subjected myself to all the juicy details. And I learned how it connected to the Appalachian Trail.

To say the term "Appalachian Trial" *seeped* into societal consciousness during the 2009 hiking season would be a gross understatement, like saying Gonad toyed with the idea of using marijuana recreationally during the 2009 hiking season.

It was during the 2009 hiking season when "hiking on the Appalachian Trail" became a euphemism – for an extramarital booty call.

You see, the esteemed Governor of South Carolina, Mark Sanford, went MIA for sex, I mean six, days in June. When he resurfaced from his six days of sex, he had some splainin' to do.

Initially, he deflected by claiming he'd been out "hiking on the Appalachian Trail." This was an untruth. What he really meant to say was something straight-shooting like, "I ran off with my soulmate to Argentina, where we bonked each other's brains out night and day. We had been planning to go hiking on the A.T. And what with National Naked Hiking Day coming up and my being a Gamecock and all, we thought it sounded like a perfect time to go pink-blazing out on the trail. But at the last minute, we decided to hop a plane to Argentina where we could copulate with impunity. That was a lot of fun, but now that I've been busted, it's time to get back to work. Heck, I haven't even resigned as Chair of the Republican Governors *Asso*ciation yet. In any case, thank you for your continued interest in all things gubernatorial in the great state of South Carolina."

Needless to say, the mass media had a feeding frenzy. The late-night smellevision talk-show hosts smelled blood. It was one Mark-Sanford-on-the-Appalachian-Trail joke after another. David Letterman, Conan O'Brien, Jon Stewart, Craig Ferguson, Jay Leno, Jimmy Kimmel, Stephen Colbert, and Jimmy Fallon – all the boys – got into the act. How could they resist? Here's a distilled compilation of the feeding frenzy:

Today the governor of South Carolina, Mark Sanford, who's the head of the Republican Governors Association, held a press conference to reveal he had an affair with a woman from Argentina. People were shocked because Republicans traditionally don't do well with Hispanic women. – Conan O'Brien

Did you hear about Mark Sanford, the governor of South Carolina? He mysteriously disappeared last week and nobody knew where he was. Today, Sanford admitted to having an affair in Argentina. I'm like, great, now we're outsourcing mistresses. – Craig Ferguson

And the jokes kept coming:

Last night, we talked about the strange disappearance of South Carolina Governor Mark Sanford. The media reported he was hiking the Appalachian Trail and forgot to tell anyone, including his wife and sons, over Father's Day weekend. We here reported that he had actually gone into the woods to chase a coyote and fuck it. It turns out, we were both wrong. I apologize to you, sir, for implying that you were a coyote fucker. Clearly, you went to Argentina to have dirty, dirty sex with a capybara, a giant rodent indigenous to the Argentine region. – Jon Stewart

Governor Sanford may have broken the law because he left the country without transferring power to his lieutenant governor. Yeah, apparently Sanford violated South Carolina's sacred bros before hoes law. – Conan O'Brien

... just another run-of-the-mill human being whose simple moralizing about the sanctity of marriage is only marred by the complexities of their own life. Well, just another politician with a conservative mind and a liberal penis. – Jon Stewart

Well, you know what they say, in the way that no man can resist the wiles of an exotic Argentine woman, those same women are equally tantalized by middle-aged, fiscally conservative Episcopalians. – Stephen Colbert

It's not a great sign when your spokesman doesn't know where you are, realizes it's National Nude Hiking Day, and thinks, well that's probably where the governor is. – Craig Ferguson

... Governor Mark Sanford just disappears for four days. Literally, takes a hike. He's out. And now he's back. And he says, "Well what's the big deal? I was just on a vacation to clear my head." You see, we never had that head-clearing problem with Bush. You know what I mean? – David Letterman

People are calling him a hypocrite, because he's another family values politician having an affair, but I don't see it in political terms. I'm just embarrassed for my gender. Ladies, if you want to know what it's like being a guy, think about the fact that there's a man, the governor of a good-sized state, who asked himself, "Hmm, can I sneak off to Argentina for a week with my lover without anybody finding out?" And somehow came up with the answer "yes." I hope that gives you a sense of what we're up against. – Jimmy Kimmel

Meanwhile, back on the Appalachian Trail, perfectly innocent humans by the score were actually hiking – and yet we were presumed guilty by association. Preemptively, many of us phoned home. Only the benign amorphous all-knowing one in the sky – if that stuff's true – knows how many thru-hikers phoned their significant other to say something along the lines of, "Honest, sweetness, light of my life, Muffin Face, I really am on the Appalachian Trail, hiking, and not fornicating with anyone. I swear. I'll take 100 polygraphs when I get home."

Weeks later, David Letterman, the grand-prize winner for most jokes told at Mark Sanford's expense, had a well-publicized sex scandal of his own. He got his cosmic comeuppance. (In New England, we call that "kahma.") His reaction was to look straight into the camera – his own camera, during his own show – and confess. This was a brilliant PR move, but it didn't stop the firestorm of unwanted attention. As his own sex scandal continued to inspire jokes, he responded in a subsequent show by looking into the camera again and this time quipping, in that well-practiced self-deprecating style of his, "I gotta tell ya, folks. I'd rather be out hiking on the Appalachian Trail right about now."

By the time of this writing, almost a year has passed, but this scandal has legs. Songs have been written. The jokes continue to flow. Sanford's ex-wife has just finished a tidy little tell-all memoir and is out on a book-signing tour. And so on.

The scandal has become part of our lexicon. The previously unambiguous and innocuous expression, "hiking the Appalachian Trail," has taken on new meaning in the Urban Dictionary. The most popular definitions, as of April 30, 2010, are:

1) Euphemism for performing oral sex on a woman.
   Mark went "Hiking the Appalachian Trail" much to the delight of his mistress.
2) Sneak away to meet your mistress.
   "Has anyone seen Jawann? I've been calling and texting him for three days and he's not answering."
   "Uh, he's hiking the Appalachian Trail."
3) Refers to someone's infidelity.
   "Did you hear about Mark's divorce? He was caught hiking the Appalachian Trail."

The number one definition for "Appalachian Trail" is: a euphemism for a long-distance booty call in Argentina. And "Mark Sanford" has become a verb meaning:

1) To preach "family values" and "good morals" only to be caught violating said values and morals.
2) To disappear ... without telling anyone where you are going.

I suppose it's just a matter of time till Merriam-Webster follows suit.

By now, the scandal has spread to the four corners of the worldwide web. A Google search reveals 21,400 sites mentioning both "Mark Sanford" and "Appalachian Trail." Meanwhile, a similar search reveals a paltry 6,410 sites mentioning both "Appalachian Trail" and "Grandma Gatewood." That's not right!

I just hope this year's class of thru-hikers aren't giving each other the disreputable trailname, "Sanford," or accusing each other of "Sanfording" or being "Sanfordish" or acting "all Sanfordly."

CHAPTER 4

Brief Encounters with Middle-aged Advice Machines☺☺☺[R]

I didn't have the honor of meeting Governor Sanford because he was hiking the A.T. in the now-infamous metaphorical sense only. So, I have no way of knowing whether he would have offered me unsolicited advice. I do know he's made a habit over the years of offering unsolicited advice to certain disgraced members of the Democratic Party, on how to live a moral and decent life oozing with puritanical spotlessness. So, it's just a hunch, but I strongly suspect he would have offered me advice if we'd met. He probably would've shown all of the standard symptoms of the syndrome.

And it really is a syndrome, I swear. I call it the MAAM Syndrome. I'm referring, of course, to the Middle-aged Advice Machine Syndrome.

You see, there's this subset of sometimes insufferable middle-aged guys on the trail whose mission it seems is to dispense advice, to dole out tipbits. The trouble with these advice machines is they try too hard, they talk too much, and much of what comes out of their mouth is unsolicited and unwelcome. And it's not usually offered as a sprinkling. It's usually an all-out deluge, a monsoon of advice. They give a litany, rather than a key tip.

What's their deal? Do they simply wish to make sure everyone is as well-informed as they? I don't know. And I won't offer an uninformed psychoanalytic interpretation, except to say these guys obviously never got enough love and they're chronically overcompensating for not making their high school basketball team.

And yet these guys were hilarious, particularly the acutely symptomatic ones. I don't mean they excelled at inducing spasmodic guffawing with each and every zinger they uttered. Far from it, these guys were among the funniest of all hikers precisely because they were virtually humorless — and hence hilarious.

∞

It's day 3 of my southbound thru-hike. Day 1 was perfect: I climbed Katahdin and slept at Katahdin Stream Campground. Day 2 was perfect: I walked to Rainbow Ledges, where I slept under the stars with Katahdin looming on the northern horizon and the Milky Way sparkling through the night. Today's been another perfect day. It's evening and the thrush serenade is underway. I'm savoring their flute-like songs, feeling fine. Best of all, I haven't seen a single hiker all day.

But, suddenly, there he is. Too late, he's seen me. He looks mildly annoyed. He's sporting a well-trimmed white mustache. His beardlessness betrays him as a section hiker. Or so I think. But then he identifies himself as one of the most legendary of all present-day thru-hikers, soon to eclipse the likes of Earl Shaffer and Grandma Gatewood and all the rest. I'll call him El Rey, because he's fast becoming the king of addicted thru-hikers.

There's no witty repartee with this guy, but he's unwittingly amusing. He doesn't try to pepper me with a laundry list of unsolicited tips, so this guy's only mildly symptomatic. He does warn me against doing 20-mile days right away, but he does this only after I've told him about my abrupt transition from long-distance biker to thru-hiker.

I don't mention that I've walked well over 20 miles today or that I'm hobbled by a torn medial collateral ligament or that I have a neurological disease that impairs my balance. I just thank him.

And then I offer my premature congratulations on finishing yet another thru-hike and on doing it so early – in June! He explains that he finishes this early every year now, because he starts his annual trek from Georgia to Maine in early January.

"Why so early?" I ask.

"To avoid the *pencil necks*," he says. "They leave their shit all over the lean-to. And they try to race me up the trail, yellow-blazing to leap-frog me. They cheat their asses off. I don't even sign the registers anymore. I'm out here for the solitude."

Wow, I think, pencil necks. That's harsh. (According to the Urban Dictionary, a pencil neck is a "weak and timid person," who "lacks courage, bravery, and shit.") El Rey seemed to use this insult in reference to anyone under the age of 30, particularly those who might want a piece of his title and who might be inclined to race him up the trail.

In profspeak, this guy's a misanthropic troglodyte, a human-hating cave-dweller. But that's OK. I get it. I've been called worse. I once spent nine months alone in a log cabin above the Arctic Circle in Alaska.

"Hey, it works both ways," I say. "I didn't come out here to join a clique of pencil necks, but I didn't come out here craving isolation either. I've experienced plenty of that in my life. But I have to say today's been great partly because you're the first hiker I've seen all day. So, while I'm sorry I intruded on your solitude, it apparently hasn't occurred to you that *your* presence is an affront to *my* thru-hike experience. If I'd seen you coming, I would have hidden behind that boulder over there and avoided this whole interaction."

"Touché," he says.

Then he walks on, no hard feelings it seems, just heading toward Katahdin and the completion of his seventh consecutive annual thru-hike. I watch him go. I catch myself admiring his gait, stride, grace. He's a pro. He's the Lance Armstrong of A.T. thru-hikers. I also find myself pitying unsuspecting southbound pencil necks coming along behind me, and I find myself wondering whether he will bad-mouth me for my flagrant pencilneckedness.

∞

A week goes by. I'm in the habit of walking alone. But hiking coalitions form spontaneously and, just for today, I've teamed up with two of my favorite SOBOs, Azul and Sphincter. Azul's one of those redder-than-red redheads, you know, with the red freckles and all. I tell him Jean Paul Sartre once argued that people like him don't actually exist. He swears he does. We chat about contradancing and *Railroad Earth*, his favorite band. He's like an old friend. Sphincter is marshmallow fluff to Azul's peanut butter. They really do complement each other. Sphincter is scathingly critical and irreverent and kind, all at once. He claims he has one of those criterion washboard physiques under his wicking T-shirt. Azul and I both ask him not to provide evidence, one way or the other. They're wicked fun and we're having a great day walking together, up and over Saddleback and beyond.

But suddenly we encounter a NOBO. I decry stereotyping and yet I catch myself profiling this guy, while he's still approaching us. He looks to be in his early 50s, which would make his mustache about 40 years old, and he has one of those auras of fierce intensity and machismo. It's just a hunch, but I'm guessing he's ex-military. And I imagine he uses his outdoor voice all the time. I can see what's coming. We haven't even met him yet and I've already renamed him, "Mello Fello."

Sure enough, he doesn't want to know *anything* about our hike, but he sure is keen to tell us about his and how we should be doing ours. He's a bona fide middle-aged advice-machine extraordinaire.

He starts predictably with a transparent boast, "That 28 miles yesterday really kicked my ass."

"Metaphorically speaking," I say, hoping to derail him.

Unfazed, he launches into an animated sermon of unsolicited advice.

He bellows, "Don't go into Rangeley! Don't go into Rangeley!"

"But we can't wait to go into Rangeley," I counter.

This just fans his flame, pumps up his volume. "Screw Rangeley, don't go into Rangeley!" he roars. "When you get to Route 4, just keep right on going until you get to East B Road. Call David from the East B Road and he'll pick you up. Go into Andover and stay at the Pine Ellis Hostel. Don't go into Rangeley."

"We'll get to Rangeley in a couple days, right guys?"

"Uh huh," says Sphincter smiling that sarcastic smile of his.

"Can't wait," Azul chimes in.

"What do you have against Rangeley?" I ask just to egg him on.

"There's nothing in Rangeley," he says. "Just stay on the trail until you get to East B Road. Skip Rangeley."

"Well," I say, "for SOBOs like us Rangeley is only the fourth trail town, so we're all really looking forward to it. Plus everyone raves about Rangeley. I've been there a few times myself. It's an idyllic little village nestled right along the lakeshore. There's a grand ole hotel and pubs and a library and an outfitter and a grocery store and a hostel. Rangeley's got it all. It may be the best trail town of all, next to The Monson. Too bad you missed Rangeley. We're all planning to go into Andover too, but that's another 37 trail miles beyond Rangeley. So there's no way we're going to skip Rangeley. Trust me, we're all going into Rangeley."

"I wouldn't go into Rangeley," he says.

"OK," I say, "I have what's known as a recalcitrant personality. If you tell me 'don't do X,' then I must do X. So, during this conversation I've gone from looking forward to going into Rangeley, to knowing that I must take at least one zero in Rangeley, to realizing that I will not simply go into Rangeley to resupply and rest and rejuvenate and reconnoiter. Nope, that might be enough for the likes of Azul and Sphincter, but not for me. No sirree, Mello Fello, *"I'll be buying a house in Rangeley — on the lake!"*

"Fine, suit yourself, go into Rangeley," he says.

"Oh, don't worry, we will," I say.

"Ledge, can we hang at your new crib in Rangeley?" asks Sphincter.

"Of course," I say, "Mi casa in Rangeley es tu casa in Rangeley. Let's just agree not to call it a crib, eh?"

Then, just when we're on the verge of extricating ourselves from Mello Fello's vortex, Sphincter sucks us right back in by asking, "Any more tips?"

"Thanks Sphincter," I say to myself.

"Yeah, one more thing," says Mello Fello, with the same ferocity, "When you get to the Whites, *don't dick around above treeline! You gotta blitzkrieg it!* If you dick around, you'll get hypothermia and someone like me will have to rescue your ass. That's what I do when I'm not hiking: I save lives."

36

"Great," I say, "now I must dick around above treeline in the Whites. I'll probably just mosey along from hut to hut, gorging on blueberry cake and taking a siesta at each stop."

We say farewell to an unfazed Mello Fello and resume walking. Azul thanks me for enriching his day, for messing with Mello Fello for our collective comedic betterment, something like that. Azul's a pretty verbal guy. Sphincter just says, "That was cold, Ledge, you're a bad man."

And then we share a group laughfest that sustains us for miles. What a day!

∞

Mile 534.7 from Katahdin. I spend a perfect night snoozing under the Milky Way on the fire tower atop Bromley Mt. In the morning, I start gliding through the dew down Bromley. It's only a 3-mile stroll to the road into Manchester Center, where I plan to zero tomorrow. About a mile down, there's a blue blaze trail that leads to a shelter, Bromley Shelter, only about one tenth of a mile off the A.T. As a compulsive reader of registers, like most thru-hikers, I reflexively veer toward the shelter. But when I get there, I stop dead in my tracks. There, alone in the shelter, sits the most notorious of all middle-aged advice machines.

He sits amid a dozen or so grocery bags strewn throughout "his half" of the 12-person shelter, with a triple drip-feed water filtration system hanging overhead. Warning bells start ringing. This guy's reputation precedes him.

He greets me. I reciprocate while groping for the register. I look for recent entries by trailfriends. But I don't get to read any of them because he starts the barrage. He's instantly in overdrive. He starts telling me about trail towns to the north, where to eat, where to resupply, where to stay, how to hike. He's unstoppable. I drop the register and start to back away. Oblivious to this nonverbal cue, he goes on and on, in his patented rapid-fire way, not letting me get a word in edgewise. I feel a panic attack coming on.

I try to pull the plug by blurting out, "I'm not even going that way."

"Oh, you're a SOBO. Well, in that case, you'll be going to the all-you-can-eat Chinese buffet this evening in Manchester Center. I didn't think it was all that great, but most of the NOBOs seemed to like it. I have to say I did like the egg rolls. Too bad you can't go for Sunday morning dim sum all along the trail. I'd eat those chicken feet and white foamy cube things every day, if I could get 'em on the trail. Have you ever had really good dim sum? You know, like you get in San Francisco or New York or Vancouver?"

Yada yada yada, blah blah blah.

This monologue started out like a sip of water from a fire hydrant. And now it's like I'm being chased by someone with a high-pressure fire hose who's hell bent on blasting me in the face with thousands of gallons of water, until my thirst is quenched. And I'm not the least bit thirsty.

"I'm not going into Manchester Center," I protest too feebly.

"Well, in that case," he says, "you'll definitely be going into Bennington. When you get there, you'll wanna eat lunch at the Mexican restaurant on the far side of town. They make their own salsa and pico de gallo and they bring fresh hot tortilla chips to the table before you even sit down. And they have a green salsa that must be made with tomatillos, and chilies too, of course. It's the best Mexican restaurant along the whole trail, except possibly for this great little place on the main drag in Elizabethton, Virginia, but most hikers never even go into Elizabethton because it's about nine miles off the trail. But if you do go into

Elizabethton, you should definitely check out that restaurant. They have great lunch specials. And they make the best flautas. I even like their flan and I don't usually eat flan. But, for one reason or another, the place is family owned and they make really fine authentic food ... at least that's what they claim. But if you're going into Elizabethton, you might as well go all the way to Johnson City. That way, you can go to the outfitter there. You wouldn't believe that outfitter. They have two stories of every imaginable gadget and gizmo. I bet they have over a thousand of those new ultra-light inflatable pads in stock. It's crazy. I spent hours there one day. And then I went back again the next day. I bet I spent five hundred dollars there. I couldn't even fit all that stuff in my pack, so I had to lash most of it to the outside."

"I'm not going to Elizabethton," I say as I backpedal.

"Anyway, you'll definitely wanna stay at the hostel in Bennington," he goes on, at the same blistering pace. "It's free. And the people who run it are amazing. The woman has these beautiful blond dreadlocks and she'll want you to be her Facebook friend. And you can shoot pool with their son, for hours on end. To get to the hostel, just get a hitch into town and ask to be dropped off at the main intersection. Don't go all the way to the Bennington College campus. That would put you way outside town, away from all the hiker services. Anyway, from the main intersection in the middle of the little downtown area, just walk half a block to the left. The hostel is the first house on the left after Friendly's. You'll see a mannequin on the front porch dressed like a hiker. You can't miss it. And be sure to tell the folks there, Arla, Chris, and Josh, I said 'hey' and that I'll be coming back for another stay in a few weeks."

"I'm not going into Bennington either," I blurt out. Then I start running, actually running. For the first and last time during the entire thru-hike, I'm running. And I don't mean loping along like a semi-professional trailrunner. I mean I'm flying, all akimbo and crazy legged.

I can't believe that guy. Talk about social ineptitude! He responded to my running away by cranking his volume. Does he have a built-in bullhorn? He's an unstoppable monologist. I can still hear him yelling a blue streak of advice as I disappear down the trail, rock-hopping and using my trekking poles to brace my daring get-away.

I just had my first encounter with the most notorious middle-aged advice machine of all time — *Dakota Jones.*

I've been charged by muskox, treed by grizzlies, shot at by tiger poachers, and evicted by black bears from my own cabin, but none of these little scares prepared me for my first encounter with DJ.

∞

What if this dormant tendency to heap advice on unsuspecting hikers lurks within my own DNA or within the psychic residue from my upbringing? To guard against any such latent predisposition toward developing this syndrome, I resolved early on in my hike to offer no more than one bit of advice per encounter with NOBOs. It was always the same advice. I perseverated.

My soliloquy went a little something like this: "Do yourself a favor. If you heed this one bit of advice, you'll be a happy hiker. When you get to Monson, the last trail town before the 100-mile Wilderness, consider staying at the Lakeshore House Inn. The rooms are clean and cozy. There's a built-in pub and restaurant and even a laundromat. The food's great. You can get bruschetta and fiddlehead ferns as appetizers. The place is right on the water and you get free use of kayaks. And you can even do a work-for-stay. I volunteered during my zero, just to help out, and I got to be sous chef, cook, server, bartender, dishwasher, tutor, backup vocalist, fire-builder, and story-teller. I had a blast.

"But what makes it one of the very best hostels on the entire trail is the owner, Rebekah. She's kind, hilarious, exuberant, and wicked smart – for starters. She'll give you a ferocious bear hug the moment you arrive and she'll say, 'Ummm, I *love* the smell of thru-hikers.' At that precise moment, you'll think, 'wow, she's about the coolest person on the whole trail.' Her honorary trailname is Double Zero because the typical thru-hiker can't resist taking at least a double zero at her place. And she'll call you by your trailname the whole time you're there, although sometimes she'll forget and call you 'Dingledoodle' or 'Pimplewood' instead. Or if she feels like teasing you, she'll veto your trailname. She sometimes calls me 'Sandals.' And her eight year-old daughter, Bella, calls me 'Lunch.'

"Go ahead and ask Rebekah why *she* thinks she's the 'perfect woman.' She'll say something like, 'Well, on a typical winter day, I can get my kids on the school bus, jumpstart my pickup truck, change the sparkplugs in my snowmobile, spend the whole day snowmobiling with friends, barter for a foot massage, help my kids with their homework, counsel a friend, make something for the church bake sale, go to the hootenanny at the general store, entertain my visiting sister, and still manage to feed the whole village prime rib that evening.'

"Plus, Rebekah has this electric brain. She can play mental ping pong like you wouldn't believe. You can't win. Just when you think you're winning, she'll blurt out something so scandalous that you'll blush all the way from your black toenails to the follicles on your scalp. She also has several encyclopedias in her brain. Quiz her about rare childhood diseases. You'll see. And you'll love her singing. She can belt out any hit pop song from the 60s, 70s, 80s, or 90s. Just don't get her started on Barry Manilow ballads.

"And when Rebekah isn't around, be sure to chat up her best friend, lovely Lindy. Ask Lindy to tell you her believe-it-or-not story about a solo snowshoeing hike that ended with a helicopter rescue. Ask how she avoided freezing to death by disrobing. Ask her whether she was lost. She'll claim she wasn't lost and then she'll admit she did get slightly disoriented, momentarily.

"And one last bragging point: each evening at the Lakeshore House Inn there's a floating bonfire!"

∞

Months later, on my northbound thru-bike from Dahlonega, Georgia (near Springer) to Millinocket, Maine (near Katahdin), I spent several days visiting with Rebekah and her family and her friends, especially Lindy, Sarah, and Bruce. She told me she had gotten "so many hellos from Ledge," that many NOBOs showed up at her place and said, "Ledge sent us." She claims she enjoyed a sizable spike in her business during the 2009 hiking season – thanks to the "Ledge Effect" and despite the global economic tsunami.

CHAPTER 5

Cultivating that Hiker-sexy Look☺☺☺[R]

THRU-BEARDS AND DOPPELGANGERS

The thru-beard confers a certain *je ne sais quoi*. Call it cachet. It's like a badge of honor. It's a diagnostic feature of *thru*-hiking men. Women on the trail are readily identifiable as hikers of one kind or another based on their trekking poles, but only the thru-beard says, "I'm a *thru*-hiker, not a section-hiker or day-hiker or weekender. I'm burly and cool and I could really use a ride to town because I'm doing the whole damn trail and I need to resupply, and I'll tell you some great stories if you just give me a ride." So, the thru-beard gives men instant credibility, while on the trail (trail-cred), while hitching (thumb-cred), and while hanging out in trail towns (town-cred).

Eventually, though, I discovered the unkempt thru-beard can become off-putting, even frightening. It raises suspicions, especially if it's too unruly or if you and your beard stray too far from the trail. You might as well go around with a maniacal grin while talking to and drooling on yourself. It can label you as a probable homicidal maniac, a serial killer, or worse.

Here's a synopsis of the disturbing reactions I got to my increasingly unruly thru-beard.

Several of us SOBOs trickle into the lovely village of Delaware Water Gap, Pennsylvania (mile 894.5 from Katahdin). After getting situated at the hiker hostel in the basement of the Presbyterian Church, we wander together down the hill in search of the biggest pizza pies and homemade berry pies money can buy. As we wait for the "Don't Walk" sign to change, a teenage lad leans out a car window and, looking unambiguously at *me*, shouts, "Yo, dude, I love your GEICO caveman bowling ads on TV! You're awesome!"

"Thanks for noticing!" I shout back as the car speeds off.

Then I protest to my trailfriends, "Nothing against Neanderthal-like cavemen, but I'm not too happy about being compared to anyone who works as a shill or spokesjerk for an intrinsically evil insurance company."

My friends think my priorities are mixed up. Why would I worry about denouncing a shill? Why fret over ethics? Don't overanalyze it, Ledge. You're missing the point, they argue. They're right, of course. The heckler's insult was simply that I look like a Neanderthal. Fine.

∞

It's early evening when I arrive at PA 94, near the midway point of the whole darn trail (mile 1075.9 from Katahdin, 1103.2 from Springer). As usual, my impulse is to stick out my right thumb. A car stops. Minutes later, I arrive at Holly Inn, on the edge of Mount Holly Springs. I head straight to the pub for my first dinner.

I get settled in with mounds of hot town food and a pint of dark ale and a crossword puzzle. And it's hootenanny night! It's a revolving door of local and professional old timey musicians. It's all fiddles and mandolins and guitars and lovely voices and ad lib collaboration. It's a wonderful scene, if you like that sort of thing.

So, I'm just sitting there having a great evening and trying to keep a low profile, when a woman approaches and says, "Hey, my friends elected me to come over and talk to you. Wave to my friends," she says as she motions toward a group of a dozen or so folks sitting together across the room.

I wave. They wave in unison. And they laugh in unison.

Then she says, "Several of us saw in the news recently that you were up for parole again, but we never dreamed you'd be released. And what on Earth are you doing here in our little town?!"

"OK," I say, "I know you're pretending to mistake me for someone else, but I'm afraid to ask ...."

"You *are* Charlie Manson, aren't you?" She asks.

"Yes, thanks for noticing," I say.

I sneak a peek across the room. The whole group's having a laughasm. Several of them look like they're about to have a minor urinary incident. I'm just glad my little sideshow attraction has added some jocularity. Glad I could be the butt of their joke.

∞

Several of us SOBOs are gathered around the breakfast table at the old Victorian manse called Sunnybrook Inn in Hot Springs, North Carolina (mile 272 from Springer). Elmer, the gentle and wise proprietor-pacifist-pastor is seated at the head of the table. We're tiptoeing around the potentially volatile notion of nonmilitary solutions, when Elmer suddenly says, "Ledge, when I met you last evening, I couldn't believe it. I don't know why but I didn't say anything then. But I have to tell you now, before you disappear forever. You look just exactly like someone famous."

"Oh, who's that?"

"Stonewall Jackson."

"Thanks for noticing," I say.

And then I mention that I've been a totally committed abolitionist in past lives. I'd rather be compared with my hero,

Henry David Thoreau, a lifelong abolitionist, except for the fact that Nathaniel Hawthorne described him as "ugly as sin."

∞

It's the first day of December in the last year of the first decade of the 21st century when I arrive at the southern terminus on Springer Mountain, Georgia. I take the requisite cheesy self-portrait with my cell-phone camera. I immediately send the photo to my sister, Luru the Guru, with the celebratory caption, "Ledge at the southern terminus!"

Moments later, Guru replies, "TED KACZYNSKI at the southern terminus!!!"

I text back, "Fine, thanks 4 noticing."

∞

OK, let's review. During my thru-hike, I was initially "mistaken for" a Neanderthal-like caveman, a superficially sensitive and benign character and yet ultimately a shameless shill for an intrinsically evil insurance company. (No offense to GEICO, all insurance companies are evil in my view.) That episode was only mildly disturbing. But then I was mistaken for a series of homicidal maniacs and mass murderers: Charlie Manson, the ever-odious one; General Stonewall Jackson, who erred on the side of slavery and whose namesake highway I later followed on my northbound thru-bike; and last but not least, Ted Kaczynski, of Unabomber infamy.

During my return northbound thru-bike, I wasn't typically recognized as someone who'd recently completed a thru-hike. After all, I had no backpack or trekking poles, just the wild beard and helmet and panniers. Without the diagnostic hiker markers, people feared me. Some folks averted their eyes and waited for the danger to abate. I had become threatening, apparently homeless, drug-addled, desperate, and possibly criminally insane.

But there were a few occasions when my residual thru-hiker look served me well. In Helen, Georgia – origin of The Trail of Trails and now a faux Bavarian village tourist trap – a woman leaving a wedding reception told me repeatedly, "You look exactly like Jamey Johnson." (He's a country singer of some considerable acclaim, apparently, and she obviously adored him.)

In Portland, Maine, a busking singer-songwriter tried to convince me that I have a long lost identical twin, comedian Zach Galifianakis. (I'm sure Jamey and Zach would be thrilled to learn that they look exactly like some hiker/biker guy, Ledge, who usually reminds people of one serial killer or another.)

Finally, back in Monson, Maine, Rebekah (aka Double Zero) said, "Don't shoot the messenger. But I have to tell you, as a friend, there's no conceivable way any woman would ever want to kiss you, ever again, for the rest of your life, unless you do something about that nasty beard."

"That's interesting," I say, "because it reminds me of what Louisa May Alcott supposedly said about Henry David Thoreau's *neck*-beard. It started at his jawline and covered his neck. Remember those daguerreotypes of Thoreau with his neck-beard? Anyway, she said it would surely fend off all suitors and guarantee his chastity for life, something like that."

"Ledge," says Rebekah, "believe me when I tell you this. It's for your own good. Yes, I remember Thoreau's beard. I've seen the pictures. Yours is worse, much worse, so much worse. It's revolting. It makes women vomit a little in their mouth. Plus, we can't tell what's under there. You're probably hideous or you wouldn't be walking around with that growth."

But just then Rebekah's daughter Bella, 8, rescues me. She announces mid-hug, "Ledge, tonight I sleep inside your beard. You won't even notice me."

SIGNIFICANT SHRINKAGE

It's not just the wild and wacky beard that makes men on the trail so ridiculous looking. It's also the way their body dramatically transforms itself as a byproduct of walking a dozen or so hours per day, day after day. The guys in their teens and twenties undergo one kind of transformation (shrinking), the middle-aged gents another kind (shriveling), and the women undergo yet another kind (toning).

Before and after photos tell the story. The lads gather with family and friends at the starting terminus for a group photo. They're moments away from the start to their thru-hike. They're beaming at the photographer. They look soft, squishy, puffy. They're neotonous. They look like juveniles. They're cute.

Fast forward two or three months. The lads who make it as far as Harpers Ferry will stand in front of the ATC Headquarters for the ceremonial photo. They look different. They look not just proudly hairy, but also lean, bony, scrawny, gaunt, maybe bedraggled and hollow-cheeked and even emaciated. They look thin and happy.

∞

As a devoted instigator, I saw fit to mess with these lads whenever the opportunity arose. I would start out by mentioning that we'd all have arms like *Tyrannosaurus rex* by the time we got to the other end of the trail.

"We'll all have spaghetti arms," I'd say. "And I'm talking angel hair pasta, not some robust noodle like fettuccini or even linguini.

But that's the way it should be. After all, by then we'll be using our vestigial forelimbs for what the trail demands: waving around ultra-light trekking poles and holding pizza slices in the neighborhood of our oral cavity."

"No way, dude," the lad would protest. "That's not gonna happen to me. I'll still be buff."

"Oh, really?" I'd counter. "Maybe you're a freak-of-nature exception, but I doubt it. It's inevitable. The trail has its own agenda and it doesn't care what you want to look like. The trail loves the ultra-marathoner physique. It loathes the linebacker physique. The trail doesn't care about all that extraneous upper-body muscle mass you manufactured while watching yourself in the mirror during 800 sessions at the gym."

"Dude, that's cold, but you might be right. Have you seen those scrawny ass NOBOs. They really do have *T. rex* arms."

"I know. It's a sad sight isn't it?" I'd say.

"It's fuckin' tragic, man. But it's not going to happen to me. Starting tonight, I'm going to do hundreds of pushups and pull-ups every evening as soon as I arrive at the lean-to."

"But that could make matters worse," I'd bluff. "You're already operating on a negative energy budget, right? You're losing weight, so increasing your metabolic expenditure will cause even more dramatic wasting. You'll just increase your deficit and so cause yourself to lose more weight than you otherwise would. And that daily strength-training regimen will backfire in a second way. It will preferentially trigger muscle-burning rather than fat-burning pathways."

"Maybe you're bullshitting, Ledge, but it sounds like you know what you're talking about."

"Well, I do play an exercise physiologist on TV."

"Very funny, but seriously, what *would* you recommend?"

"Well, I wouldn't squander my evening recuperation time doing something counterproductive like breaking down muscle tissue, that's for sure. My recommendation would be to stop fretting about it. All that pointless neuronal activity is energetically expensive. You'll end up losing five to ten pounds from all that worrying alone. Besides, no matter what you do you're sure to end up looking like a NOBO. That's an understatement, because by the time you get to Georgia, you'll bear a striking resemblance to one of those bicycle rickshaw drivers in places like Delhi. You know those guys who waste bit by bit because they can't balance their daily energy budget on 42 cents a day in purchase power. You'll probably weigh less than your girlfriend, if you even still have one.

"But here's the good news," I'd say. "When you get back home after the hike, you should go to your old gym and let them see what's become of you. They'll probably offer a full reimbursement of your aggregate membership fees."

"You're a bad hombre, Ledge."

"I know, but while I'm on a roll I'd like to mention how silly that barb-wire tattoo is going to look after all that shrinkage."

"I hate you, Ledge."

"No you don't."

∞

The middle-aged gents routinely undergo an even more dramatic shrinkage. They start the trail thinking they look fine and fit. They consider themselves to be "solid" and "rugged," not fat. A few weeks later they've lost something on the order of 40 pounds. And let's not kid ourselves: this is virtually all subcutaneous adipose tissue. That's a lot of lard, especially considering that it took, say, 35 years or 420 months to accumulate it and just one short month to shed it. So just like that, lickety-split, these gents revert to what they weighed at their high school graduation, when they fancied themselves quite the elite athlete. And all it took – to lose more weight than if they had stayed home and fasted – was one dubiously planned hiking vacation.

This extreme overexertion combined with inadequate nutrition causes serious shrinkage. It's remarkable to see someone's body decrease in volume – deflate as if stuck by a pin – by more than a third in just a few short weeks, simply by shrinking those fat cells that took so long to swell.

But does this dramatic shrinkage imply a faithful return to the high school physique? Sure, go ahead and tell yourself that. Just do the rest of us a favor and, please, keep your shirt on at all times. Thank you for your cooperation on this important matter. We do not wish to gaze upon your shriveled prune-like integument, saggy man breasts, and stretch marks. Let's face it, you actually look worse now that you've lost all that lard. But fear not, thanks to the notorious boomerang effect, it'll take only a couple of months after your thru-hike to regain every last pound, to swell those fat cells to their pre-hike volume.

∞

For many thru-hiking women, the makeover is more subtle. Virtually all thru-hiking men lose loads of weight, but many thru-hiking women lose precious little weight. Why? Several reasons, I think. First, women, on average, have a lower basal metabolic rate and so may avoid caloric shortfall more easily. Second, women who hike with a male partner tend to share meals, with nearly egalitarian portions. Third, women, in general, probably start the hike in better shape, with less extraneous tonnage to lose.

This last point relates to a sex difference in planning for the trail. Whereas many women give the possibility of a thru-hike very serious consideration and then train quite hard in advance, lots of young men are so cocky as to *assume* they are well-suited for a thru-hike. When asked how they came to the decision to attempt a thru-hike, these guys sometimes confess that they had never even considered the possibility. But when they found out one of their buddies was planning to do a thru-hike, they responded instantaneously by declaring, "Yo, dude, I am *so* there!" In other words, men often seem to spend just a fraction of a second impulsively deciding to do the trail. There's no need to deliberate. Of course they can do it. Of course they don't really need to train for it. Of course they'll succeed. This observation helps explain, I think, why the attrition rate for male thru-hikers is well over 90% and the attrition rate for female thru-hikers is closer to 50%.

If women often don't undergo hilarious shrinkage on the trail, what do they undergo? What kind of morphological shift do we see? They become denser, transformed in shape, toned. They look like members of the USA Olympic soccer team. What we see in them can be summed up by conveying what Sad Hands saw happening to *her* physique. A few weeks into her hike, over dinner in Hanover, New Hampshire, she said, "Ledge, you know those undergrad granola chicks at places like the University of Vermont, with their blond ponytails and their bubble butts and their washboard bodies and their insanely muscular calves?"

"Uh, yeah, I guess so. I think I know the phenotype."

"Well, I've hated them my whole adult life. I mean, the way they walked around campus, looking all superfit and perfect and aloof. Of course, I never dreamed I could look like that. But, dude, check it out! It's happening. Promise not to hate me, but I'm becoming one of them!"

∞

Although the human physique can follow variable trajectories as it travels along the trail, there's one commonality – a near universality – among thru-hikers. It's more nearly universal than trekking poles or the thru-beard or the eye-watering olfactory cues. The one feature that nearly all thru-hikers share: *a tiny bum.*

Fellow SOBO Urban Walker even bemoaned his virtual asslessness. But I reassured him that I had better-than-shaky empirical evidence of some non-negligible bit of flesh that could be construed as a vestigial derriere. "Several times," I explained, "when the wind has been just right and the fabric of your shorts pressed against your body just so, I thought I could make out what looked like two small grapes dancing side by side." He was no buttless wonder, in the strictest sense possible.

And whenever we spotted a hiker approaching us, we succumbed to temptation and speculated about which kind of hiker she or he was.

"Thru-hiker?" one of us would ask.

"Not a chance. That guy's a day-hiker, weekender, possibly even a long-distance section-hiker. But he's definitely *not* a thru-hiker. Guaranteed."

"How can you be so sure?"

"There's no possible way he's a *thru*-hiker: *His bum's too big!*"

CHAPTER 6

Fuel for the Hiker Furnace☺☺☺[R]
day six as SOBO
one hundred mile wilderness
please don't say pizza

What's a thru-hiker to do? How do you prevent complete recrudescence of your gluteal tissue? In plain English, how do you prevent your bum from vanishing? The answer: eat. Eat more. Eat bigger meals. Eat more often. Eat better food.

Not surprisingly, thru-hikers obsess about food.

I started out telling myself I'd probably be immune from the phenomenon known as "hiker hunger" because I'd cycled 15,000+ miles in the year leading up to my hike. I even arrived in Millinocket by bicycle. I reasoned my metabolism was already so sky high that I wouldn't notice any increase in chronic hunger level.

I was wrong.

My hiker hunger, despite all that pre-hike cycling, seemed real enough. I noticed it mostly on zero days, especially if I was hunkered solo in a motel. I would binge – like it was my job. I worked a double shift. I probably deserved hazard pay. I would even wake during the night and eat some more.

To generate concrete evidence of this trail-induced gluttony, I quantified my caloric intake during one of these zero days. At the stroke of midnight, I dumped the waste basket in my motel room in Buena Vista, Virginia and took an inventory of the wrappers I'd thrown out that day. I also generated a mental list of the hot meals I'd eaten that day. Tabulated with caloric estimates, here's the obscene discovery:

Meal/mouthful/morsel	Quantity	Calories
Hungry Hiker Breakfast (including eggs, home fries, toast, pancakes, grits, biscuits with gravy, orange juice):	1	2450
Power/energy/protein bars:		
KIND: Macadamia & Apricot	2	380
KIND: Almond & Apricot	2	340
KIND: Almond & Apricot in Yogurt	2	420
KIND: Fruit & Nut Delight	2	340
KIND: Fruits & Nuts in Yogurt	1	210
KIND PLUS: Mango Macadamia	1	190
Odwalla Super Protein	1	230
Clif Builder's	1	270
MET-Rx Big 100 Meal Replacement	1	360
Tiger's Milk Protein Rich	2	280
Tiger's Milk Peanut Butter	1	150
Savory snacks:		
Planters Cashews (3 oz.)	1	150
Planters Trail mix (3 oz.)	2	300
Sunchips Multigrain Original	1	210
Planters Mixed Nuts (3 oz.)	2	1020
Sweet snacks:		
Nature Valley Nut Clusters	2	300
Snickers Bar	1	271
Nutella (26.5-ounce jar)	1	4000

Dinner #1:		
Vegetarian pizza (14 in.)	1	2300
Dark ale (pint)	2	480
Dinner #2:		
Vegetarian submarine sandwich	1	460
Lemonade	1	200
Banana	1	105
Late-night snacks:		
Muscle milk	1	220
Ben & Jerry's Cherry Garcia	1	252

GRAND TOTAL   15,888

As you can see, I ate prodigiously. In one day, my intake was a whopping 15,888 calories. That's more than a week's worth of food for a typical person, with an average daily energetic requirement of 2000 calories. Rather than walk 20 miles that day, I ate the equivalent of 20 meals. In one day, I had ingested well over 100 dollars' worth of food and beverages. (Please don't mention my unsustainable food footprint.) And I was hardly sated. I ate ice cream just before midnight.

Why did I eat so much on zero days? The most obvious reason: I was overcompensating for the deficit of prior days. The less obvious explanation: I ate so much on zero days because my hands weren't gripping trekking poles all day. Instead, they were free to open wrappers – 27 of them on this particular zero.

With this second point in mind, I briefly considered emulating Gonad and jettisoning my trekking poles. Not so I could roll joints, mind you, but so I could open wrappers on the fly. That way, I could satisfy my addictive cravings for Tigers Milk® and KIND® bars without breaking stride. I could do big miles *and* remain fat and happy.

∞

Upon completing a thru-hike, you'll find you've entered a lifelong Q-and-A session. Curious minds demand answers to all sorts of questions about your experience. They want to know how many times you had bad encounters with bears, whether you were scared "out there," particularly during encounters with homicidal maniacs, and whether you carried a gun. My stock answers were all affirmative: Yes, I was mauled by a bear, but only twice and I was able to escape with all of my limbs attached; yes, the maniacal nocturnal laugh and fiendish "tickle fits" of serial killers in shelters gave me nightmares; and yes, I carried a double-barrel twelve-gauge shotgun, but hardly ever used it.

Curious folks also ask lots of questions about food. Some of them imagine you spent much of your time foraging for wild edible plants and fungi and angling for brook trout all along the trail. Nearly everyone eventually asks, "What did you eat? You must have had a really healthy diet, right?"

"I mostly ate a steady diet of gas station snacks," I always say.

They laugh politely, I suppose because they're afraid it's true. And so it is.

∞

Patronizing gas stations sounds like an implausible way to refuel the hiker furnace, I suppose, but it worked for me. Having opted out of the car culture years ago, you might think I wouldn't be caught dead in a gas station. But gas stations these days double as convenience stores, with often vast arrays of power bars and trail mix and Little Debbies and sugar wafer cookies and mystery meats, including Spam Singles and Grandma Gatewood's favorite, Vienna sausages. Long gone are the days when gas stations sold little more than guzzleline and cigarettes.

These days it's more feasible than ever to resupply opportunistically simply by hitching or walking to nearby stores. I did so with regularity, sometimes twice in the same day. This allowed me to carry no more than two days' worth of food, except in Maine. This slowed me down, but I got to meet lots of hilarious bipedal types along the way. And my pack was always light, usually less than 20 pounds. (I never once felt the urge to slackpack, which is anathema to my green hiking mandate.) I traded off pack weight against the minor inconvenience of visiting convenience stores.

Some thru-hikers still take an old-school approach to resupplying. Dirt Crab and Stay Put, for example, relied on mail drops, which was a common practice on the A.T. decades ago. Before their hike, they sent a food box to themselves c/o General Delivery at each of about 25 post offices along the way. This approach worked fine for awhile. But eventually they regretted their approach because every food box had the same contents. That's right, they ate a monotonous diet for 2179 miles.

I once ate pinto-bean sludge for 48 straight days while overwintering in a cabin in northern Alaska, but I didn't plan it that way. No, my diet became monotonous only after I'd polished off all the goodies, like dried mangoes and papaya spears, crystallized ginger, gourmet chocolate, carob bits, and cashews.

So, my monotonous diet was the byproduct of lack of discipline. Dirt Crab and Stay Put's monotonous diet was intentional.

I was present when they opened one of their boxes, near the Partnership Shelter in Virginia. It was quite entertaining. Stay Put ceremonially announced each item as he pulled it from the box and held it overhead, and Dirt Crab voiced her harsh disapproval right on cue. It was like a well-rehearsed skit.

"Five pounds of peanuts," announced Stay Put.

"Gack, I'm developing a fatal peanut allergy," said Dirt Crab.

"Three pounds of raisins," said Stay Put.

"I vow never to eat so many as three individual raisins – ever again, in total, for the rest of my life," said Dirt Crab.

"Twenty packages of Swiss Miss hot cocoa powder," said Stay Put with an apologetic glance.

"Bleck. Gag. Patooey. Boo."

"Four pounds of oatmeal," announced Stay Put.

"Perfect. I hate goatmeal. Why not forty pounds? I'd rather carry forty pounds of oatmeal than eat four pounds of it."

"And, for the big finale," said Stay Put, "twenty packages of always delicious, totally nutritious Ramen noodles!"

"I hate my life and I wanna go home, seriously, right now!" concluded Dirt Crab.

Oozing empathy, I offered to share some of my bounty, having just hitched back to the trail with a restocked food bag. They refused. I escalated. They refused again. They were dug in, so I walked on, feeling smug about the smorgasbord of gas station snacks I'd just scored.

While walking along thinking about the wisdom of refueling at gas stations rather than post offices, my thoughts turned to more extreme refueling strategies. I thought of two friends, who both happen to be Mainers and who attribute their success to

"Mainer ingenuity" (not to be confused with the much weaker form known as "Yankee ingenuity"). This phrase is common parlance in Maine, where people accept at face value the mythological notion that they are somehow more resourceful, resilient, and clever than "Flatlanders." You be the judge.

My friend, Sashimi, says he had "no flow" (cash flow) when he did his thru-hike (in 2008), so he couldn't rely on either gas-station or post-office refueling. Instead, he relied heavily on hiker-box refueling. No kidding. He specialized on scrounging from hiker boxes along the way. A typical score would be something like six packages of Ramen noodles, a few stray fossilized marshmallows, and a couple Ziploc bags full of that off-white mystery powder. The rest of us joked about these bags. What did they contain: soy protein, dehydrated potato flakes, nonfat dry milk, or cocaine? For us, these bags were a substrate for humor. But for Sashimi, they contained precious, if unidentifiable, sustenance. With his latest hiker-box score in hand, Sashimi would head straight back to the trail, crunching on raw Ramen noodles and pouring the mystery powder into his mouth as he walked. Using this dubious refueling strategy, he made it all the way to Katahdin, every white blaze.

But he also had some miserably lean stretches. He was below 3% body fat at Trails Days in Damascus, Virginia. He ran out of food in the 100-mile wilderness. And he struggled at various points along the way. He was low on calories and essential nutrients and morale. But just when things looked bleak, a small miracle would intervene to save his hike.

One day, in the surreal Empire State, he arrives at a road and surveys the scrounging opportunities. He knows of no nearby hiker box. A successful dumpster dive could save his hike right about now. He walks along with dreadlocks almost down to the manskirt he had designed and sewed himself. A van stops. He's so relieved. It's an act of trail magic, a free shuttle ride to a hiker feed perhaps. He'll gorge and get back on the trail tonight. Perfect.

As he climbs into the empty van the driver asks him whether he's "from the city." Sashimi plays along and says something cryptic like, "We're all from the city, right man?"

Minutes later the driver pulls up to a building. Sashimi sees a sign above the doorway. Lo and behold: *it's a rehab center!*

This isn't an act of trail magic after all. No, the driver's mistaken Sashimi for a drug-addled homeless guy, a desperado from the mean streets of New York City. Sashimi tells him, "I'm a thru-hiker on the Appalachian Trail. I need pizza, not methadone."

The driver apologizes profusely. Then he drives Sashimi to the nearest pizza place, buys him a large pie, and delivers him and his pizza back at the trailhead.

OK, so maybe that was trail magic after all?

Whether you think being mistaken for a homeless addict qualifies as ingenuity I'll leave to you. But you must admit Sashimi's hiker-box refueling combined with opportunistic scrounging constituted a successful refueling strategy. He's humble and deflects all praise. He swears it's nothing more than Mainer ingenuity.

But don't try this at home, especially if you're not a Mainer and a fully legitimate one at that. Disclosure: I was born and raised in Maine, but I'm not a real Mainer because both complimentary strands of my DNA, maternal and paternal, come from Massachusetts. Mainers are very firm on enforcing this loophole. The old metaphorical punchline, courtesy of comedian Tim Sample, is: "if your cat had kittens in the oven, would ya call 'em biscuits?"

∞

The grand prize winner for extreme refueling strategy by a fully legitimate Mainer goes to Blazy. Talk about Mainer ingenuity! I met Blazy one gorgeous day in Grayson Highlands State Park, North Carolina. I was perched atop an outcrop enjoying the panorama and trying not to fret about the tax dollar-subsidized pony-grazed balds. Suddenly, a mysterious sylph approached. I said "hey," she looked up and flashed a smile. She was wearing a little black dress and shit-kicker work boots. She had a hawk feather in her hair, a ring in her nose, and an old-school bedroll under her arm. She had me at "yo." We were instant friends.

Out for a stroll for a few days and not the least bit concerned about mileage, she sat cross-legged on the ground and told me her thru-hike story. A few years ago, at age 19, she arrived at Springer with an ancient backpack she'd bought for two dollars at a thrift store. Lashed to the outside of her pack, she carried a kerosene lantern. On the inside, her food bag was filled with potatoes she'd grown in her garden in Maine. She caused alarm. Everyone who met her gave her a speech, "You need to get off the trail immediately. You don't know what you're doing. You don't have any of the right gear. You'll never even make it to Neel's Gap. You should turn back now. You can call for a shuttle to come get you off the trail back at the last trailhead. You do have a cell phone at least, right? Can I call for you? Do you want me to hike back with you? Do you need any food or clothes? Do you even have a sleeping bag? Do you know about hypothermia? Don't you know it's supposed to snow for the next three days?"

She would say, "Hey, don't worry, I'm a Mainer. And I have plenty of potatoes."

Six months later, all but a precious few of those would-be rescuers had washed out, dropped out, gone home. They'd "attritted," as Bush Forty-one, Dubya's daddy, would have put it.

But penniless Blazy walked all the way to Katahdin, passing every white blaze along the way.

How'd she pull it off? She didn't use my gas-station refueling strategy, Dirt Crab and Stay Put's post-office strategy, or Sashimi's hiker-box strategy. Nope, she used an ecologically sustainable approach I'll call the organic-farm refueling strategy. She did impromptu work-for-stay stints along the way. She would hitch to an organic farm and volunteer for two or three days. Her hosts would fill her food bag, put her back on the trail, and help her arrange the next gig with friends of theirs farther up the trail. That's green ingenuity.

Again, don't try this at home. Blazy's a rock star. She'll walk around the world, eventually. She walks to Hot Springs, North Carolina, each spring just to plant Elmer's organic garden at the Sunnybrook Inn hiker hostel. Then she walks home. She spent last winter playing her fiddle in a Roma encampment in the shadows of the Frankenstein castle. This year, rumor has it, she's walking to Bolivia. Think twice before you try to emulate Blazy. She's a fully legit Mainer, from the Abenaki nation no less, and she's fearless and feral.

CHAPTER 7

All Things Scatological☺☺☺[R]

infatuation
it's love at first sight of the
heart-shaped privy seat

Desecrate this book, please! You have my blessing to tear out pages, preferably after you've read them. Butt don't fold, spindle, or mutilate them, particularly if you're reading an eBook version. Instead, please use them as TP. Nothing would be more gratifying than to find these pages composting in moldering privies all along the trail.

∞

Early on, I eavesdropped on daily chatter about feces. Many SOBOs seemed to have a Sigmundian fixation on their stools. They volunteered all-too vivid descriptions of color (too yellowish), consistency (not nearly viscous enough), odor (shockingly and appallingly toxic), and massiveness (bigger than a Dachshund). I just grimaced and waited for the topic to shift to one befitting my squeamish sensibilities.

Why this fecal fixation? My take is that some of my fellow thru-hikers had hardly ever done as bears do, and as humans have done through their entire evolutionary history. This was a near-novel experience, to defecate in the woods, and they mistakenly thought the trail experience was somehow transmogrifying their stools into something satanic. In any case, this initial obsession mostly faded away within the first few weeks. Yet, inevitably, some scatological amusement would crop up every few days or so. Here's a little sampler of stool stories – a stool sample.

∞

Olfactory molecules travel downwind, creating an odor gradient. Likewise, information on the trail travels in a unidirectional way, creating a gossip gradient. Day after day, by word of mouth and via register entries, you hear news of friends who are ahead of you on the trail. But you hardly ever hear news of people behind you. So, if a friend ahead of you does something scandalous or gets befallen by a humbling act of god, you hear about it because you're traveling against the gossip gradient. Usually, these stories are short-lived. As you pass through the gradient, you stop hearing the rapidly evolving story. But, occasionally, one of your friends who happens to be a week or more ahead of you will do something truly scandalous. These stories tend to have a long shelf life. In such cases, you might get regaled with tales of your friend's foolishness or misfortune day after day.

Here's a prime example. My friend, Sphincter, through dogged determination and a reluctance to zero, managed to outpace me down the trail. Eventually, I lagged behind by a couple of weeks. This was ideal because I got to hear many versions of the same scatological story, which went a little something like this. It seems Sphincter began having issues of the gastrointestinal sort, *Giardia* perhaps, somewhere in Pennsylvania. He soldiered on, despite frequent bouts of explosive diarrhea. He was dehydrated. He couldn't digest anything. He was down below 3% body fat – and perhaps above 25% *Giardia*. What was he thinking? That he was somehow superior to the unfriendly microbes that multiplied exponentially and thrived within his lower GI?

In retrospect, it should have been obvious that he was brazenly flirting with disaster. Apparently, on day two or three of this volcanic unpleasantness, he was struggling along the trail when he was once again overcome with intestinal burbling. In keeping with his now-standard protocol, he pivoted to race off the trail a respectable 200 feet or more, to explode in private. But this time he tripped right on the trail and the impact detonated the bomb. He exploded. He scrambled to salvage the situation. Too late, he wallowed in his own sewage. The details are unspeakable. He was in poison ivy from the waist up and sprawled in the trail from the waist down. He yanked down his shorts. He screamed a blue streak of expletives that would have made Gonad blush. And he exploded again, right *on* the trail.

But things got worse.

As he lay there with his shorts to his knees trying to clean himself, and so exhausting his precious supply of Baby Wipes®, along came a Christian youth group. Luckily, one of their leaders was a bit out in front of the group and saw Sphincter in his full volcanic predicament – face down in Humiliation City – before anyone else got a close look.

She panicked.

She reversed direction and corralled her group, attempting to shield them from the horrific scene and so protect them from permanent emotional scarring. She was then heard to say to another leader, "Oh my gosh! Don't look! We're turning around. We're going back. ***That man was touching himself!***"

Months later, we still refer to this episode, without any hint of malice or ridicule, as "The Incident" or "Sphincter's Volcanic Sphincter Incident."

∞

Sphincter's Incident brings to mind what could be called "The Bob Peoples Incident." But there's a key difference between these incidents. Whereas Sphincter defecated on the trail and mostly on himself, Bob defecated the trail itself.

To clarify I need to tell you that Bob's a legendary trail figure. He's the owner of Kincora Hostel, just two-tenths of a mile off the A.T. in Tennessee (mile 412.8 from Springer). He's a trail angel and trail builder extraordinaire and an all-around mensch. He's so admirable that he's been credited with superhuman powers, some of them scatological.

Por ejemplo, one particular graffito on a shelter wall in Tennessee offers this testimonial, a possibly apocryphal A.T. creation story:

> "Back in the early 1930s, a young Bob Peoples took a dump and out came the entire Appalachian Trail, white blazes and switchbacks and shelters and all."

Presumably to minimize the hiker's urge to scrawl such gems on shelter walls, local volunteers routinely equip virtually every shelter with a register, typically a spiral-bound notebook stored in a Ziploc bag. So, unlike Bob's creation story, nearly all of the literary efforts in the scatology genre are deposited for posterity in these registers. These contributions include some pretty erudite stuff. Not!

Here's an example, courtesy of the always pithy and sardonic SOBO called Praise, who daily entertained fellow hikers with his own creepy brand of Deep-Thoughts-by-Jack-Handy-like humor: "If I were to take a dump in this shelter, it would be right over there, in that corner … hypothetically."

∞

Given the breadth and depth of this fecal fixation, it may come as no surprise that hikers are also fascinated by the feces of nonhuman species. Take the moose, for example. The population density of these enormous browsing herbivores in Maine is higher than it's been in centuries. So too is the density of their droppings. Imagine pile after pile of fecal nuggets each the size of a mutant hybrid supergrape on growth hormone. Imagine these deposits strewn along the entire length of the trail in Maine. My back-of-the-envelope guesstimate suggests an astronomical total of at least 10 million droppings along the trail in Maine. And since hikers take only about half a million steps while trudging through Maine, it should be feasible to adjust the placement of each footfall and thereby step in moose droppings with virtually every stride.

Why anyone would want to do this is beyond me. But hikers do love extraneous challenges. (Like the trail isn't challenging enough!) We love the various ice cream challenges (especially the 14-scoop Summit Sundae Challenge at the A.T. Café in Millinocket), the Four-State Challenge (PA, MD, WV, and VA in 24 hours), the Pennsylvania Pizza Challenge (daily pizza while in PA), the 100-Mile-Wilderness-in-50-Hours Challenge, and so on.

I hereby issue a new challenge: *The Maine Moose Dropping Challenge.*

Here's my recommended computational recipe. Because it would be tedious to tally all of the successful and unsuccessful strides for the whole state of Maine, I suggest this quick-and-dirty alternative. It's wicked easy. Simply tally the successful strides for your first 100 steps each morning. And then compute a daily average when you get to Katahdin, if you're a NOBO, or when you get to New Hampshire, if you're a SOBO (one of the cool kids).

Let me know if you beat my sterling performance of 90.8%?

∞

Just imagine yourself sashaying down the trail in your skirt, striding gracefully from one pile of moose droppings to another, all the while rocking a pair of dangly moose-dropping earrings. I kid you not, you can purchase this fine jewelry from David at the Pine Ellis Hostel in Andover, Maine. David, you see, knows how to piece together a living in the hinterlands. He's a backwoods entrepreneur. He has the true entremanure spirit. (Groan.) But, seriously, he'll gladly help you with errands, give you a semi-professional haircut, take you fishing, drain your blisters, shake down your pack, mend your tent or sleeping bag or raingear, translate Native American place names to English or French or Spanish, tell you stories about his adventures in the Canadian Arctic, and even sell you some of his fine hand-crafted jewelry. Don't worry, the droppings are well-plasticized and the jewelry is hypoallergenic.

One of my trailfriends, Moose Deuce, bought a pair of these earrings as a gift for his life-partner back home in Georgia. Apparently, he reasoned that fecal jewelry would be adequate compensation for his abandoning her for six months. Rumor has it she wears those earrings with blissful naiveté. You see, to this day she has no idea who made them – or from what! He can't confess now, of course. There could be repercussions.

∞

If I've done my duty, this little collection of stories has conveyed that thru-hikers are strongly inclined towards scatophilia. But they're no homogeneous bunch, of course. Far from it. Consider, for instance, the subset of thru-hikers who succumb to what I call privy madness. These folks tend to have a hypertrophied capacity for appreciation of privy esthetics. They're privy savants. And they often become self-appointed privy-raters. These obsessive folks use their supple, discerning minds to critique privies all along the trail.

Upon arriving at a shelter, they head straight for the privy. Upon returning to the shelter and after a healthy slathering with Purell® hand sanitizer, they grab the communal ink pen and jot down their review in the register.

Like professional movie or restaurant critics, these unpaid privy-raters can be ruthless. They'll pan a privy over the slightest grievance. And they rarely give four stars. A privy can get three stars because it's a composting privy and it's new and clean and stocked with TP, provided it also has some special feature like a heart-shaped seat or skylight or funky door handle or fake flush handle or homemade curtain. But to get four stars a privy must have that certain *je ne sais quoi*, a super-extra-special intangible quality that only a truly legitimate privy-rater could ever appreciate.

∞

The typical SOBO privy critic must have been beside herself when she got to Tennessee. She'd hiked 1719 miles, almost 80% of the trail. Along the way, 97% of shelters, or all but 5 of 179, had an accompanying privy available for her rating pleasure. But now that her feet have brought her into Tennessee, where all reason seems to have been suspended, she'll soon discover that the percentage plummets – to zero. It's an outrage, an out-house-rage. But at the moment, still riding high from her stay in Damascus, she's totally unsuspecting. She has no idea what's in store. After all, it practically goes without saying that shelters have privies and vice versa.

She hikes southward, overconfident, relaxed, oblivious, and smug. And then, 6.5 miles into Tennessee, she arrives at the first shelter. She drops her pack and heads for the privy. But where is it? She can't seem to find the customary little sign pointing the way. She can't find the familiar little side-trail leading to the privy. But in the process of searching, she does discover that fellow hikers have been defecating here and there and everywhere, in a pattern radiating out from the shelter. There's a feces-free zone immediately around the shelter, but beyond lay concentric rings of declining bum-wad density. She retreats to the shelter, tiptoeing through the scatological minefield. She digs out her data book and, sure enough, there it is in black and white: "Abington Gap Shelter (1959) —Sleeps 5. *No privy.*"

How could this be?! It must be an anomaly. She consults her data book, scanning for the next shelter just to be sure it has a privy. But, no, it's privyless too. What the bleep?! She keeps scanning. More bad news.

She discovers this is just the first of 10 consecutive privyless shelters. The nearest privy is 74 miles away, at Overmountain Shelter. And that's followed by a 56-mile-long privyless stretch encompassing six shelters. In the next 130 miles, there are 17 shelters but just one privy. And when she gets there she'll discover that it's a crappy privy-rating opportunity. It hardly qualifies as a reprieve from all that privylessness. You see, the privy at Overmountain Shelter doesn't even have a roof – or walls, for that matter.

Without warning, her hobby has become obsolete. Without privies to rate, what's the point of going on? This jolt could put her right off the trail.

Let's pause to empathize with our hypothetical privy-rater. The rest of us, the non-privy-raters, can easily adjust to this entry into a privy vacuum. We know how to defecate in the woods. And we know how to camp under the stars or in a tent or hammock. We don't need to stay at the shelters with their surrounding minefields and makeshift bum-wad-trails, exposing ourselves to all that stench and contamination. But it's easy for us, by comparison, because our self identity isn't all wrapped up in privy criticism. For the privy-rater, though, this is her *raison d'être*. And her reason for living has just been cancelled, for a week or more.

But as she continues hiking south toward the next privyless shelter, her outlook begins to brighten. She realizes this is just a hiatus from her avocation. You see, a string of 10 consecutive privies begins with Bald Mountain Shelter at mile 1856.1. She'll be back in business in just a few days, she realizes. And she'll have a renewed appreciation for the privy-rating opportunities that await her. She'll never again take for granted the existence of those nasty little shacks.

CHAPTER 8

United States of Appalachia☺☺☺[R]

Thru-hikers are provincial. Most of us hail from one of the 14 trail states. So, not surprisingly, lots of discussion revolves around what hikers like or dislike about individual states. The geopolitical boundaries are nothing more than arbitrary byproducts of history, of course, but every thru-hiker is keenly aware of which state she or he is in at all times. We lose track of time. I rarely knew the date or day of week and even sometimes lost track of the month, but I always knew which state I was in.

Here's my quirky take on state-specific kudos and qualms. Here's what struck me funny as I walked through each of the trail states.

MAINE: The Way the Whole Trail Should Be

After leaving Maine, I encountered waves of NOBOs daily. I was super-chatty with them. We'd exchange trailnames and synopses of our life stories. This little meet-and-greet usually took a minute or two, during which I would try to win them over with my palaver. If I managed to suck them in for a few more minutes, they would usually end up asking, "Ledge, every SOBO seems to think Maine is the hardest state. Why *is* that?"

I couldn't resist messing with them. So, my standard response went something like, "We'll, you've asked two questions, one hard and one easy. I'll answer the hard one first. You asked 'Why?' It goes without saying, that's a conundrum, one of the great imponderable riddles for the ages. We could commission 1000 fully credentialed philosophers of just the right ilk and we'd surely get 1000 unique and yet uniformly unsatisfactory answers. So, I'll just punt and say 'Why not?'

"Your second question was, 'Is Maine the hardest state?' My answer is, 'Yes, Maine is the hardest state.'"

"That's cute, Ledge. You gonna answer our question or not?

"Sure, why not? First of all, in Maine, virtually every time you put your foot down you'll be stepping on a root or rock or both. And if you wanted to, though I'm not sure why you would, you could step in moose droppings with nearly every stride all the way to Katahdin. You see, the moose population in Maine – about 30,000 of 'em – exceeds the combined human population of Maine's trail towns by a wide margin. So, you'll be stepping on moose droppings by the jillion every day.

"Anyway, you'll discover the trail in Maine often feels hypothetical, with the white blazes indicating roughly where the trail might have been built, if the CCC workers in the 1930s had done what you might think they were supposed to do. Sometimes the next blaze is on a house-sized boulder, as if to say, 'the trail could have been here and it could be here someday, but for now just do the best you can.' But I think Myron Avery, the trail legend most responsible for putting the trail through Maine, wanted it this way. Maybe you've even seen his famous quote about how the trail should be remote and narrow and meandering? Well, mission accomplished! Compared to every other state's segment, Maine's is quite remote and pretty sinuous too. Up north, it meanders around giant lakes, day after day. You'll love it!

"And when hiking in Maine, just keep reminding yourself: it's a foot path through the forest, it's just a footpath through the forest, it's nothing more than a footpath through the forest. Then you can entertain yourself with one of those chronic internal debates we have on the trail. You can subvocalize something like, 'A foot path? Oh please! That's a flagrant insult to proper footpaths the world over.'"

"Anything else, Ledge? Maine's not getting any closer."

"Well, as you've probably heard, the trail towns in Maine are great, but they're also few and far between. You'll be hiking through one unorganized township after another. Unlike every other state, Maine has no roads that parallel and crisscross the trail. On average, it's 30 miles between paved roads. Every other state has a much higher road density. Anyway, because the trail in Maine is so much more remote than in any other state, you need to carry more food.

"Finally, I can't emphasize this last point enough. It trumps all others. The number of switchbacks in Maine is identical to the number of poisonous snake species in Maine: zero!"

New flash: One set of switchbacks was built during the summer of 2009. It seems the MATC has set a worrisome precedent. If this newfangled notion catches on in Maine, the A.T. could be doubled in length, just from all that extraneous zigzagging.

NEW HAMSHIRE: Live Free or Hike
I'm ambivalent about crossing my first state-line, into New Hampshire, the Granite State.

I grew up in Maine but left for Alaska decades ago because Maine wasn't Maine enough – no glaciers, no grizzlies, no genuine wilderness. But now I'm nostalgic to be hiking through Maine and downright sad to be walking south, *away* from home. Many thru-hikers walk toward their childhood home. They follow their homing instinct. But I'm doing the opposite. It's an uncomfortable feeling. And it gets stronger when I arrive at the border.

Other SOBOs paused for celebratory photos at the border, but I'm tempted to turn back and walk north. The sign to the south reads, "Maine-New Hampshire Border." Turning around I read the perfectly shabby, hand-painted sign greeting northbounders. It reads, "WELCOME TO MAINE: The Way Life Should Be." If you're a Mainer, this inside joke warms your heart. You recognize this sign as a mini-replica of the one that greets northbound motorists entering Maine from New Hampshire on I-95. If you're from elsewhere, this must trigger your gag response. You must think, "Come on, Maine, get over yourself!"

I've been stalling for days now. I even hitched into Bethel, 19 miles off the trail, pretending it was a regular trail town. I did so just to keep myself in Maine for another couple of days. But then I got back on the trail, hiked up and over Old Speck and through the boulder scramble of Mahoosuc Notch, where I once led a hiking group of eleven 11-year-olds. They loved it, of course. And so did I. I still do. It's like a mile-long playground, with cabin-sized boulders rather than monkey bars.

Now I'm here at the border, heading south. The trail through Maine is like one long practical joke for some hikers. But I soon discover New Hampshire has a few tricks up its sleeve as well. It starts with a practical joke: there are virtually no blazes! And the trail goes hard up. I love the ups, but I don't like hiking on the wrong trail. So, up I go, studying every tree and rock for the first white blaze. Nothing. I consider turning back and exploring a couple of inconspicuous side trails. Maybe I missed the first white blaze. I'm unconvinced this is the A.T. partly because the trail is overgrown with balsam fir thickets. In Maine, the superabundant twig-eating moose perform pro bono trail maintenance year-round, keeping the balsam fir thickets from encroaching on the trail. Still no white blazes, but I persist. Southward, southbound, always south. No turning back now.

Finally, I come upon a telltale sign. It's a weather-battered memorial plaque. It says nothing about the A.T., but I'm comforted by the fact that someone died here. This must be the trail. I continue on, through the first mile or so of overgrown trail in the Granite State. And then I finally see a faded white blaze and, eventually, another, and then another. Good one, New Hampshire. I admire the primitive nature of your trail so far, but please give us SOBOs one white blaze, eh?

I'm keen to hike on through New Hampshire, but I also know what's in store. I know the road density quadruples in New Hampshire. I know the trail towns become tourist traps. I know there will be billboards enticing me to "Come See the Trained Bear" and frolic at the world's most thrilling waterpark and visit Santa's Village.

And I know a bit about the AMC huts in The Whites. I know they offer work-for-stay arrangements for thru-hikers. I know I'll be allowed to sleep on the floor and eat at a special table, sufficiently distant from the nostrils of the section-hikers who pay full freight. I've heard rumors about skits put on by the staff, with the Hut Master acting as emcee. But I have no way of anticipating that one of these Hut Masters is a multi-time "Strongman" champion or that he makes his "mad cheese" (real cash) during the off-season "working" as a nude model. He assigns me the following task in exchange for a place at the table and a spot on the floor: "tell me stories about Alaska." And I have no way of anticipating that the maestra of another hut has three kidneys, all of them functional. So, the hut experience is overtly funny. The AMC must recruit their hut staff from comedy clubs in the big city.

And I know all about the hideous autoroad and cog railway and gift shop atop Mt. Washington. As a child, I spent way too many excruciatingly boring Sunday afternoons fidgeting in the backseat as our family cruised in the woody station wagon with its "This Car Climbed Mt. Washington" bumper sticker. As a teenager, I chose to do all of my hiking on Mt. Katahdin, which has been spared from this sort of development. Indeed, in keeping with the terms of its bequeathal by Governor Percival Baxter, Baxter State Park is to remain in its wild and road-less state in perpetuity. The Whites, unfortunately, were not deeded to the people of New Hampshire with any such proviso. So, I brace myself for the physical challenge of The Whites and for the shenanigans of New Hampshire, especially atop Mt. Washington.

I'm not disappointed.

I go up and over Mt. Washington on July 4th. It's a refreshing day, with ferocious gusts and driving rain. We thru-hikers flirt with hypothermia. Bent at the waist, bracing for the next gust, we barely pause long enough to exchange trailnames. We just grunt as we pass each other in the rain and sleet and hail, while trying to ignore the racket from the autoroad and cog railway. At the summit, "pukers" who arrived by motorcar or train or helicopter or hovercraft line up at the gift shop to purchase memorabilia to celebrate their momentous feat. Oh please! I want to brag about my little feat and whine about my not-so-little and still-expanding feet, but I refrain. I want to ask these folks, "If you didn't want to hike up the trail, why didn't you at least walk up the autoroad?"

Two days later, a certain someone did walk up the autoroad. Believe it or not, that someone was a camel named Josh. (I'm not joshing.) It was quite a day for Josh and his entourage, two hominids, two horses, and one Irish wolfhound. You're anticipating, perhaps, that the whole entourage got arrested for criminal trespassing, after Josh spat in someone's eye. Au contraire, the outing was sanctioned by the proper authorities. It was a photo op, a PR stunt, *not* an extralegal prank. Josh was even presented with a "This Camel Climbed Mt. Washington" rumper sticker when he got back down to the visitor center at Pinkham Notch. Classy, eh? I know, you can't write fiction like that.

But if you think that's priceless, get a load of this: Josh also received a Certificate of Appreciation – for his "hard work and dedication" – from none other than US Senator Jeanne Shaheen.

This raises all sorts of uncomfortable questions, like didn't the Irish wolfhound deserve the same kind of highfalutin kudos? And didn't Senator Shaheen appreciate the teachable moment here? Didn't she see this as an opportunity to begin a dialogue about shutting down the autoroad, about how it's anathema to anyone who cares about ecological sustainability, about how it's linked to our addiction to oil, our contribution to global warming, our permanent military installation in the Persian gulf, and the global extinction crisis?

And this raises one more question: where's *my* Certificate of Appreciation? When will *I* be recognized for *my* dedication to hiking a green, car-free hike? Do I need to ride a unicycle backwards up the autoroad? If that's what it would take, I'd do it.

But wait, I have an answer to my own rhetorical questions. I predict I'll be recognized next year, 2011. Here's my plan to get Senator Shaheen's attention. It's perfect. You see, the sesquicentennial of the autoroad is next year, according to the autoroad's very own website. So, pretty soon I'll draft a proposal seeking permission to venture up the autoroad with an entourage of my own. It'll be an ark-like procession. I'll lead the way on a unicycle, while juggling three jars of Nutella®. Behind me, fine furry and feathered friends will walk and hop two-by-two, 2179 species in all, from Pinkham Notch to the summit.

I'll do a little lighthearted speechifying about the evils of the autoroad and the continued religious-like celebration of the gasoline-powered automobile. I'll start small and talk about how it's an affront to the thru-hiking experience. Then I'll go big and explore the linkage between global warming and the biodiversity crisis. It'll be fun. And then everyone who decides to divorce their car will be invited to join our merry trek back down to Pinkham Notch, where we'll receive our richly deserved accolades.

VERMONT: Ben Cohen for President

It's late evening, well past hiker midnight and just about the stroke of town midnight, when I cross my second state-line, into Vermont, the Green Mountain State.

I've strolled across the bridge spanning the Connecticut River between the bustling burgh of Hanover, New Hampshire, home of Dartmouth College and the Green Mountain Hiking Club, and Norwich, Vermont. Norwich is immaculate. Every house is white. All the kittens are white too, no doubt. And everyone's been in bed since 8 PM, including the constable, I suspect. I tiptoe through the snoozy village, trying not to disturb a soul.

I'm glad to be in Vermont. In my imagination, I've been in Vermont ever since Glencliff, New Hampshire, where the trail transformed dramatically. It became easier, easier on our feet, livers, and minds. The trail became soft and smooth. Our bodies healed on the fly. We SOBOs walked bigger miles. Our feet felt fine for a change. Our patellar tendinitis faded into a dim memory. We took fewer ibuprofen, so our livers healed as well. We felt mental relief because we could stride gracefully, without focusing so intently on foot placement and foot pain.

I took full advantage of this new freedom to walk with head held high. I spent the days as a self-appointed ecological detective. My head was on a swivel. I used my limited forensic powers to study the landscape, searching for clues to explain all this underfoot pleasantness. I detected two key clues: stone walls and massive trees with a shrub-like growth form.

Meanwhile, I surveyed fellow SOBOs. Universally, they reported a similar experience. They loved the trail, their feet and knees felt better, they stopped popping so many pills, and they noticed the trail was soft and smooth. But they were oblivious as to why that might be so. This isn't a criticism. The thru-hike is a mesmerizing experience. Most of us didn't recognize that we'd walked into a whole new biome, never mind the subtle ecological clues lurking in Vermont's reclaimed forests.

The stone walls and giant shrub-like trees tell the tale. The trail through this stretch of Vermont is so soft and smooth for a deceptive reason. It's not because the Green Mountain Hiking Club has done such a fastidious job of trail construction and maintenance. It's not because Vermont's bedrock is intrinsically soft and spongy. It's not because our pain receptors have given out and so we no longer realize how hard the footing really is. No, there's an elegant and parsimonious explanation based on ecological history.

The main reason the trail is so soft and smooth is because it bisects a mosaic of historical family farms. This isn't pristine or logged forestland as in Maine and most of New Hampshire. No, the trail crosses what was once a broad patchwork of fields and pastures. The stone walls contain the very rocks that would have hurt our feet, if not for the unintended latent contribution of Vermont's early farmers to trail construction.

And the enormous shrub-like trees further reveal that the forests here are reclaimed pastureland. These trees grew in open pastures, in the absence of light competition, and so didn't grow in the usual tree-like form. They invested in early reproduction rather than verticality. The linkage is clear: where you see stone walls along the forest floor and giant shrub-like trees scattered about, your feet will feel fine and you will glide along the trail.

Rather than demanding a senatorial commendation for myself, I think I'll petition US Senator Patrick Leahy (D, VT) to sign one of those snazzy Certificate-of-Appreciation forms in recognition of the contributions of this region's historical farming community. They should be commended for their "hard work and dedication," even though they knew not what they did. Unwittingly, they groomed the future A.T. with their back-breaking work. They removed the pain-inducing rocks and used their masonry skills to stack them into those esthetically pleasing stone walls. As a positive byproduct of the Law of Unintended Consequences, they altered the whole landscape in a way that ultimately led to one sweet stretch of hiking trail for generations of fellow Earthlings to enjoy.

∞

I also surveyed fellow thru-hikers, asking them to identify the most famous Vermonter of all time. Some hikers balked. Everyone else gave the same answer: Ben Cohen. And then I asked them to name their *favorite* Vermonter. Same answer. "Not Bill Lee or Helen and Scott Nearing?" I'd ask.

Why is Ben so beloved among thru-hikers? Is it because of his anti-war activism through *True Majority*? No. Is it because he's a philanthropist of the nth degree? No. Is it because he's a Deadhead and because so many thru-hikers still mourn Jerry Garcia's premature demise and love Dead-inspired jam bands? No. Is it because he's an icon for Vermont's reputation as a haven for countercultural refugees, including hairy hikers and Bill "Spaceman" Lee? No. Is it because he's a master communicator who uses Oreo cookie metaphors as a rhetorical device to explore solutions to social justice? No. Thru-hikers clearly love Ben so much simply because they were weaned on Ben & Jerry's ice cream, mostly Chocolate Chip Cookie Dough and Chunky Monkey and Phish Food.

You see, thru-hikers, even those with mild lactose intolerance, love ice cream. And just as thru-hikers might be oblivious to the underlying ecological history of Vermont and how long-defunct farms made the trail soft and smooth, they also ignore the fact that they're addicted to a frozen confection that starts as baby food in the mammary glands of a nonhuman mammalian species. Udderly ridiculous, I know.

I suppose I should ask Senator Leahy for a Certificate of Appreciation for Ben as well. He too, like the people who ruined their backs long ago removing rocks from the incipient trail, has contributed mightily to thru-hiker betterment. I figure my own Ben & Jerry's consumption fueled roughly 412.7 miles of hiking.

MASSACHUSETTS: How Would Henry Hike?

"... in Wildness is the preservation of the World."

"... I cannot preserve my health and spirits unless I spend four hours a day at least ... sauntering through the woods and over the hills and fields absolutely free from all worldly engagements."

"... our only true names are nick-names."

— Quotes from Thoreau's (1862) essay, *Walking*

As I saunter across my third state-line, into Massachusetts, I start reminiscing. This feels like a homecoming. This state, one of the commonwealths, is a lot of things to me. It's the source of my DNA. It's also the source of my childhood heroes. My baseball hero was Bill Lee, lefty pitcher for the Boston Red Sox, later a half-hearted lefty Presidential candidate, and always a countercultural gadfly. My intellectual hero was Henry David Thoreau (1817-1862), author, poet, abolitionist, philosopher, conscientious objector, tax evader, conservationist, back-to-the-lander, organic gardener, hiker, voyageur, naturalist, surveyor, and proto-ecologist. He championed such lofty notions as abolitionism, wilderness preservation, nonviolent resistance, and environmentalism. He was a saint.

As a pre-pubescent lad, I listened to Bill's exploits furtively with transistor radio under my pillow, and I struggled to read everything Henry ever wrote, including his prolific journals. I even fawned over his handwritten surveying plans. And I communed with his ghost and picked up litter around his cabin site at Walden Pond. There I walked among some of the same trees he had walked among and I listened for the descendants of *his* ovenbirds and wood thrushes. I pondered transcendentalism at this hallowed spot, where he had lived simply and deliberately for two years, two months, and two days (and, presumably, two hours, two minutes, and two seconds).

Years later, I would replicate Henry's "experiment" by living simply, deliberately, and alone in backwoods log cabins, first in Maine, later in arctic Alaska, and most recently in Ontario. Like so many like-minded people of my generation, I have always imagined myself to be Henry's kindred spirit and vice versa.

Henry's birthplace, Concord, happens to be the precise source of my DNA. It's where my lovely Aunt Shirley and cousins still live, all just a few minutes' stroll from Henry's birthplace, his cabin site on Walden Pond, and his gravesite, where his stone is labeled simply "HENRY." For a thru-hiker, it's also an easy one-day's stroll, just 18 flat miles from Bill's former jobsite, Fenway Park. But now I find myself 146 walking-miles from Concord, 146+1 years after Henry's death, in the northwestern corner of the state.

As I glide down the trail towards Williamstown, I catch myself fantasizing about how much Bill and Henry would enjoy the thru-hike experience. They're both pre-adapted.

Bill, 63 years young, already has a nickname that would be an apt trailname, "Spaceman." He often sports a reasonable facsimile of a thru-beard and did so even during his playing days, when it was considered an egregious infraction of team rules. He'd be gregarious. He'd be great at doling out trailnames. (He called his manager, Don Zimmer, "The Gerbil.") He could barnstorm his way down the trail, pausing in trail towns to hurl a few innings for local pick-up teams. Plus, he's always had a passion for wild places, long-distance running, and THC-laced pancakes. His flamboyant personality and scofflaw ways and iconoclastic wit would make him an instant trail legend.

Henry we could call "The Hankster" or "Tree Hugger" or
"Nature Lover-boy," although these possibilities seem wholly
disrespectful, even sacrilegious. I would offer him the trailname,
"Saint Henry." He'd probably accept "Hank." He was an avid
pedestrian, to say the least. While the poet ee cummings claimed a
day without laughter was a complete waste, Henry obviously
thought a day without walking was a complete waste. He
preferred to spend at least half of each day sauntering and
meandering through woods and fields around Concord. This was
considered eccentric, even in the mid-nineteenth century when
Americans still routinely walked more than 200 feet at a stretch.

But would he walk the trail? Would he do a thru-hike? He
wasn't one to follow the herd. But if he did join us and I'm sure he
would, he'd be the A.T.'s best naturalist of all time. (Of course, you
could count on one hand the number of thru-hikers each year
who know their trillium from their hermit thrush, their trout lily
from their ovenbird, their botanical ass from their ornithological
elbow.) Perhaps he'd sully his intellect and stoop to jot down a
few pearls of wisdom in the registers, in that stilted style of his
day. Perhaps he'd even deign to do a little privy criticism. And
he'd finally get to summit Katahdin, successfully this time. He'd be
a SOBO, of course. That way, he could walk solo, living in his head,
without the distraction of fellow hikers telling him about the next
place to get pizza or weed or a shower. He'd arrive on his bicycle
in Millinocket, sporting that burly Amish-style *neck*-beard, which
made him so unsavory in his day in Concord but would make him
ultra-hiker-sexy on the A.T. He'd spend the first night at the
Appalachian Trail Lodge, with Navigator (Jamie) and Ole Man
(Paul). He'd opt for the black-bean burrito entrée at their
Appalachian Trail Café, where they don't serve moose tongue or
brook trout or wild cranberries or wintergreen tea or any of the

other wild edible fare that comprised his "victuals" when last he was in Maine.

On the trail, Hank would be earnest, but I don't think he'd be antisocial. After all, even during his sojourn at Walden, he took meals at his parents' home in town and gave public lectures and chatted with his uncouth, philistine neighbors. He was a part-time, half-hearted hermit. So, he'd probably be flexibly social on the trail, sometimes pausing to chat with a fellow traveler, but sometimes walking right on by and not even bothering to mumble a greeting. He surely wouldn't turn into one of those verbose middle-aged advice machines.

He'd be funny too, not jocular and goofy, but wry, ironic, facetious. His erudite tongue-in-cheek witticisms would rely more heavily on Greek mythology than flatulence. He'd use tropes, not puns. By his standards, puns were never punny. He'd hike his own hike, that's for sure, and he'd do so with integrity and humor aplenty. He'd be Thoreauvian, thru and thru.

The trail in Massachusetts remains nice-and-easy going. With my attention undivided, I catch myself spending lots of time communing with Hank's spirit and pondering the question, how would he hike? Would he charge along like I'm doing or would he linger to botanize and berry-pick and really explore Mt. Greylock, as he once did? I imagine writing a book titled, *Henry Hikes the Appalachian Trail* or perhaps *How would Henry Hike?* While entertaining these thoughts, I find myself giving Hank an update, all the way to the Connecticut border.

Before I mention anything about my little A.T. adventure, I need to get him up to speed on some major developments. A lot has happened since his untimely demise. "It's mind-boggling, Henry, but you died just as all sorts of major historical stuff was about to go down." I begin by praising his rant in favor of John

Brown's raid on Harpers Ferry, an attempt to instigate a slave uprising. I tell him about the Civil War, the abolition of slavery, and the civil rights movement that's still ongoing. I tell him about his influence on Martin Luther King, Jr. and Mahatma Ghandi. I tell him about the human population explosion and validate his concerns about materialism and free enterprise capitalism and development and wilderness preservation.

I imagine telling him about my career as a professor of ecology, a field that some of my colleagues think he might have "sired" if only he hadn't died so young. I tell him that his contemporary, Chuck Darwin, whom he admired, is the real intellectual hero of my field, even though he had no algebra. I tell him about the universities where I've worked, none of which existed when he graduated from Harvard as a teenager. I tell him about my research in Alaska, a state he's never heard of. And I tell him about the invention of baseball and the Boston Red Sox and how much the New York Yankees suck.

I even tell Henry about his posthumous fame and imponderable developments such as television and the internet. He's appalled, in my imagination, to learn that I've just paused beside the trail to use my cell phone to do a Google search for "Henry David Thoreau." And then I tell him the result: a whopping 1,620,000 hits! In his death, he's become a celebrity. He's become famous for being famous. (The *incognoscenti* think he lived in the remote wilderness, not on the edge of town and just 1.5 miles from his mom's kitchen.) To keep him humble I do Google searches for "Charles Darwin" (5,630,000 hits) and "Jesus Christ" (40,700,000). This cracks him up. He's a patient listener and he asks precious few questions. Throughout, he's mostly rapt, though not so much about baseball.

I imagine his saying, "Methinks baseball is an opiate of the masses and I would vastly prefer a solitary slog through any leech-infested swamp than to sit amongst throngs of humanity with my legs crossed watching grown men in pajamas play with sticks and balls."

At long last, I turn to the topic of hiking. I tell him about my "yo-yo SOBO thru-hike and return NOBO thru-bike on the Appalachian Trail." He's baffled, of course. This jargon is all futuristic whimsy to him. At the time of his death, the Appalachian Trail didn't exist, bicycles and yo-yos were still unavailable, and even the term hobo, the root of SOBO and NOBO, hadn't come into vogue.

"Dr. Ledge," says Henry, "you might think me perverse, but I wonder whither you might agree, perchance, to do me the courtesy of clarifying some of that strange language you used. I do not know which language that was, but I am certain it was not the vernacular of my day. I can only assume it was the vulgar slang of to-day."

"Good one, Hank," I say. "You do have a sense of humor! And I'd like to thank you for making me the target of your good-natured sarcasm."

It's a heady thing to be zinged by Hank, even if only in a daydream.

"Perhaps you would kindly start by telling me about this so-called Appalachian Trail?" asks Henry.

"Well, Henry, the world's a messed up place, but damn it there are good things. And the Appalachian Trail is one of them. It's a 2179-mile continuous foot path that hikers use for recreation and spiritual renewal and adventure. It was put in place about 70 years after you died. It was championed by a guy named Benton MacKaye, who went to high school in Cambridge, MA, and studied the natural history around Shirley Center, MA, which he mapped extensively. He then studied forestry at Harvard. He might have been your protégé if you hadn't kicked the bucket at such an unripe young age. But you clearly inspired him. He cited your work extensively in his writing. So, it seems pretty clear you inspired the creation of the Appalachian Trail."

I step off the trail and do a Google search for websites mentioning both "Thoreau" and "Appalachian Trail": 14,300 hits. Remarkably, this exceeds the number of sites mentioning both "Benton MacKaye," the trail's inventor, and "Appalachian Trail": 13,600. I imagine telling Henry these factoids and his being bemused.

"Anyway, Henry, the southern terminus of the trail is at the summit of Springer Mountain, in Georgia. The northern terminus is at the summit of Mt. Katahdin, which I happen to know you tried to reach on your adventures in The Great North Woods. There's a spring named after you. It's on the tableland, above treeline in the alpine tundra, and just one measly mile from the summit of Katahdin. Most folks seem to think you turned back near this spring. Otherwise, the summit, called Baxter Peak, might have been named after you. Instead, it's named after a former Governor of Maine, Percival Baxter, who was born a few years after your death. He climbed Pamola Peak on Katahdin when he was almost the same age as you were when you died. Ultimately, he bequeathed the mountain and 300+ square miles of surrounding uninhabited forestland – a dozen times bigger than the township of Concord – to the people of Maine, to be protected in its wild state in perpetuity."

I imagine Henry raving about this trail. And then he asks, "Dr. Ledge, does the Appalachian Trail pass through Massachusetts?"

"Sure does, for southbounders the trail goes over Mt. Greylock and down through the Berkshires. You might be gratified to know that quotes from your writing are preserved on plaques on the Greylock summit."

He seems more embarrassed than gratified.

I them explain what I meant by the inscrutable phrase, "yo-yo SOBO thru-hike and return NOBO thru-bike." I explain the thru-hike phenomenon first. He's astonished that ordinary people – and extraordinary ones like Grandma Gatewood and Bill Erwin – walk all the way between Katahdin and Springer every year and have been doing so for half a century now.

"In fact, Henry, the number of people purportedly attempting a thru-hike on the Appalachian Trail this year exceeds both the number of students at Harvard when you were there and the number of townsfolk in Concord in your day."

He's incredulous for all kinds of reasons. Henry was considered an oddball in his day for his skulking along the hedgerows, trespassing on neighbors' farms, as he made his way through the fields and woods on daily rambles of upwards to 20 miles. And despite his bold adventurous spirit and passion for traveling through wild places by foot and canoe, on self-propelled wilderness treks he never ventured farther from Concord than the "Ktaadn" region. And he did most of that mileage while fidgeting in trains, steamboats, and horse buggies. So, it seems inconceivable to him that an army of hikers would choose to walk 20 or so miles a day for months on end.

It's also hard for him to imagine these hikers would wish to begin or end their hike in The South. In his day, the pull was to The West, which he used as a metaphor for "wild." And New Englanders in general and especially abolitionists, felt thoroughly estranged from The South. So, naturally, he gravitated to the west

(Mt. Greylock) and north (The Whites of New Hampshire and The Great North Woods of Maine) whenever he went venturing beyond the confines of Concord. I suspect the thought of hiking into the Deep South hardly occurred to him.

I imagine his asking me about my experience in The South, so I explain what I meant by a yo-yo. He couldn't begin to intuit the meaning of this word because the yo-yo was patented in 1866, four years after his death.

Finally, I tell him about my thru-*bike* experience. This too was cryptic because he died about 30 years before the advent of the bicycle. And he can't conceive of how I could have traveled by bicycle, except along gravelly horse roads and frozen rivers and lakes. So, I tell him the bad news – not the catastrophically bad news about global warming and warfare and the biotic holocaust, just the bad news about automobile addition and paved roads.

"Here's some good news, Henry. You'll be pleased to know The Great North Woods of Maine remain ostensibly wild today. The A.T. passes through many still-unsettled unorganized townships and minimally settled plantations. You'd hardly notice any change in the landscape. The few villages along the way remain small and tidy. In fact, if you began a southbound thru-hike at Katahdin, you'd spend a week or more hiking through what's now affectionately called the 100-mile wilderness. You wouldn't encounter a single town until arriving in Monson, which you referenced in *The Maine Woods*. Monson had a big fire in 1860, two years before your death, and it's never really recovered. The town's still-modest population is a macabre 666. And the next town along the trail, Caratunk, is even less populous, with just 108 people. So, the trail in Maine, I'm glad to say, would give you that 'tonic of wilderness' you craved."

I imagine he's comforted to hear the trail in Maine passes through mostly intact industrial paper-company land and that precious few roads penetrate what he knew as The Great Maine Woods.

But then he asks about the roads and the state of the trail in his native state. I fill him in: "Massachusetts, I'm sorry to say is overrun. The trail never gets farther than a mile from the nearest paved road! One of these roads goes to the summit of Greylock. The 90-mile segment in Massachusetts crosses 34 paved roads. And the road density remains high all the way to the Smokies, I'm afraid.

"But here's a more positive spin, Henry. I recall you wrote that you could wend your way 20 miles in the fields and woods around Concord without passing through a single town. The A.T. does the same thing. It meanders. It sticks to the mountains and ridges, shunning cities and towns. The A.T. is over 2000 miles long, 100 times longer than your daily walks and, remarkably, there are only a handful of places where it passes through a town. In Massachusetts, it goes through Williamstown and Dalton. In New Hampshire, it goes through Hanover; in Pennsylvania, Port Clinton and Duncannon; in West Virginia, Harpers Ferry; in Virginia, Damascus; and in North Carolina, Hotsprings. That's about it, though. So I think you wouldn't be too put off by this aspect of the trail. And not that you'd go in for taverns and ice-cream challenges and other such shenanigans, but you might even come to love the trail towns the way most thru-hikers do.

"But the roads, Henry, the paved roads, that's what I'm afraid you'd hate. You see, the road density here is about a dozen times higher than in Maine. In Massachusetts, there's a paved road crossing every 2.6 trail miles, on average. In Maine, it's 31 miles between crossings. This alone captures the dramatic transition

SOBOs experience. Compared to Maine, where there are just 0.6 road crossings per 20 miles, the road density is four times higher in New Hampshire (2.6), five times higher in Vermont (3.6), and nearly a dozen times higher in Massachusetts (7.6). So, here in Mass, where the next road's never far away, you can easily visit three or more trail towns in a single day. This means the trail here isn't remote enough to bother carrying much food or water. You can refuel your body directly, several times a day, when you get to a town."

As if to prove the point, on my first full day in Mass I eat breakfast in Williamstown, pause for a sandwich and salad atop Greylock at midday, enjoy a brief excursion into Cheshire for ice cream in the afternoon, and make it to Dalton for an evening feast. That makes four town meals, three trail towns, 23+ easy trail miles, and one scintillating hallucinatory conversation with Saint Henry – in just one day.

Late that night, I'm about to doze off in the loft of the barn called "The Birdcage," Rob Bird's free hiker hostel in Dalton. But I have one last little chat with Henry: "So, what do you think? If you were alive today, would you do a thru-hike on the A.T.?"

"Yes, Dr. Ledge, it is safe to say, if you could dig me up and breathe life into my corpse, I would rove thither to Georgia on that footway you call the Appalachian Trail. I would probably live on the trail through all seasons, walking to and fro, pausing now and then to read at a library or give a public lecture at a lyceum."

"Surely," I ask, "you wouldn't own a car if you were alive today?"

"I didn't even own a horse in my day," scoffs Henry.

"How would you get to the trail-head in Baxter State Park? Would you travel by train, steamboat, and buggy? Or would you ride a bicycle, like I did, leaving Concord after midnight and arriving a few days later in Millinocket?"

"Yes," says Henry, "I would do the same. This bicycle contraption seems like a good device for fast travel, but it would be otherwise vastly inferior to walking."

"Yes," I say, "I'm afraid you'd hate the speed. Just as traveling by horse-and-buggy precludes the leisurely botanizing you loved, traveling by bicycle is even worse. Bike-speed is about three times faster than horse-speed. It's too fast, too detached. But it's a beautiful way to cover great distances, like from Concord to Millinocket or from Georgia to Concord."

"Dr. Ledge," says Henry, "if I had my druthers, I should prefer to paddle a canoe and walk all the way to Baxter's park. My main reservation about using a bicycle for long-distance travel is whether it might be unduly difficult to balance, never mind master. Is it harder than *Latin* or the piano?"

"No," I say, "don't worry. It's easy and not easy like ballroom dancing is supposedly easy. It's actually easy. I could teach you how to ride a bicycle in just a few minutes. And you'd never forget. We even have an expression for this phenomenon. We say, 'it's like riding a bicycle,' which means if you've ever learned skill X, then you will never forget how to perform that skill."

"Well, that settles the matter, Dr. Ledge. I would travel by sitting on a bicycle all the way to Governor Baxter's park. Then I would climb to my namesake spring and continue on for the extra mile to Baxter's peak. And then I would turn around and walk to Georgia."

"OK, Henry, thanks for chatting with me today. And stop calling me Dr. Ledge. If we're going to be friends, you must call me Ledge. Can we agree to that?"

Back on the trail in the morning (forenoon to Henry), I channel Henry and resume my dialogue with his ghost. All that news yesterday, much of it devastating, must have been overwhelming. Today I resolve to steer the conversation in a new direction. I'll try to cheer him up. I begin by sharing news about recent legislative initiatives in the Bay State. Considering his adamant views on civil disobedience, I try to steer the conversation in this direction, hoping to pique his imagination or rile him if not tickle his funny bone.

"So, Henry," I begin, "in light of your contention that we should violate any law we see as being truly unjust, because to obey it is tantamount to supporting it, I wonder what you think about this scenario. I have before me a superabundance of opportunities to jaywalk, given the high road density in Massachusetts. I happen to view the state's frivolous jaywalking law as an unjust affront to my thru-hike experience, so I plan to take advantage of every one of these opportunities."

"Ledge," Henry asks, "is it really a crime to jaywalk in modern-day Massachusetts?"

"No, it's not a crime. Whereas you got jailed for refusing to pay your poll tax and thereby tacitly support an unjust war and slavery, I won't get jailed for jaywalking. But I still hope my little anarchic protest might trigger the repealing of the silly law."

"Is there a fine for jaywalking?" Henry asks.

"Yes, the fine for jaywalking as a first offense is a hefty $1. That's right, one US dollar bill. A buck, isn't that hilarious?"

"No, it's outrageous," says Hank.

"That's for the first offense," I say. "It's also a dollar for each of the next two offenses and then the fine doubles. With 34 road crossings in Massachusetts, these fines could mount up. A devoted jaywalker could accumulate fines totaling $65, and even more if she or he were to go haywire and start jaywalking all willy nilly during visits to towns. As for me, with 23 road crossings between here and the Connecticut border, I could accumulate fines totaling 43 dollars."

Henry's indignant. He thinks the law's unjust because he's shocked by the sticker price. He points out that $43 is more than it cost him to build his cabin at Walden Pond. That cost $28.12, including a penny he spent on chalk and thirty-one cents he squandered on hair, presumably horse hair used as a plaster-strengthening material.

So, I have to tell him about inflation. "Hank, don't roll over in your grave – if that stuff's true – but you won't believe this: these days you can buy a replica kit of your Walden cabin online. The company will prefabricate and deliver it to the spot of your choosing for the tidy sum of $15,800."

Henry scowls and then steers us back to the jaywalking topic. "You've convinced me, Ledge. Even though the fine is nominal, this jaywalking law should be repealed. What's the legislature been doing all these years? Why hasn't this law been repealed?"

"Well, on a positive note, the Massachusetts legislature, in its finite wisdom, did recently decriminalize marijuana. This is what we now call the cultivar of *Cannabis* with psychoactive properties, not the feral hemp you called cannabis. By the way, Henry, you might be gratified to know your views on civil disobedience are routinely invoked by those in favor of legalizing marijuana. So, the fact that thru-hikers can now carry up to an ounce of marijuana on the trail in Massachusetts without threat of imprisonment is arguably part of your legacy." (I step off the trail and do a quick Google search. Sure enough, a search for websites mentioning "Thoreau" and "marijuana" yields a whopping 59,300 hits.)

"I even read recently that US Senator Barney Frank invoked your views on civil disobedience in announcing his plan to introduce a federal bill proposing to decriminalize marijuana nationwide, as has been done so far in individual states, not just in Massachusetts but also in Maine and Alaska and a few other states that you've never heard of."

"That is gratifying," says Hank, "except I dreamt, too grandiosely perhaps, for a government that would govern minimally or, ideally, not at all. Tell me is there still a fine for possessing this variety of hemp you call marijuana?"

"Yes, but it's now just a civil offense, subject to a $100 fine. This happens to be the same as the base fine for operating an automobile in an unsafe way, like driving faster than the speed limit or failing to come to a complete stop at an intersection. The marijuana-possession fine also happens to be the equivalent of five bicycle-related infractions.

"Unfortunately, Henry," I say, "I can't smoke the stuff. It triggers an asthmatic response. Within a few days, I'm sick with bronchitis and even pneumonia."

"That's unfortunate, Ledge," says Henry. "I think I probably died from complications following recurrent bouts of bronchitis."

"Rumor has it," I say.

"You know how I died?" asks Henry.

"Of course. How, where, when."

"That's curious," says Henry, "to think that generations of men [sic] would concern themselves with such trivialities.

"But tell me, Ledge, did the Massachusetts legislature decriminalize marijuana because it was unjust or because it was somehow the expedient course of action?"

"I don't know, Henry, but I have my suspicions. I'd like to think your influence played a role. I suspect the legislators recognized, at least tacitly, that the rate of compliance was so low as to suggest it was an unjust crime. But I also suspect they were being pragmatic. Before decriminalization, more than a thousand townsfolk in Concord and the other towns of Middlesex County had been arrested annually, for years running. Just imagine the expense to taxpayers – for an indiscretion. So, I suspect they were pandering to those who argued it was no longer economically feasible to enforce prohibition.

"Or maybe the legislators had more pressing matters on their docket," I add. "Maybe they had better things to do with their precious time. For example, believe or not – and try not to blow a gasket, if you even know what that means – the Massachusetts legislature will soon consider a bill proposing to make the Fluffernutter the Official State Sandwich."

I tell Henry about this marshmallow-and-peanut-butter sandwich and then a few lowlights of its recent history. He's more annoyed than amused, but I persist. "The Fluffernutter has been a political football in Massachusetts for a few years now."

"What's football? Is it something like baseball?" ask Henry.

"Football's another opiate of the masses. But if baseball is chess, then football is a violent form of checkers, played by ginormous men wearing form-fitting long underwear. You'd have to see it to believe it."

"Anyway, Henry, I just meant that politicians have been using the Fluffernutter in self-serving ways. One seemingly well-intentioned state legislator, who shall remain nameless, recently made a grandstanding attempt to have it banned from school lunches throughout the state. There was an outcry. He was vilified.

"Meanwhile, Henry, the legislature has repeatedly considered petitions to make The Fluffernutter the Official State Sandwich. I'm not kidding."

He says nothing. His ghost is fading fast. I'm afraid I'll lose him with this goofball nonsense, so I try to reel him back in: "Henry, I don't want to distract you from your wont thoughts, as you would put it. I don't want to annoy you with trivialities. I don't want to pollute your chaste mind with silliness, but I do want to entertain you. And since this is my daydream, I get to decide what we talk about. So let me finish this little Fluffernutter story?"

"I'm listening," says a contemplative Henry.

"Well, I should reveal that this frivolous proposal originated with a group of schoolchildren. This has been going on for some time now. In years past, the legislature has passed lots of such bills, adding to the growing list of official state symbols. Believe it or not, Massachusetts has lots of official foods. I won't bore you with the full list, but the Official State Bean is the navy bean. You might approve of that one since you grew them in your garden. Other official state foods include: Boston crème donut, corn muffin, chocolate chip cookie, and Boston crème pie. The Official State Beverage is cranberry juice. The Official State Folk Song is "Massachusetts" by Arlo Guthrie, who happens to live in a trail town. And the Official State Polka Song is a rousing little number called, "Say hello to someone from Massachusetts." The Official State Colors are green and cranberry. And the Official State Blues Artist is the great Taj Mahal. I'm thinking of nominating myself for Official State Thru-hiker.

"I'm sorry to say, Henry, you're not the official Massachusetts state anything. And once again this year nobody promoted you to be a state symbol. Not the Official State Author or Philosopher or Abolitionist or Conservationist or Surveyor or Saint. Nothing.

"Meanwhile, Henry, schoolchildren from around the state promoted not just the Fluffernutter as the Official State Sandwich but also the elephant as the Official State Mammal, and six as the Official State Number."

"Did any of these attempts succeed?" asks a frowning Henry, who seems bemused by the prospect of elephants roaming freely in the commonwealth.

"No," I say, "the legislature opted not to draft bills for any of these, perhaps because they feared a media backlash, laced with ridicule."

"Well," says Henry, "methinks it will not be long now until groups of schoolchildren in Massachusetts begin petitioning their legislators to draft a bill to make marijuana the official state medicinal plant."

"Good one, Hank! A few more doozies like that and I'll be nominating you for Official State Humorist!"

CONNECTICUT: The *Counterfeit* Nutmeg State

A couple days later, I cross my fourth state-line, into Connecticut, the state with the medial silent <c>, the Constitution/Nutmeg State.

I won't be here long. I've never been one to dally in Connecticut. I spent a night in Danbury once. That was too long. (There were too many Yankees fans.) And before that I once played in a 64-team, *triple*-elimination indoor soccer tournament at the University of Connecticut in Storrs. We expected to spend the weekend. But fresh off the bus, we suffered one of those demoralizing losses, this one to the NCAA Division 1 National Champion UConn Huskies, one-to-nil, on a last-second goal. At 9:30 AM, our record stood at 0-1. We then dropped two more games in rapid succession. We were showered up and back on the bus by noon and out of the state by 2 PM. Compared to that brief foray into the Nutmeg State, this time I'll be here long enough to qualify for resident status.

Actually, my stay will be brief this time as well because the trail's easy and it's even shorter than it is easy. It's only 52 miles to the New York border. The trail's short meander across the northwest corner befits the Nutmeg State, though, which after all is tiny itself. It's 48th of 50. It's not Rhode Island or Delaware tiny, but Rhode Island and Delaware aren't really legit states, so you wouldn't really want to brag about how much bigger than Rhode Island and Delaware you are, right? Anyway, with 52 trail miles inside its borders, the Nutmeg State claims 2.4% of the entire trail, which is more than it deserves based on its miniscule area. You see, Connecticut comprises just 1.4% of the combined land area for the trail states. So, Connecticut, your trail segment is already excessively long. Let's not get greedy.

Speaking of greed, Connecticut and New Jersey put all other trail states in their place when it comes to wealth. Don't get me wrong, the folks in trail towns to the north aren't exactly lining up for bread or soup or to donate blood so they can buy lunch. And even Monsonians and Caratunkians are wealthy on a global scale, considering that half of our fellow Earthlings have less than $3 per day in purchase power. But the trail townsfolk in Connecticut are especially well off. The per capita income in the trail towns here ($41,332) exceeds that of Maine's Monson, Caratunk, Rangeley, Andover, and Stratton ($16,789) by 246%. By Nutmeg standards, this is equivalent to saying that the folks in Maine trail towns switch from paid to volunteer positions each year on May 28th. Ouch.

I'm still a few days' walk north of bona fide Appalachia (pronunciation: \ⵊa-pⵊ-ⵊla-chⵊ\), but even so I imagined the trail here in the northwest corner of the state would pass through something vaguely akin to quasi-Appalachia. Not so much, although I was bamboozled for a couple hours on day one. I had just finished walking alongside and photographing the first *corn field* of my thru-hike. I labeled the photo – "Come on, CT, you're better than that!" – and e-mailed it to a trailfriend. I then crossed US 7, climbed several hundred feet up the little ridge pretentiously called Easter Mt., and walked on toward West Cornwall Road. Still unsuspecting, I began hearing a racket off in the distance. It got louder as I walked southward. I was baffled by the whining and roaring and screeching. What an incongruous cacophony. This was the wrong time (seven decades too late) and place (a half dozen trail states too far north). What I heard sounded like a sensationalistic, made-for-TV Appalachian stereotype. It sounded like moonshiners outrunning revenuers. Maybe locals were using that corn field as their source for mash? What next, a still? I continued on, trying to make sense of it all. Why hadn't anyone warned me about this?

Believe or not, I soon came to realize there's an auto racetrack just a fraction of a mile from the trail. Talk about an affront!

But any misguided impression about being in moonshining-cum-NASCAR country was abruptly recalibrated when I hitched into the next trail town, West Cornwall. This town, like the others here, is a Richie Richville. My brief confusion about the racetrack notwithstanding, the whole Connecticut segment feels more like the Affluenzan Trail than the Appalachian Trail.

The trail townsfolk here would never self-identify as Appalachian Americans. Their cultural history has little to do with economic injustice, tobacco farming, black lung disease, or fiddle music. They don't even sound Appalachian. I don't want to perpetuate positive stereotypes, but these folks enunciate like their former headmasters at the area's elite prep schools, where they lettered in lacrosse and fencing. Of course, it's true some of the locals were underprivileged. I even met one woman who had to attend – gasp – a public university.

But these townsfolk are like townsfolk everywhere along the trail in at least one way: they're bursting with civic pride. You don't even need to prompt them to talk about their favorite topic. Not the ecology or cultural history along the trail. Not the Native Americans who preceded them. Not the key historical players post "European contact." No, they talk spontaneously and proudly about the obscenely wealthy celebrities who live in their town. In Salisbury, they brag about their "neighbor," the great actor Meryl Streep, as if they sometimes help her review scripts. In Sharon, they talk about movie-star couples – Kyra Sedgwick and her hubby Kevin Bacon and Tracy Pollan and her hubby Michael J. Fox – as if they just might go golfing or sailing or antiquing with these beloved neighbors over the weekend. In Cornwall, they regale me with tales of partying with Whoopie Goldberg "back in the day" and then they report that Tom Jones – the composer of *The Fantastiks*, not the Welch crooner with the tight trousers – stopped by for a sandwich just a few minutes ago. I *just* missed him. And, in Kent, they either rave about or downplay their role in harboring Henry Kissinger, winner of the Nobel Peace Prize and noted warmonger. It's a syndrome, this trail town obsession with celebrity.

To compensate, I developed a counter ploy. Every time someone started namedropping about local mansion-dwellers, I'd say, "Hey, do you happen to know why Connecticut is called the Nutmeg State?" They all took the bait. They bluffed. They told presumably apocryphal tales about sailors carving counterfeit nutmegs out of wood for months on end while at sea, duping unsuspecting buyers once ashore and thereby making windfall profits. Maybe this explains how Connecticut Yankees became so rich, I mean originally, before the recent massively unethical hedge-fund payday.

And if the townsfolk tried to shift the topic back to their favorite local celebrities, I'd blurt out, "Hey, did you hear about that recent bank robbery in Cornwall Bridge?"

Again, everyone took the bait and they all had their own unique corrupted version to tell. Here's an example.

"How much did the robbers get?" I ask.

"Two lousy dollars," she says in an authoritative tone.

"Why so little? What went wrong?" I ask.

"Well, the guy who did the robbery got a whole bag of cash, but when he ran to the getaway car, which his girlfriend – she's from Sharon – was waiting in out behind the bank, he fell down a steep bank and the gun went off and the bullet went right though his femur. The money, all but two dollars, fell right into the river. His girlfriend tried to swim after it, but the current was too strong. Plus her boyfriend was in the process of dying, so she turned back. She helped him into the car and drove to the hospital. The cops around here usually aren't too swift, but they put two and two together and actually got four this time. They arrested him in his hospital bed. What a jackass!"

"What about the woman, the getaway driver? She was an accomplice, right? Did she go to prison too?" I ask.

"She's probably out now, on probation, but I did hear she was arrested for conspiracy to commit stupidity."

"Good one! But tell me, did the judge make them return the two dollars to the bank?" I ask.

"Not as far as I know," she says.

"Well, that's not a bad haul, then," I say. "In Massachusetts, that's enough to pay off two jaywalking fines. Of course, he probably won't be doing much jaywalking with that shrapnel in his leg, even after he gets out of the big house."

Maybe some schoolchildren will petition the state legislature to honor these two trail townsfolk with the recognition they so richly deserve: Official Connecticut State Bank Robbers.

NEW YORK: I'm Walkin' Here

As I cross my fifth state-line, into New York, I'm prepared for anything. Or so I thought. I'd heard rumors, of course. But I had no idea that I'd spend the next few days having this one recurrent thought: "This is so surreal." Or as some of the kids on the trail would say, "dude, this is like literally so surreal."

On day one, I arrive at NY 22, at the "Appalachian Trail" stop on the New York City commuter train, Metro North. How surreal, I think. I could hop on the next inbound train, switch to the C-line at Grand Central, and I'd arrive at the American Museum of Natural History in not much more time than it will take me to walk to the seedy motel up the road, in the town of Wingdale. I opt for the seedy motel.

Wingdale is surreal too. I'm not in Connecticut anymore, that's for sure. Wingdale is one of those angry broken-down upstate New York towns that had its heyday a while back. According to locals I meet, Wingdale flourished "before the prison shut down." Folks would arrive in droves on the commuter train, especially on weekends, to visit their incarcerated kin. The place was a bustling burgh, a going concern. Now it's a strip of liquor stores, literally.

The next day, back on the trail, I arrive at a quiet country road, the West Dover Road, and I can't believe my eyes, figuratively. It's the biggest oak tree I've ever seen, in my whole life, literally. I continue on, pausing to read the register at the Telephone Pioneers Shelter. That's what it's called, literally. Then I tiptoe along the shoreline of Nuclear Lake, site of a decommissioned nuclear fuels processing facility, literally. I arrive at the RHP Shelter well after hiker midnight. The place is packed. All the bunks are occupied. I wake everyone, literally, by cranking the very squeaky water pump. The water is liquid rust, literally. I sleep under the stars – figuratively, because the sky's completely overcast. I end the day listening to traffic on I-87. It's so loud that it feels like I'm camping in the median strip.

The next evening I arrive at the Graymoor Spiritual Life Center, a Franciscan monastery where the monks graciously welcome thru-hikers to camp at the ballfield pavilion. Is that surreal or what? New York has just ratcheted up its surrealism a few notches.

In the morning, I stroll down the hill from the friary and stop at the convenience store at the US 9/NY 403 junction. I'm sitting outside, eating back-to-back breakfasts, when who should appear but one of my favorite SOBOs, Lil' Quantum. She yells with joy when she spots me. Distracted by our imminent reunion, she injudiciously darts out into heavy traffic. She nearly ends her thru-hike right on the spot. But she's nimble and manages to jump backwards and so lives to hike another day. With me!

We cruise along together, lost in the moment, savoring each other's company and chatting like it's our job. She's verbal and bright and, like her fellow Quakers, she might not speak in tongues, but she sure does think in tongues. I admire her brain, athleticism, boldness, kindness, and most of all her unwavering positive attitude. A lot of hikers say they love the trail, but when Quantum says it, she really means it. She loves the whole thru-hiking experience, privies and all.

A few miles down the trail we're suddenly confronted with the biggest dose of surrealism yet. It feels like we've just stepped through the looking glass. We've arrived at the Hudson River and its enormous bridge, once the longest suspension span bridge in the world. We pause at the midpoint, flanked by Sing Sing Prison a few miles downriver and West Point a few miles upriver. But the bizarre juxtapositions are just beginning. When we get to the other shore, we'll be walking straight through a zoo. I kid you not. After crossing Bear Mountain Bridge, we'll follow the white blazes right through Bear Mountain Zoo, past Bear Mountain Inn, and then up and over Bear Mountain, which just so happens to be in Bear Mountain State Park.

Lil Quantum and I detect a pattern here. We notice that virtually everything around these parts is called Bear Mountain something or other. We discuss the possibility of going to Bear Mountain Outfitters in the town of Bear Mountain and getting some Bear Mountain Ice Cream along the way back to Bear Mountain. We rename Sing Sing the Bear Mountain Correctional Facility and West Point the Bear Mountain Military Academy. While we're on a roll, we speculate that every little hill between here and the New Jersey state-line is called Bear Mountain. Little did we know: no fewer than 11 hills in the state of New York bear the name Bear Mountain. Eleven. That's a bunch.

Passing through the zoo –Bear Mountain Zoo, that is – we pause to commiserate at the lowest point on the entire Appalachian Trail. It's the lowest point both literally because it's just 124 feet above sea level and figuratively because it's right in front of the maximum-security enclosure where the black bear inmates are held, just upriver from maximum-security Sing Sing. So surreal.

Minutes later, Lil Quantum and I pause at Hessian Lake, a blatant misnomer, at the far side of zoo. She plans to power up and over little Bear Mountain and continue on for miles and miles. She's chasing down one of her platonic trail husbands. I love hiking with her, but I have my own agenda and so we hug huge and say fare thee well and miss you already. I do an about-face and then march solo toward town, just for fun, just to see what trail-town absurdities might materialize.

Bear Mountain, the town, doesn't let me down. I spend the evening chatting with a local fellow who spent years as a homeless troll living under the Bear Mountain Bridge. He now lives in town where he's turned his home into a shrine to Benedict Arnold, literally.

In the morning, I walk back through the zoo, along the shore of Hessian Lake, and then up Bear Mountain. As I'm racing along I overtake a middle-aged hetero-couple apparently out for a day hike. I gather they're still in the honeymoon phase as I approach from behind. I stop and chat for a few minutes. They're curious about the thru-hike phenomenon and want to ask loads of questions. I'm curious about them too, but I want to ask just three questions. I ask whether it's their first date, whether they met online, and whether they met in person for the first time just an hour or so ago. They're blown away. They want to know how I intuited all of this. "Easy," I say, "the give-away was the very high frequency of stopping and putting your tongues in each other's mouth. If we thru-hikers were to engage in foreplay like that, it would take two calendar years to complete the hike."

A few minutes later, I arrive at the top of Bear Mountain. More surrealism: I can see the Manhattan skyline, but I can't seem to find the next white blaze anywhere. I find some blazes, but they don't seem to be official A.T. blazes. They don't meet specifications. They're white but not two inches wide. They're two skinny. And they have an unfilled red circle superimposed on the white background. I tell myself, that can't be the trail, it must be some sort of side-trail, don't follow it, keep looking for the real trail. To prevent myself from chasing those irregular blazes, I sit down and drink some water. And I think about the general direction the trail should be heading over the next day or two. Those funky blazes seem to lead too far off course. I keep stalling. Finally, in one last search around the area, I notice a legitimate white blaze – under a parked car! The car is parked illegally. You guessed it: Massachusetts license plate.

I write a "tactful" note to put under the windshield wiper. And then I follow the legitimate white blazes. Back on the proper trail, I'll be in Jersey and shit before you know it.

A couple of days later, along came my trailfriend, Zamboni. Apparently mesmerized by all this Bear Mountain surrealism, he made the gaffe I'd barely avoided. He followed those curious white blazes, the too-skinny ones with the red circle. He followed them, even though he knew he shouldn't. He kept telling himself he shouldn't be following them, even as he continued to do so. The skinny-blaze trail didn't seem to be heading in the right direction, but he didn't have a map. Besides, he knew the A.T. sometimes meanders off in a strange direction but eventually turns back toward Georgia. And those funky blazes were the only white blazes he could find. And everything about the trail here was so weird anyway, so why would he expect the blazes to remain the same as they'd always been? Besides, these blazes were white and white blazes have always been the proper blazes to follow. So, he continued following the skinny white blazes with the open red circles.

Suddenly, he saw a lake. Not just any lake. Not an unfamiliar lake. It was Hessian Lake, the lake next to the zoo, on the northeast side of Bear Mountain. It was the lake he had just walked alongside before climbing Bear Mountain, only to follow some bullshit trail back down to it – in the wrong direction, toward Katahdin.

He lost it. He had a meltdown. He cried. He cursed a blue streak. He threw his trekking poles into the lake, flinging them like javelins as far as he could. He thought they'd float. They didn't.

Even in this state of mind, he noticed a family of four hominids scuttling away, with the parents shielding their offspring as if they were newborn muskoxen and Zamboni was a half-starved wolf.

Next he threw his pack, like a hammer-thrower spinning round and round and grunting mightily as he heaved it. Kerplunk. The pack sank too.

Then, with nothing left to throw, he turned and glowered at his onlookers. Needless to say, he was quite the spectacle. A whole Peter Pan busload of torons had stopped photographing each other long enough to watch his spontaneous improv performance. He bowed deeply at the waist and then swam out to fetch his pack and poles.

Once back on dry land, Zamboni quickly regained his composure. He spent a few minutes wringing out his gear. He repeated his mantra. He walked over to a vending machine and bought two cans of soda. He guzzled them one after the other, belched as loudly as he could, waved to his fans, and trotted away from the scene. He claims he rescaled Bear Mountain in record time, despite all of that extra "water weight."

Zamboni doesn't know it yet, but I've renamed him. His new trailname is "Bear Mountainman." I think I'll petition the state legislature to have him designated as New York's Official Bear Mountain Climber.

NEW JERSEY: We Don't Expect Too Much

As I cross my sixth state-line, into New Jersey, the Garden State, I can't help but sing John Gorka's lyric, "I'm from New Jersey, I don't expect too much."

That lyric suggests a sound policy for thru-hikers: leave your unrealistically high expectations at the state-line, you've just entered Jersey and shit, and we're not making any promises. Sure enough, immediately upon crossing the state-line I can see Jersey's bad attitude in full display.

You see, there's a do-not sign for virtually every imaginable human activity. It's all banned. In some of the northern states, there's effectively a laissez-fair policy on human activities. In Maine, it's anything goes. In New Hampshire, there's a single sign at each trailhead listing rules and regulations, but the font is so teensy that the sign might as well not exist. I wasn't about to dig out my reading glasses just to read the minor infractions I'd soon be committing. In New Jersey, there's no wiggle room for claiming ignorance about the rules. Signs are posted everywhere. I didn't keep a running tally, but I'd bet $74, one for each Jersey trail mile, these signs vastly outnumber white blazes.

I know what you're thinking. "Come on, Ledge, get on with it. Stop being all hyperbolic and just tell us already what's banned along the trail in Jersey."

OK, here's a brief rundown. In New Jersey, don't even think about lighting a fire. Forget about it. And there's no swimming. And even camping is totally out the question for much of the Jersey segment. In Alaska you can camp on the front lawn of the administration building on the Alaska Pacific University campus, in Anchorage. (My brother, The Barnacle, has done it – after the campus police suggested it.) In Jersey, you can't camp along the A.T., except along special sections with very specific restrictions. Where the C-word is ever so grudgingly permitted, it must be done within 50 feet of the trail or within a narrow band: no closer than X feet and no farther than X+Y feet. But this doesn't apply if there's a posted "danger zone," in which case you must stay on the trail at all times. Even glancing in the direction of a danger zone is verboten. And whether near a danger zone or not, hikers are repeatedly warned against bear-hunting. (I decided not to poach a bear because I wouldn't have been allowed to light a fire to cook it.) And another thing, while hiking along the trail in Jersey, don't even think about shooting narrow-tipped arrows. I'm dead serious, there's a strict ban on narrow-tipped arrows. Now, I don't wanna get all epistemological, but my inference is that it's perfectly OK to use *broad*-tipped arrows, to your heart's content. Just don't shoot 'em within 30 feet of the bonfire next to your rogue campsite inside a danger zone.

And if you get busted for any of these transgressions, whatever you do, don't smile at the law enforcement officer. There's no smiling, of course. And don't be tempted to laugh or hitch-hike. This is Jersey and shit.

But I'm a scofflaw, so starting with my first night, I began breaking the rules. I camped under the stars atop a massive glacial erratic boulder within arm's reach of the trail. I was out of view, but I still didn't sleep well. I tossed and turned worrying that I'd be busted at first light for snoring in a danger zone.

OK, I know what you're thinking. "Man, Ledge, you're pretty down on Jersey. There's gotta be *something* good about hiking the A.T. in Jersey. For instance, how 'bout if you tell us which trail town you hated the least?"

Funny you should ask. It just so happens I spent the next night in the best trail town in New Jersey. Which town is that, you ask? Well, it's unanimous. Every thru-hiker agrees the best trail town in New Jersey, by far, is: Unionville, **New York**. That's cold, I know, but it's true. We all wandered four tenths of a mile into Unionville and gathered at The Mayor's free hiker hostel, "The Outhouse," to get pampered and inspired for a night or two or three.

That's where I met Sarsaparilla, a seemingly harmless NOBO. I asked about his stunning white dreadlocks. He said nothing. I asked why he'd fallen so far behind the bulk of the NOBOs. This got a reaction. He explained he was actually a superfast hiker, but he'd fallen behind due to his time-consuming habit of going into each trail town and sacrificing one human life. I laughed. He didn't.

I didn't sleep well that night.

Back on the trail in the morning, I walked for a few hours with Jelly Belly and Beagle. We were models of rule-abiding hiking. Beagle peed on the trail, like he always does, but we saw no sign explicitly banning that uncouth behavior. We arrived at Culver's Gap (US 206) early that afternoon and decided to have lunch together at the local biker bar. I had a ketchup-on-cardboard pizza-like concoction and a watered-down, artificially carbonated, cat-pee-style domestic draft beer. Bellies full, Jelly Belly and Beagle got right back on the trail, but I had my own agenda so I lagged behind.

The first item on my agenda was to find a better eatery and have a second "linner." I wandered over to Kevin's Steak House, which lived up to its billing as a hiker-friendly establishment. I jotted down a brilliant aphorism or, more likely, some truly pedestrian observation in their hiker register. I ate my second linner and quaffed a legit ale.

Then I shifted my attention to the second agenda item. I walked over to the deli right next to the trail. I'd been warned against going there. But I had to see for myself. I just had to check out the infamous ogre who runs the place. His reputation is so bad that his deli, despite being practically on the trail, wasn't listed in my trail guide. And the word on the trail is all bad. But, for me, all the admonitions against patronizing his place had the predictable unintended effect: they backfired. I couldn't boycott him because I needed to know whether he was really as bad as everyone claimed.

I prop my pack against the outside wall, take a deep breath, and open the door.

"Put your pack on the other side of the door!" He barks.

"Oh, sorry, yes, of course," I say, trying not to sound like a sycophant. And I think, wow, that's priceless. Rumors confirmed, just like that!

I move my pack and try again. This time I'm in. I start grabbing candy bars and piling them on the counter, so as to avoid getting evicted for loitering or pumped full of lead projectiles for looking like a ne'er-do-well shoplifter.

Then I start chatting him up. I have a plan. My goal is not to hug him or take his photo or convince him to sing a "Kum Bay Ya" duet with me. Nope, my goal's modest. This is Jersey after all and I'm trying not to expect too much. My goal is to get him to do two things: 1) smile and 2) utter that quintessential Jersey expression, "and shit." It takes a while, maybe 10 minutes, to get him to do #1. But I prevail. He smiles. OK, maybe it was a smirk, but it definitely bordered on a smile and it wasn't a grimace. But I can't seem to induce him to do #2, to say the verbal tic "and shit." I finally give up. I say so long and head for the door. And then, as if right on cue, he orders, "Eat on the bench around the corner, where no one can see you and shit."

He's not smiling now. But I am.

Sitting on his hiker-dedicated bench, I ponder that expression. Is it really endemic to Jersey or is that just an urban myth? I pause long enough to do 14 Google searches. The first one, for "jersey and shit," yields 61,000 hits! The next 13 searches, one for "Maine and shit," another for "New Hampshire and shit," and so on, ending with "Georgia and shit," yield virtually no hits (0-8). Imagine that, just when you think the whole country's become one bland homogeneous place, it turns out New Jersey's cultural uniqueness remains intact.

And maybe the fine folks from Jersey are onto something with their low expectations. I heard recently that a researcher in the emerging area of Happiness Studies discovered that the happiest nation in the world these days is Denmark. Why? Well, apparently, Danes are so happy because, like their grumpy counterparts from Jersey, they don't expect too much. By keeping their expectations realistically low, they tend not to get derailed by life's little and big inevitabilities.

As I glide along the Kittatinny Ridge toward the southern end of Jersey's segment, at Delaware Water Gap, I think about two of my favorite trailfriends, Sad Hands and Chin Music. They happen to hail from the happy Garden State. They're lagging behind, by two or three days. I send 'em a text message to ask when they're going to catch up. Chin Music texts back twice in rapid succession. The first message contains unhappy news: Sad Hands has suffered a hike-ending foot injury and so they're both off the trail. But that's OK because they didn't expect too much from the thru-hike experience. The second message contains happy news: they're "movin 2 boulder & shit."

PENNSYLVANIA: Where Hiking Boots Go to Die

As I cross my seventh state-line, into Pennsylvania, the Quaker/Keystone State, I have a pretty good idea what's in store. Or do I?

We SOBOs have already entered the Ridge-and-Valley region of the A.T. We've become ridge-walkers. We've spent the past couple of days walking along the ridge of Blue Mountain, beginning in northwestern New Jersey where the ridge was affectionately called the Kittatinny Mountains. Nearly all of us have ignored this nomenclature *and* we've overlooked the fact that we've begun migrating slowly along a single distinct ridge.

After dipping down to Delaware Water Gap and popping back up, we'll spend the next 150 miles walking along this single narrow ridge of Blue Mountain. We'll spend most of our time within a narrow range of elevations, between 1400 and 1700 feet above sea level, on this single mountain. And we, most of us, won't even notice. We won't notice a lot of things it turns out. We'll hike with heads down, disconnected from the natural world, oblivious to miracles around us. We'll hike on autopilot.

The NOBOs we met weeks ago warned us about the pointy rocks of Pennsylvania. And we've joked about Pennsylvania's being as flat as a pancake. We've known for weeks now that the number of times we'll be climbing above 6000 feet or 5500 or

5000 or 4500 or 4000 or 3500 or 3000 or 2500 or even 2300 feet is the same: zero!

We've also heard about the unwild nature of the trail, the high density of roads and humans and pizza places that deliver to shelters. And we've heard rave reviews of some of the trail towns, including Delaware Water Gap, Port Clinton, and Duncannon.

Remarkably, though, nobody's told us that, for the first time along the trail, we'll be walking along a single very long, narrow ridge – for weeks. Nobody's told us we're on the verge of this dramatic switch from hiking mountain-to-mountain throughout each day to hiking on a single mountain for days on end. Since that first day on Katahdin, we haven't spent anywhere near a full day hiking on a single mountain. But now we'll be residents on a single mountain, while slowly migrating toward Georgia along this skinny ridge. And no one says a word? Go figure.

Satellite imagery would make us thru-hikers look like barely visible smurf-hiking homunculi walking single file along a rib on corduroy pants, where the cuff corresponds to Big Gap, near Shippensburg. This mountain ridge, our new home away from home, is a hundred times longer than it is wide. And we'll be marching along this rib without realizing it.

This ridge-walking means the trail is straighter here, and in Maryland, than anywhere else on the trail. Actual trail miles (232) exceed the straight-line distance between the ends of the trail in Pennsylvania by 52%. In Maine, where the trail meanders around massive lakes, the trail is 102% longer than the straight-line distance covered. Likewise, in North Carolina and Tennessee, where switchbacks are the rule, the distance walked is also twice as long as the straight-line displacement. But no one mentions how straight the trail will be.

Thru-hikers are oblivious everywhere, but especially so in Pennsylvania. They're oblivious to their own near-linear pathway along a single ridge, perhaps because they're walking with head down focusing on foot placement like they haven't had to do since New Hampshire. Here the trail demands this kind of attention because, as the joke goes, the folks who maintain the trail here do so with a file in each hand. And they use these files to sharpen the rocks, to make the trail challenging. They do this to make your feet hurt, to distract you so much that you don't even realize there are no mountains, other than the little narrow rib-like one you're living on.

But as we stumble-marched over all those pointy rocks, we were oblivious to more than our own pathway along that ridge. We SOBOs were also oblivious to a parallel migration event, taking place right overhead along the Appalachian migratory flyway. That's right, nearly all of us were oblivious to 20,000 or so raptors – hawks, eagles, and falcons – also migrating south right above the trail.

But while our migratory pathways were one and the same, any resemblance ended there. While we few hominid SOBOs stumbled, the multitudinous avian SOBOs soared. We fumbled; our aerial counterparts glided. We blabbed; they made nary a peep. They rode thermals and glided gracefully and silently, most of them hardly flapping a wing. And they traveled down the A.T. right along the same narrow ridge in this graceful, presumably pain-free aerial way, in just one day.

The buteos, in particular, ascend by spiraling in thermals right above the trail and then set their wings and glide southward following our ridge, their ridge. By repeating this spiral-ascent-and-glide process, they travel all the way to Maryland – in one day. That's *their* Pennsylvania Challenge.

During the middle two weeks of September 2009, 6585 raptors summed across 17 species were counted by observers as they passed overhead at Hawk Mountain Sanctuary, a blue-blaze hop and a skip from the A.T. Accounting for nearly half of this total were the 2928 broad-winged hawks that passed overhead, southbound, in a two-day period, September 16-17. The thermals were filled with swirling raptors on those days. I noticed.

I also noticed that none of the other terrestrial SOBOs noticed. Heads down, grimacing with foot pain, they gingerly stepped on or between Avogadro's number of pointy rocks, missing the raptorial splendor overhead. They were hiking through Rocksylvania while I stumble-hiked through Hawksylvania.

But all of us observed a different sort of aerial display in Pennsylvania. It's not like we're permanently incapable of glancing skyward, even while negotiating all those pointy rocks. No, it turned out we remained perfectly capable of looking up and did so each time the US military suddenly induced us to do so. I'd be walking along, loving the trail, pausing now and then to enjoy the overhead parade of avian SOBOs. And then, when I least expected it: yet another deafening strafing attack. Talk about Homeland Insecurity! These fighter jets caught us unaware not just because we had our heads down but also because they traveled just a shade under the speed of light. One instant they didn't exist, the next instant they were just above the canopy and every molecule in our bodies got jittered. Needless to say, getting repeatedly staggered by the sonic boom of strafing jets was an affront to my thru-hiking experience. But these flyovers did make the trail in Pennsylvania less challenging, by shocking the scat out of us and taking our mind off our foot pain. As a bonus, the lingering physiological effect of each of these jolts was on par with two 20-ounce cappuccinos. And we didn't even have to carry coffee to reap this benefit.

Eventually, the A.T. would turn away from this ridge and cross miles of corn fields on the way to the Maryland border. I would enjoy this reprieve from pointy rocks and look forward to lovely footing all the way to Springer.

MARYLAND: Come Camp at Camp David

As I arrive at my eighth state-line, at the Pennsylvania-Maryland border, I realize I'm straddling the historic Mason-Dixon Line and the present-day starting line for SOBOs attempting the Maryland and Four-State Challenges.

Ahead, the trail cuts straight through the skinny panhandle of Maryland. It's just 41 miles to the Potomac River where the trail crosses ever so briefly into Harpers Ferry, West Virginia. Because the trail through Maryland is so short, straight, and easy some thru-hikers choose to power through in a single day. That's the Maryland Challenge.

Alternatively, thru-hikers with machismo to burn stage here just inside Pennsylvania and cross into Maryland at the stroke of midnight. Walking with headlamps, they pass through about half of Maryland before sunrise. They do the remaining miles in a few more hours. That evening, they cross over the Potomac into Harpers Ferry and then right back across the Shenandoah River, arriving at the border of Virginia before midnight. They cover 43.5 miles, crossing three state-lines and setting foot in four states, in one day. That's the Four-State Challenge.

I decide to take a different approach. I challenge myself not to accept these challenges. I have nothing against seeing Maryland in the light of day. I decide instead to dilly and dally and poke along rather than blast on through. I will not be accepting the Maryland Challenge, never mind the Four-State Challenge. I'm not tempted.

Meanwhile, trailfriends, Zamboni and Strawberry Shortcake, did the Four-State Challenge without me. According to Zamboni, I faked a chronic injury (shin splints). He called me names and trash talked and otherwise hurt my feelings.

The truth is I just wanted to walk alone.

They completed the Four-state Challenge with time to spare. So, Zamboni made a sales pitch: "Hey, Strawberry, we've walked 43.5 miles already today, right? And we're feeling OK. Not great, but OK, right? So, why not go another 6.5 and make it an even half century. Fifty miles in one day, that'd be pretty cool, right? Come on, come on, whaddya say, Strawberry, let's do it?"

Strawberry Shortcake, the less-talkative one, said, "OK."

But when they reached the 50-mile point, they realized the next shelter was just another 1.7 miles farther down the trail. Naturally, Zamboni cajoled Strawberry into continuing on to the shelter, which completed their 51.7-mile day, with 18 minutes and 7 seconds to spare.

Zamboni then went off the trail for five days, which he spent shopping with his mommy while his feet were on the mend. Strawberry limped southward through Virginia, which takes more than 24 hours to walk through. It takes more like 240 hours. But I digress.

I'm still glad I didn't join them. My leisurely solo stroll through Maryland's short straight segment gave me time for contemplation. I was entertaining myself thinking about the young hetero-couple who did the Maryland Challenge together a few years ago. As I heard the story, they hadn't been seeing each other very long, but the guy took a chance and proposed marriage somewhere around Mile 29. She answered in the affirmative. And this story makes me think of the Greg Brown lyric, "Betty Ann, Betty Ann, marry me while you can."

But then I had an epiphany! I got to thinking about Camp David, the nearby Presidential retreat. I recall hearing about Dubya (or "Shrub," as Molly Ivins nicknamed him) spending oodles of time there while he was in office. He liked to chill there, when he wasn't on the ranch in Crawford. He'd ride around Camp David on his mountain bike, listening to country music on his iPod and making up little white lies about weapons of mass destruction and his face-to-face meeting with Jesus and so on. But these days, Camp David doesn't seem to get much use. As far as I know, Obama buzzes over in the helicopter for church service once a week and that's about it. I'd hate to see the place fall into disrepair.

Meanwhile, Maryland's A.T. segment is much too short and too straight as well. You see where I'm headed?

OK, here's my proposal. I'm just floating the idea. Let's start with a little background. Camp David was built in the 1930s by the CCC, like the A.T. itself. It was a camp for federal employees, until FDR sequestered it for his own private use as a health spa. He had terrible sinus problems, you see. Well, as far as I know, Barack has perfect sinus health. Isn't it high time, then, to restore the camp's original public function? I think so.

Just imagine Barack dispensing with that tired old tradition of hogging Camp David as an exclusive retreat. With one left-handed stroke of the Presidential pen, he could open the grounds to hikers a la the Graymoor friary in New York. The white blazes could lead right up to the front door of the main Presidential cabin. But if they don't want a bunch of filthy thru-hikers besmirching the good linens in the main Presidential cabin, we'd be glad to slum it in the smaller outlying cabins or just sleep under the stars on the putting green or driving range.

Now before you naysayers start listing cons, let's review some of the pros. Rumor has it Camp David features babbling brooks and excellent views. FDR supposedly called the place "Shangri-La," before it got renamed for Eisenhower's grandson. And just think of the built-in recreational opportunities at the Obama A.T. Retreat: swimming, basketball, tennis, mountain biking, billiards, ping pong. Presumably, there's a decent library. After all, some of our Presidents since FDR have been learned. And, finally, the grounds are already under jurisdiction of the National Park Service, like the A.T., so this plan shouldn't turn into one of those bureaucratic nightmares you hear about.

OK, presuming Camp David will soon put out the welcome mat, this seems like a good time to consider how best to reroute the A.T. Currently, the trail passes within about a mile and a half of the western edge of Catoctin Mountain Park, which encompasses Camp David. The presidential compound is about three miles farther into the park. So, we could reroute the A.T. by making the white blazes run right through the compound and then loop back to the original trail, which would add about 11 miles to Maryland's segment.

This new meander would go a long way towards legitimizing Maryland as a trail state. Its segment is currently 41 miles long, surpassing only West Virginia's, but West Virginia isn't really a trail state. Lengthening the trail from 41 to 52 miles would get Maryland out of the cellar, putting it in a tie with Connecticut for last place among trail states.

To keep the total length of the A.T. fixed at 2179, 11 miles could be trimmed from some other state's segment. I nominate Virginia, where 11 miles could be trimmed simply by straightening some of those extraneous puppy switchbacks. And Virginia would retain its #1 ranking for trail miles, by a very wide margin. Everyone wins.

∞

I won't bother Barack with this admittedly frivolous request right now. I know he's busy (squandering his mandate). He has a very long to-do list. Let's see, there's the fixing of the corrupt-from-the-start health care system, the getting out of Iraq and Afghanistan, the moving toward a steady state economy and thereby saving millions of species from extinction, the broader need to move toward true ecological sustainability, and so on. Big things. And this proposal, my little idea for A.T. utopia, would be at or near the bottom of that list. Maybe I'll pester him with this proposal during his second term, when he starts sweating the small stuff.

And I truly do appreciate how busy he is. The last I heard he was up half the night filling out his bracket for that men's March Madness basketball tournament thingy.

WEST VIRGINIA: Almost 0.1% of the Trail

As I cross my ninth state-line, across the Potomac River and into *West* Virginia, I'm also on the verge of crossing my tenth state-line, back across the Shenandoah River and into Virginia.

West Virginia is simultaneously both the least prominent and most prominent trail state. Let's face it, West Virginia is really just a mighty fine trail town, Harpers Ferry. It's not really a trail *state*. At its deepest point into West Virginia, the trail is less than three quarters of a mile from the borders of both Virginia and Maryland. It never veers more than a few hundred feet from the banks of the Shenandoah River. It doesn't even leave the little peninsular municipality of Harpers Ferry. And yet West Virginia is one of the most prominent of the trail states because it's the ritualistic midpoint for many thru-hikers.

Forget about the fact that Harpers Ferry is arguably the nexus of US history. Forget about its harboring the likes of Stonewall Jackson. Forget about John Brown's raid on Harpers Ferry, which aimed to trigger a slave uprising. Forget about its role in the civil rights movement. Forget about all that. Thru-hikers care most about the tradition of marching to the ATC headquarters to get their Polaroid mug shot taken so it can be added to the photo album.

Once inside the building, thru-hikers love to leaf through the album perusing for trailfriends. Each photo is labeled with the date, trailname, and other bits of information, including the hiker's "town name," the name on the birth certificate. This makes hikers downright giggly as they page through and discover the real names of friends. It's routine practice to point out a trailfriend's photo and then read the town name out loud. And then laugh, hard.

Why is this so funny? Well, just imagine knowing someone by her trailname only. For months, you've known her as Lil Quantum. Then you see her "real" name. It's going to strike you funny, no matter what it is. After knowing someone for months by their trailname, her town name seems preposterous. It's like finding out that your best trailfriend has been holding out on you. She's not Lil Quantum after all. She's Mildred Butterfield. And with a town name like that, you're not sure whether you can be her friend anymore.

∞

For me, West Virginia, even this tiny little corner of it, feels like home. I've been looking forward to Harpers Ferry for a long time.

I started thinking about this place when I was still in Maine. I hadn't even started hiking yet. I was still biking toward Millinocket to begin my thru-hike when I stopped off one evening to hear live music. I was keen to see the brilliant singer-songwriter, Peter Mulvey, for the first time. I arrive at the venue early and, looking for a place to lock my bike, bump into the star of the show. Peter and I hit it off immediately. We're kindred spirits. We have dinner together. He tells me about his upcoming bicycle tour and invites me to join his entourage, as team scientist, and help spread the word about green travel. He'll be pedaling from his driveway in Milwaukee to Boston, doing about a dozen gigs along the way. I'd love to join him but I have a gig of my own, the A.T. gig.

And then he tells me about his favorite gig ever, an annual show in West Virginia. He tells me about these supposed geniuses at something called the National Youth Science Camp. He says each summer West Virginia hosts the top two science- and math-oriented high school graduates from each of the 50 states, plus some other "world geniuses." And they have lectures and play ultimate Frisbee and visit the White House and go whitewater kayaking and so on. And one of the best things they do is a spelunking trip. The entire camp – delegates, counselors, visiting lecturers, staph [sic] – goes together. They're led through a series of narrow passageways. Eventually, they arrive at a giant room with stalactites and stalagmites all around. And then a spotlight is turned on and – voila! – there sits Peter Mulvey with his guitar. It's an annual surprise, a well-guarded secret. He plays a gig right on the spot. It's a beautiful surprise for the campers and an honor for him.

At this point, I can't hold back any longer and so I say, "When I was a National Youth Science Camp delegate from Maine in 1977, we went as a group to that very cave, your venue, but you weren't there!"

"Well, I was only 7 years old. My parents wouldn't let me tour yet. All my performances took place in my bedroom in Milwaukee. But wait, what are you saying? Are you bullshitting? Were you really a delegate at NYSC? Really?

"Yep."

"I don't believe it," says Peter, "that's one helluva coincidence!"

"I know, it's crazy, right?"

"Yeah," says Peter, "I guess that's an example of the small-world phenomenon everyone talks about, but I don't think I've ever heard a better example than that."

"Same here," I say. "I guess we'll have to be friends now."

"No shit," says Peter.

So, it's a beautiful thing to be here in Harpers Ferry again, after all these years, this time singing Peter Mulvey lyrics to myself as I stroll through town, "The trouble with poets is ... they talk too much." And it occurs to me that the trouble with singer-songwriters is ... they sing too much and don't hike enough.

For even better examples of the small-world phenomenon see **A Match Made in A.T. Heaven, Our National Social Trail,** and **Hitch-hiker's Guide to the Trailaxy.**

VIRGINIA: We're for Switchback Lovers

I cross my 10th state-line, into Virginia. I'll be here awhile. I'll be living here, maybe even voting here. The trail in Virginia is a most impressive 544 miles long. If smiles are directly proportional to miles, then this section should be 10.5 times funnier than Connecticut's section, 7.3 times funnier than New Jersey's, and 3.7 times funnier than Vermont's. It won't be.

So, why is Virginia's A.T. segment so long? Is it simply an inevitable byproduct of Virginia's expansiveness? Is it because Virginia is the largest trail state of all? Nope, 'fraid not. Virginia's in a virtual tie with Tennessee for sixth largest trail state. Virginia represents just 11% of the combined land area of the 14 trail states and yet its segment represents a full 25% of the A.T.'s total mileage. If trail miles were directly proportional to area, Virginia's segment would be just 242 miles long, less than half its current length.

This raises the more accusatory question, why is Virginia's segment *excessively* long? Is it because its segment is excessively wiggly? This sounds like a plausible way of explaining away some of the excess. It's true that Virginia's segment has switchbacks galore. And they're so shallowly graded that some thru-hikers – well, me anyway – like to joke that Virginia's segment would be much shorter if some of these puppy switchbacks were eliminated. In Virginia, you get the sense that you're rarely walking south at any given moment. Instead, you're zigzagging. The vector points to Springer, but you often feel like you're making only glacial progress thanks to all those extreme switchbacks.

It's also true that the trail seems to meander excessively even where there are no switchbacks. Consider this one little factoid: the trail crisscrosses the Skyline Drive 51 times. I'm not kidding.

But these wiggles can't explain away the excessive length of Virginia's segment. Even if it were converted to a perfect line that would pass through tunnels where necessary, it would still be excessively long at 290 miles.

If it's not the zigzags and wiggles, then, once again, why is Virginia's segment so excessively long? I didn't want to say anything, but isn't it obvious? Presumably driven by greed and some residue of historical animosity, Virginia's segment is so long because *West* Virginia's is so short. As a SOBO, this seemed obvious. The trail crosses the Potomac River from Maryland into Harpers Ferry, West Virginia. It could stay in West Virginia for the next 200 or 300 miles. But it doesn't. Instead, it hugs the bank of the Shenandoah River for a mile or so and then crosses over the Shenandoah to the Virginia border. The trail stays in *West* Virginia for a macroscopic 2.4 miles. It then skirts along the Virginia side of the border for a shamelessly bloated 544 miles, which means Virginia has 99.5% of the combined mileage for these two states, which once comprised a single unified state.

Virginia's a trail hog. Where its trail segment could straddle the Virginia-West Virginia border and even penetrate into West Virginia, it doesn't. Unlike Tennessee and North Carolina, which share the trail, Virginia doesn't play nice with West Virginia. If you're a West Virginia sympathizer, that's just plain unfair.

I get the sense there's something that isn't being said. If you're anything like me, you probably suspect Virginia's selfishness stems from some deep-seated resentment over West Virginia's separation in 1861. And it may reflect Virginians' obvious superiority complex over *West* Virginians. Virginians don't call themselves *East* Virginians now do they? Clearly, they view themselves as being the true Virginians and view *West* Virginians as being subhuman. And Virginia's tourism campaign brags about

130

being "for lovers" – yeah, like West Virginia and the other 48 states are strictly for loveless losers.

This superiority complex can arguably be traced all the way to the early 1600s, when Virginia putatively became the first place settled by British "illegal immigrants," who decimated Native Americans and enslaved African Americans.

But regardless of the root cause of Virginia's selfishness, I have a win-win solution. I'm not calling for reunification. I'm just saying Virginia should stop bullying *West* Virginia and hand over about half of its trail miles. I'm too busy writing scat stories to take the lead on brokering this accord. But I hereby offer my consulting services pro bono to the folks at the ATC in Harpers Ferry.

Before you start poopooing this proposal, consider some of the not-so-obvious benefits of rerouting much of Virginia's segment through *West* Virginia. First, as a welcome byproduct, this rerouting would move the trail away from the Skyline Drive and so eliminate those 51 road crossings. Imagine spending more time walking in the forest and less time dodging SUVs. Second, NOBO thru-hikers would no longer whine about the Virginia Blues. Third, Virginia could restore its own reputation. It could gain loads of respectability points simply by turning over half its mileage. This kind of reparation might even lead to reconciliation between Virginia and West Virginia. You never know. At a minimum, I predict Virginia will change its name to *East* Virginia.

TENNESSEE: We Don't Need No Stinking Privies

As I cross my eleventh state-line, into Tennessee, I catch myself singing an old Grateful Dead tune, "Tennessee, Tennessee, Ain't no place I'd rather be, Baby, won't you carry me, back to Tennessee?"

And I reminisce about the first and only time I've hiked the A.T. through the Smokies. It was Spring Break, 30 years ago. Hobbit, Dark Star and I arrived at the trailhead at 3 AM, all full of cockiness. We were all 20. That's 60 years of combined cockiness. We planned on sunburn and snakebite, we got windburn and frostbite. It was a blast. We spent a week hiking in knee-deep snow, trudging and laughing. Whenever one of us wiped out, the other two would take turns reenacting the pratfall. We exaggerated each spill as much as we dared. We bounced our bodies off trees and did spectacular flips with our packs on. We laughed hysterically. We peed ourselves.

But then the blizzard hit. The drifts were spectacular. We trudged on. Dark Star was miserable. His frayed ACL was now fully torn. He hobbled through the drifts, grimacing and sucking it up like the Jersey boy he was. It was our last night out. The temperature plummeted to 8°F. All of our gear was frozen solid. There were eight of us section hikers in the shelter. We wore our boots and parkas to bed. We huddled in a big wad of hypothermic humanity and told stories through the night.

At first light, Hobbit managed to light a match held with his teeth. We had communal goatmeal and hit the trail. Twenty-some miles later, excruciating miles for Dark Star, we made it down below snowline where it had been raining all week. The trail was mud soup. For our comedic benefit, Dark Star flopped face down and swam. He really swam down the muddy trail. Hobbit and I joined in. We swam most of the last half mile. And we laughed and laughed.

An hour later, we arrived in Gatlinburg and started looking for the cheapest motel in town. They turned us away. No room at the inn for the mud-caked trio. We hatched Plan B: at the next place, we would ask the desk clerk to hose us down and then rent us a room for the night. It worked. She lined us up in the parking lot and sprayed us. It wasn't one of those high-pressure hoses like they use for crowd control, but she managed to remove the first few layers of muck. We laughed till we peed. She laughed too.

Ever since, the word Gatlinburg has made me laugh out loud.

Gatlinburg still makes me laugh. It's the same absurd tourist trap now that it was then, only more so. I hitched into town to see for myself. I wasn't disappointed. Gatlinburg was hilarious three decades ago. If anything, in the interim, it's become a caricature of itself. That makes it genuine, I suppose.

You don't even need to visit Gatlinburg in person to see how funny it is. An e-visit is guaranteed to entertain. The town's website is a hoot and a half all by itself. It describes G-burg in this exalted way: "Amid the splendor of the Smoky Mountains, Gatlinburg embodies the simple goodness of small town life. **Gatlinburg** is where we gather together and stand in awe of nature's glory. Here, we fill our spirits, seek inspiration, and continue the journey toward what we know is right. In **Gatlinburg, Tennessee**, we *Reach Higher Ground*." Oh please! I know, I know, it's too easy, this stuff writes itself. Seriously, it's like shooting clay pigeons in a barrel.

But an actual visit is even funnier than a virtual one. As you stroll through the throngs of spheroid tourists, you can't help but notice the place is teeming with pancake houses. I counted 10 of them. These are just the places with the word pancake in the establishment's name. There are many other places in town where you could get pancakes. But I'm talking about pancake specialists. I counted 'em and, just to confirm, I Google Mapped 'em. Again, ten places filling the pancake-specialist niche.

To put this in perspective, ten also happens to be the number of T-shirt stores in G-burg, which means that both pancake houses and T-shirt stores are twice as plentiful as Baptist churches and wedding chapels. Ice cream parlors (9) and putt-putt golf courses (7) outnumber Baptist churches. Impressively, though, Baptist churches do outnumber fudge shops (4), suggesting G-burg is a pretty pious place after all.

Ten also exceeds the number of shelters (9) – all of them privyless – we SOBOs encountered in our first few days in Tennessee. In case you're keeping score, here's the list complete with miles from Percival's Peak, the northern terminus.

Mile 1725.8, Abingdon Gap Shelter – **No privy**
Mile 1734.1, Double Springs Shelter – **No privy**
Mile 1741.7, Iron Mtn Shelter – **No privy**
Mile 1748.5, Vandeventer Shelter – **No privy**
Mile 1755.6, Watauga Lake Shelter – **No privy**
Mile 1764.4, Laurel Fork Shelter – **No privy**
Mile 1772.3, Moreland Gap Shelter – **No privy**
Mile 1781.9, Mountaineer Shelter – **No privy**
Mile 1791.2, Apple House Shelter – **No privy**

What's the deal with this concentration of privylessness in Tennessee? Is it just a colossally unlucky coincidence? No, I've calculated the probability that 227 (93%) of 244 shelters elsewhere would have a privy, but none of the nine shelters in Tennessee would have one. It's infinitesimal. It's 3.1×10^{-10}. That's smaller than your chances of meeting Grandma Gatewood while hiking with Moses on the PCT and getting hit on the noggin by a meteorite and winning the MegaBucks Lottery all on the same day. Clearly, this isn't a chance event. There's something conspiratorial going on. I have no idea what. Perhaps it was just a practical joke perpetrated on the early hiking community back in the 1930s. But, really, we don't care about the historical details. We grant you amnesty, Tennessee. We appeal to your sense of decency. We beseech you, give us some privies.

I'm just joshing, Tennessee. Trust me, your privylessness is nothing compared with what I saw in India. Arriving at first light on a night train in Delhi, I witnessed the phenomenon I'd read about in Arundahti Roy's *God of Small Things*. The poorest of the poor, the pavement dwellers, have no defecation rights. In megacities like Delhi, the people in the mega-slums, literally millions of them, simply have no privy access. The men and boys defecate communally each morning right along the train tracks. (The women and girls defecate in interstitial spaces, like parks, throughout the city.) In India, this ritual is a social opportunity. They squat together, sometimes with legs touching. Universally, they face the train, watching the richer people while the richer people try not to look. I looked. I stared. I counted. In an hour, I saw penis-scrotum-feces, penis-scrotum-feces, penis-scrotum-feces tens of thousands of times, perhaps over 100,000 times. And this was a tiny fraction of the pavement dwellers lacking defecation rights that day. They lacked the option, which Tennessee provides freely, of simply wandering off into a big quiet forest and defecating privately and with dignity.

Besides, all that privylessness is ancient history by the time you land in G-burg. Arriving mid-day, you'll have plenty of time to gorge on crepes, blintzes, and Belgian waffles at one of the pancake houses, attend church, go ziplining with Dolly Parton, play a couple rounds of putt-putt golf, eat some fudge, visit the wax museum, get yourself a classy T-shirt that reads "Kiss me, I'm from Dixie," gorge on ice cream, and get married – all in time to hitch back to the trail before hiker midnight.

And, just so you know, unlike the trail in Tennessee, Gatlinburg has privies galore and even a few toilets of the indoor flush variety.

NORTH CAROLINA: Come Get Licked by Ponies

As I arrive at my twelfth state-line, the one the Volunteers share with the Tar Heels of North Carolina, I can't reasonably expect an instantaneous rebound from Tennessee's flagrant and fragrant privylessness. The trail straddles the border with Tennessee for the next 150+ miles. And as much as North Carolinians may wish to distance themselves culturally from the privyphobic Vols, it's only natural that some of that Vol influence would diffuse across the permeable border.

In the border stretch, there was a partial rebound. Tennessee's influence was still evident, but 61% of (18) shelters did have a privy. That's almost civilized. In the Great Smoky NP, an almost identical 58% of (12) shelters had a privy. In the North Carolina section, where the trail veers away from Tennessee, the percentage rebounds nicely: a whopping 87% of (15) shelters had a privy. In Georgia, it's 12 of 12. So, the rebound was complete, in the end.

But while North Carolina spared itself from the full embarrassment that arises from all-out privylessness, it did distinguish itself in another unflattering way. North Carolina provided thru-hikers with the opportunity to hike with quadrupeds. I don't mean the tax-payer subsidized, introduced, nonnative, grazing-machine ponies and cattle of Grayson Highlands. I don't mean the "feral" ponies that licked us on the balds. I don't mean clip-clopping horses on the trail in the Great Smoky NP. I don't mean the domestic-dog partners that some hikers bring along. No, I'm referring to the four-legged hiking companions provided unwittingly by North Carolina's bear hunters, namely their own mangy half-starved hunting dogs.

Now don't get me wrong. I'm not denigrating these domestic dogs. They're innocent. They deserve not one iota of blame for their role as accomplices in this unbearable enterprise. They don't know whether their humans are poachers. They don't know whether their prey's gall bladder and paws will be used medicinally on the other side of the planet. They just work for crunchies.

Besides having a clean conscience, these domestic dogs are clearly more domesticated than their human partners in the bear-killing hobby. They don't chew tobacco indoors, leave their socks on the floor, pick their teeth while eating dinner on the couch, drink beer after beer from cans only, or watch NASCAR for hours on end. (They're not even allowed indoors.) And their humans don't seem to realize it, but these dogs don't even seem to like *hunting*. Gasp.

But they sure do love *hiking*.

I discovered this while walking solo one morning. I was cruising up a series of switchbacks, when I started to get that uncomfortable sixth-sense feeling that I was being watched. I turned and there she was right on my heels, a half-starved hound complete with GPS collar. I was being dogged, by a dog. We started chatting. I said brilliant things like, "hey buddy." She just panted. She stayed right on my heels. When I stopped to get a drink of water, she stopped and waited, not mashing against my leg or begging for food, just waiting. On we went. A mile or so later we were joined by two more dogs. They too walked right on my heels. We continued as a pack of four for another mile or so. But when I stopped for lunch, they went back down the trail. I learned later that they joined one of my SOBO trailfriends and repeated the hike they'd just done with me. And they did so again the next day. I went on to hike with other hounds on subsequent days. Over the next week or so, I accumulated a mountain of evidence that these bloodthirsty hounds would rather hike than hunt.

The hunters themselves could have gathered corroborative evidence for this hiking-over-hunting preference, if only they'd been a bit less prideful and a bit more vigilant. They stood right on the Appalachian National Scenic Trail proudly displaying their GPS units, belt buckles, and shotguns. Of course they were proud: they were using state-of-the-art, satellite-based, remote-sensing technology to "harvest" a natural resource – voluntarily, for God and Country and North Cackolacky. They stood there cradling their "unloaded" guns, waiting for their dogs to chase a bear up a tree. Then they'd use their GPS unit to home in on the bear and fill it full of lead or just wound it and let the dogs finish it off.

If only they'd been a bit more mindful. If only they'd tapped into the real potential of their GPS technology, they could have monitored the precise pathways traveled by their "hunting" dogs. They would have noticed a curious zigzag pattern. If they had superimposed this pathway on the map of the A.T., they would have found perfect overlap. They might have realized their dogs were walking on the Appalachian Trail, walking to and fro on switchbacks. Then they might have got suspicious and wondered whether their dogs weren't really hunting at all. They might have come to realize that their half-starved hunting dogs were hiking with hikers.

These dogs were day-hiking trailfriends. They walked right on our heels, like certain human smurf-hikers we know. But unlike hominid smurf-hikers who nip at your heels all the way to

Georgia, these canid smurf-hikers would usually pant at our heels for just an hour or two at a time. Sometimes, though, they stayed overnight in the shelters with us. When they did this, I gave them trailnames.

Why did they so readily attach themselves to us? Could it be they felt a connection simply because we were almost as lean as they were? We were lean from months of self-imposed marching. They were lean from being starved under the premise that a hungry hound is a good hound because hunger makes it extra bloodthirsty and more driven to chase bears. Maybe there was some weird cross-species fellowship based on our scrawniness? These dogs looked mangier than the typical thru-hiker, though. You could see their ribs. Their humans, the real bear executioners, meanwhile were not deprived, as suggested by their girth. I confirmed this fact through close-up personal observation. They were depraved, yes. They were deprived too, but not *food*-deprived. They tended to be built according to the average American floor plan: 5 foot 8 inches, 340 pounds – about the size of three thru-hikers put together.

I know why bear hunters in North Carolina don't resort to starving themselves so as to sharpen their senses and prep themselves for the big hunt. You see, North Carolina is not one of the ten remaining states where bears can be baited with donuts. So, the hunters here, law abiders that they are, do the only sensible thing: they eat the donuts themselves. This is cruel and unusual behavior. It's altogether inhumane, but at least it's self-inflicted.

∞

I sense you might concede there's something mildly amusing about bear-hunters unknowingly providing canine hiking companions for thru-hikers and thru-hikers unintentionally intervening on behalf of bear welfare. But surely you'd argue there's nothing funny about the unbearable blood sport of bear-hunting, with or without dogs, *n'est-ce pas?*

Au contraire, I've always found the standard rationale for bear-hunting to be laughable. Hunters and managers don't always see eye to eye and yet they're in cahoots. Both groups argue like zealots that hunting is *necessary* to keep the bear population in check, to maintain it at healthy stable level. They simultaneously argue that hunting doesn't jeopardize the viability of the bear population because hunting-related mortality is compensatory. This means the same amount of mortality would occur naturally, in the absence of hunting. In practice, this is almost impossible to achieve. But for the sake of argument, let's concede this point. Let's suppose they're right, that hunting mortality substitutes perfectly for the mortality that otherwise would have occurred. If this were true, hunting would have no impact on the population, all else being equal. So, it's unnecessary, by their laughably vehement argument.

Leaving aside the fallacy of the typical population-based argument, their argument is laughable for another compelling reason. It's unethical. Why? Because by focusing solely on what may or may not be good for the bear population, it completely ignores what may or may not be good for the individual. Should the concerns of the individual be dismissed entirely in favor of what's supposedly good for the population? Would it be OK to hunt species X with GPS-collared dogs based on a fallacious rationale about how killing individuals with lead projectiles is better for the population's health than the alternative of allowing natural mortality. Would it be OK to ignore the welfare of individuals if species X were chimpanzees?

I didn't claim the rationale for bear-hunting was funny ha-ha. I said it was laughable.

Just for the record, I'm not trying to pick on North Carolina. Nationwide, 28 states permit bear-hunting and 17 of them permit the use of dogs. Of the 14 trail states, all but Connecticut and New Jersey currently permit bear-hunting. And seven of these 12 states permit the use of dogs. Along with North Carolina, bear-hunters could unwittingly provide canine companions for thru-hikers in Maine, Vermont, West Virginia, Virginia, Tennessee, and Georgia.

But only in North Cackolacky can you become an official "Bear Cooperator" simply by turning in the upper premolars of your prey. Exploiting the same carcass, you could also become a Bear Scumbag by selling the paws and gall bladder for medicinal use in a faraway land. Or you could become a Trail Cooperator simply by staying home. While hunting bears with hounds on the trail constitutes a major affront to the thru-hike experience, we sure would miss those hiking companions you so generously provide.

GEORGIA: On Your Mind

As I walk across my thirteenth and final state-line, into Georgia, a peach of a state, I wonder whether the NOBOs were right. I wonder whether Georgia will be tough going. It won't be. From the glass-half-full perspective, the Georgia segment has a fairly low road density. Except when the marines get rambunctious at their nearby training facility, it has a semi-remote feel that's most welcome. Overall, the trail's nice and easy for SOBOs and it almost provides that Thoreauvian "tonic of wilderness" we crave.

Springer itself is cute. I think my heart beat eleven times on the "ascent" to the "summit" of Springer "Mountain." To recover, I lay on the near-level ground next to the plaque and posed for the prerequisite I-did-it photo.

Flashing back a few days, I find myself slowing down and trying to savor the last few days of thru-hiking, before beginning my thru-bike back to Maine. So, I'm already in the mode of looking for excuses to stall when I hear about a trail town, Helen, that's called "The Gatlinburg of Georgia." Sold! Say no more. I'm there. This should be très amusing.

Helen proves to be roughly 42 times funnier than G-burg, and G-burg was a laugh factory.

What's so funny about Helen? Well, for starters, it's one of those fabricated tourist-trap towns. This one happens to be a faux alpine Bavarian village. The store fronts have gingerbread trim. The alleys are covered with cobblestones. The folks in the sidewalk oompah band are sporting embroidered lederhosen and those knee-high socks with snazzy tassels. I can't resist. To play along, I wander around the village speaking rusty Germanglish to the villagers, asking the shopkeepers where I can buy lederhosen [*Wo kann ich kaufen lederhosen?*]. I figure I'll finish the thru-hike in style, in leather short pants with suspenders and all. But I'm shocked and appalled: nobody here speaks German. It's a sham.

But it's a funny sham. During my visit, the toy town was overrun with bipeds flashing their platinum cards. They overindulged on bratwurst, schnitzel, sauerkraut, and giant ales. They ate massive wedges of Bavarian chocolate cake, flown in yesterday from Germany according to the server. They went tubing on the Chattahoochee River. They purchased genuine imitation fake knock-off Bavarian cuckoo clocks made in Vietnam. They pretended to enjoy the offerings of the sidewalk oompah band. They did all this and more – with a straight face.

I watched and laughed my non-Bavarian ass off.

And I wondered how all this faux Bavarianess had come about. If Helen felt it needed to reinvent itself, why didn't it do so in an authentic way? At a time when the whole world was tripping over itself trying to Americanize, Helen decided to Germanize. (As absurd as Gatlinburg is, at least its excesses are authentic American commercialism run amok, with a vaguely sensationalistic Dixie theme that seems somehow true to its roots.) The Helen facelift was planned in 1969, the summer of love [*der sommer der liebe*]. It was a capitalist plot, of course. The Chamber of Commerce brags about Helen's miraculous transformation, but what kind of success is it really? Let's take a quick look. Census records reveal that 430 faux Bavarians lived in Helen in 2000. This must represent only a modest increase over the number of Helenites who lived here during the late 1960s when the town was given mouth-to-mouth resuscitation. But since 2000, the local population has exploded. As of 2009, there were 791 Helenites. Don't laugh, Helen is now bigger than Monson (population: 666), its counterpart near the northern end of the trail. Let's pause to bask in the faux glow of Helen's booming population.

And by 2000, Helen's median per capita income, $22,281, had eclipsed Gatlinburg's, $19,678. This stunning reversal of fortunes suggests G-burg will soon begin calling itself "The Helen of Tennessee," despite the fact that Helen has nary a single dedicated pancake house.

Let's celebrate Helen's prosperity while resisting the urge to dig deeper. After all, who really wants to know how many of the 791 Bavarians are working poor who have no health insurance, who wash dishes and perform other honorable yet menial minimum-wage tasks "for a living" and then go on the dole during the off season. Let's back off the Helen of today and bask in the faux glow of its booming population and humming economy, even if it is a mirage of unsustainability.

But we simply must ask the uncomfortable question: *why* did the Helen of yesterday give itself this facelift? What was it trying to hide? Well, it probably wasn't its inglorious economic history based on unsustainable logging and gold-mining. No, the dirty secret here is what Helenites refer to euphemistically as their "rich history." You see, Helen is the origin of the Trail of Tears. That's right, the faux Bavarians of today's Helen live in the heart of the ancestral homelands of the Cherokee, who were "removed" and "relocated" to present-day Oklahoma in accordance with the Indian Removal Act of 1830. Purportedly, 4000 of 13,000 Cherokee died en route. This death-march toll was the price these indigenous "thru-hikers" were "asked" to pay to open the southeast to white settlers, ultimately faux Bavarians.

Helen's population prior to this horrific episode in US history was 100% Native American. Then it plummeted to 0%. But maybe Helen's recent boom reflects an influx of Native Americans resettling in their ancestral Homeland? Not so much. As of 2000, 0.23% of the local population self-identified as Native American. How many individuals is this? It's one: 0.0023 multiplied by the town's population size, 430, = 0.989. (Because *Homo sapiens* come in whole units, we assume the discrepancy between this estimate and 1.0 is simply a rounding error.) So, it's hard to make a compelling argument that Helen's Cherokee population has begun a miraculous recovery from the forced removal. With all that cultural guilt to wallow in, it's no wonder Helenites today live *in cognito* in a fantasy land.

CHAPTER 9

Trail Towns as Hiker Havens☺☺☺[R]

best trail town of all
free pizza new boots dancing
too bad Goose got jailed

I could easily have written a book's worth of stories about trail towns. Some of these stories I've told elsewhere. But I'll add a few stories here to help convey just how fun and funny it can be to arrive at a trail town – and then to stay for one or two days or weeks or years or decades.

Thru-hikers love trail towns. Some would-be thru-hikers become the guest who never leaves. They drop out right on the spot. They get a J-O-B. They find a place to crash for the winter. Or they complete their thru-hike and then return to their favorite trail town. They love that town so much that they end up settling there. Trail towns are littered with former thru-hikers. There was the lovely couple who run the hostel in Millinocket, the gent who runs the canoe-ferry service in Caratunk, the fellow who owns the laundromat and the other guy who ran a free hiker hostel in his apartment in Rangeley, the woman who works as a server at the restaurant in Damascus, the gaggle of fine folks who've settled at Mountain Crossing, the other lovely couple who run the hostel in Dahlonega. The list goes on and on.

Be forewarned, if you're nice to us, we just might reciprocate by moving to your town. I had such a wonderful time in Millinocket before getting on the trail that I entertained the thought of settling there. Then my experience in Monson was the same, only more so. I thought I'd finish my thru-hike in Georgia and pedal right back to Monson to overwinter. (I did pedal back, but I didn't overwinter.) And so I expected to get swept away by the next trail town too.

It's early evening when I finally skirt along the "outskirts" of Caratunk, Maine. This is one of those frozen-in-time places. The settlement proper is just a small gathering of white clapboard houses, with a post office. The local human population stands at a robust 108, up marginally from four decades ago when there were just 90 residents. Caratunk is *not* showing off.

I reach the Arnold Trail (US 201), the two-lane paved road that runs along the Kennebec River, which I'll be crossing by canoe ferry in the morning. For the next couple of days, I'll be retracing the route taken by Benedict Arnold and his ragtag troops who passed through on their way to invade Canada during the Revolutionary War in 1775. They started in Massachusetts on a now-ominous date, 9-11. They struggled mightily to get themselves and their ultra-heavy bateaux – rather than ultra-light canoes – up to this point on the Kennebec. Then they took a left at present-day Caratunk. They went overland to the Dead River. They had to carry their absurdly heavy bateaux and all their gear. Their supplies ran low. They suffered from diarrhea. They were as scrawny, hairy, and smelly as thru-hikers. Many men died. Many others defected. By the time they arrived at Quebec City, their numbers had depleted from 1100 to 500. They spent the winter encamped outside the fortress walls, holding the city under siege while burying their dead. It had been one helluva macho march through the wilderness of present-day Maine. It turned out to be a feeble attack on British-held Quebec. The invasion failed. So, what might have become the major portion of the USA – Canada – remains little more than the source of our wintry weather and hockey goons.

I'll be following Ben's route over to Stratton, but not till morning. Tonight, I'll luxuriate indoors. I decide not to head north along 201, where a clique of SOBOs plans to soak in the hot tub at Northern Outdoors Resort. I'm not jumping on that bandwagon. Not one to follow the herd, I head south along Arnold Trail, just a mile to the Sterling Inn. It's a massive white clapboard house, built in 1816 as a stagecoach stop. According to the caretakers, it housed a dancehall and post office in its heyday. It was a vacation lodge for aristocrats from Boston and New York. Families would travel by train and then stagecoach, arriving for weeks of trout fishing, boating, swimming, berry-picking, and other such wholesome activities. I'll be here for just the night and I won't be doing anything active or wholesome. Next week the place will be filled to capacity when bicyclists in the Trek Across Maine pass through, but tonight I'm the one and only guest. I have the cavernous great room to myself, where I can sprawl out, watch an NBA playoff game, and shed a toenail in private.

And the evening's solitude gives me time to ponder Caratunk's "rich history." Not only did Benedict Arnold and his motley crew pass through on their way to invade Canada, but Canada supposedly returned the favor 225 years later by providing a safe haven for the 9-11 terrorists. You may recall the barrage of news reports that the hijackers staged in Quebec. On September 10th, Muhammad Attah and his co-conspirators entered Maine, passing through the US Customs and Immigration checkpoint near the metropolis of Jackman (population: 718). Waved right on through the border crossing, they then sped along 201, downstream along the Kennebec, on their way to martyrdom.

There was an outcry, a backlash against our too-gentle ginormous neighbor to the north. Sure, security might have been lax at the US border crossing, but it was Canada that had provided the safe haven. This wouldn't do. Canada may get away with stunts like sending a *single* battleship to the Persian Gulf, during Dubya's daddy's war. It may get away with chronically committing troops in a "peace-keeping" capacity. It may get away with being kind and gentle and oh so polite, in stark contrast with its loudmouthed warmongering neighbor to the south. But harboring the 9-11 terrorists, that was too much! Fingers pointed northward. Canada was blamed, vilified, and scolded by the media and by high-ranking American politicians. It was time for Canada to grow up.

The only problem with making Canada the scapegoat: it didn't happen. None of the 9-11 terrorists had even set foot in Canada. But myths like this are hard to debunk, almost impossible to eradicate. We all love to believe false allegations, especially when they're levied against a patsy like Canada, eh?

The initial news reports seemed plausible to me. You see, I'd passed through that very border crossing a few weeks before 9-11. I saw with my own eyes just how porous the border was. I arrived on my bicycle in the evening. There was no line-up of cars. I pedaled right up to the front door. The lights were on, but nobody was home. Nobody was there to greet me, to interrogate me. I waited a few minutes. I thought about leaving a note. Finally, a man appeared in the doorway.

I thought, man, he looks like my dad. He was squat and rotund. He was about 5 feet 5 inches, 340 pounds. His shirt was untucked, with one of the belly-buttons missing. He hadn't shaved in a few days. He was unsteady on his feet. He was chewing tobacco.

"State yuh puhpose!" he orders.

"I've come to Maine to visit my dad."

"Has he lived here all his life?" he asks.

"Not yet," I say, doing my part to deliver the punchline of a familiar Maine joke.

He laughs, waves me through, and quips, "If you had the sense god gave a donut, you'd get rid of that pedal-bike and get yuhself one with a motah."

∞

In Caratunk, the town itself was tiny and strictly residential and I was back on the trail first thing in the morning, so I didn't have a typical trail-town experience. It was atypical because I didn't get to interact with locals, to pester them with all sorts of annoying questions. And they didn't get a chance to love me up, to heap trail magic on me, to hikernap me.

Sometimes I went into a town just to resupply and ended up spending a night at a sleaze motel. In the south, in places like Pearisburg, Virginia, these motels often house people awaiting sentencing, others on disability benefits, and others who work itinerant construction jobs. These places tend to be lively and interesting. But the rooms can be unsavory. So, whenever I got a chance, I would ask fellow hikers in advance: "How was the room? Did you sleep in your sleeping bag?"

Usually I would go into a trail town and hilarious encounters with naked apes would ensue. The trail townsfolk were unfailingly amusing and usually überkind to boot. Every town has a story. Every town yielded at least one comedic vignette.

Bethel, Maine was no exception. From Grafton Notch, I hitched into town and went straight to the pub for dinner. There would be live music that evening. Bonus! Sure enough, a fellow arrives, takes a seat on a stool, tunes his acoustic guitar, and starts dazzling the audience. He plays effortlessly, with virtuosity, in a distinctly jazzy style. He has a vast repertoire that includes hundreds of Bob Dylan and Grateful Dead songs, the "Snoopy theme song," and many originals. You name it, he can play it.

When he finally takes a break, I sidle up to him and ask, "What are *you* doing *here*?"

"I could ask you the same question," he says.

Despite this awkward start, we hit it off. It turns out he's Denny Breau, brother of the late great Lenny Breau, who was murdered in Los Angeles thirty years ago. Denny lives here and makes a living by playing hundreds of gigs per year at local pubs. And he doesn't want to tour anymore. He's happy.

I'm happy too. I have a great evening listening to Denny and getting to know some of the Bethelites. At closing time, one of the locals says, "Hey, Ledge, we're going to my house to eat eggs and smoke weed. You're invited and we won't take 'no' for an answer."

"Well, I accept, but I'd rather smoke eggs and eat weed."

"That can be arranged," she says. And then she announces to her entourage, "Ledge accepts. He's coming to our slumber party."

∞

A few days later, in Gorham, New Hampshire, I rendezvoused with Sad Hands and Chin Music, two of my favorite SOBOs. And I finally got to hear the song Sad Hands had written for me while hiking in Maine. We were walking together back to the hostel, "The Barn," in the wee hours of the morning. Walking arm-in-arm, with her boyfriend, Chin Music, on one side and me on the other, Sad Hands suddenly threw back her head and belted out in a bluesy style, *Oh Ledge / You're living on the edge / You've teetered on a ledge / You've hidden in a hedge / You can identify a sedge / Between us there's no wedge / That's what I pledge / Oh Ledge.*

I cried. She sang it again. I laughed.

"What's funny? Are you laughing at me or my song?" asked Sad Hands.

"I'm not laughing *at* you, I'm laughing *with* you. I'm laughing at the rhyme scheme."

"Good, you get the joke. I knew you would. For the record, the rhyme scheme is: A-A-A-A-A-A-A-A."

∞

In North Woodstock, New Hampshire, I finally arrive – on foot. It's a different world here. It's touristy. Unlike Maine, where hitching was easy as blueberry pie, here it's harder than granite. Folks around here don't seem to realize that while thumbs-up ordinarily means "OK," in the current context it means "please pull over and give me a ride into town." The torons speed by with tunnel vision, heading to the waterpark, menagerie, gift shop, or fudge factory. I try hitching but have no luck. I end up walking all the way to town. That's 7+ miles of unplanned road-walking tacked onto 20+ miles of trail-walking.

But I finally arrive, well after hiker midnight. I enter the lobby of one of the little mom-and-pop motels. I'm their only guest for the night. How do they stay in business, I wonder? The desk clerk is in his PJs. He seems annoyed by my interruption of his marathon TV-watching session. He doesn't say a word. I hand over my credit card and fill out a registration card. It's all so perfunctory. He doesn't ask anything about my hike. He doesn't say anything at all. He slides the room key to me and finally speaks. He orders, "Don't empty your pack in the room."

"Huh?"

"Don't empty your pack in the room."

"What?"

"I said, 'Don't empty your pack in the room.' Hikers always do that and get forest debris all over everything."

"Forest debris?"

"Yes, forest debris."

"But I'm a hiker and surely you must realize that everything I own is inside my pack. Is it OK with you if I empty the contents of my pack *outside* the room? I'd be glad to do that. It's just an unusual expectation. Should I go buy a new toothbrush? Maybe I should leave my pack here with you? It would stink up the whole lobby and your living quarters, but at least I wouldn't get so much as a spruce needle on the carpet in Room 4."

He says nothing. Not one word.

I slink over to room 4, where I remove my forest debris-filled boots outside the door. It's a most impressive deposit. Bracken fern fragments, spruce needles, and pulverized duff galore. Then, for the first time ever, I dump the entire contents of my pack in the room, right on the pristine carpet. I shake the emptied pack vigorously. Nothing comes out. There simply is no appreciable forest debris inside my pack, which of course is why his demand was so puzzling in the first place.

Then I settle in for the night. But instead of writing in my journal, I write the desk clerk a letter hinting ever-so-tactfully at my dissatisfaction. I acknowledge it was unfair of me to expect much from him. He's inert, inanimate. He's devoid of personality. He's not going to hug hikers and rave about how he loves the smell of thru-hikers, and he's not going to call you by your trailname or tell you to help yourself to the nonexistent hiker box. He's homozygous for apathetic and boring. I get that. But I thought he should know the definition of "hiker friendly," since the trail guide identifies his motel accordingly, even though his behavior personifies the antonym, hiker *un*friendly. I also thought he should know that hikers don't go into his rooms and dump all of the contents of their pack on the floor and then turn their pack inside out and shake it. And if they did, virtually nothing would happen. Why? Because the "forest debris" he loathes with every fiber of his being resides in our boots, not our packs. So, what he should do in the future is ask hikers, nicely if he can muster that, to leave their boots outside. This is a routine request and one that hikers are only too glad to comply with.

I sign off my letter by wishing him all the best in future opportunities to treat his paying guests like crap, to drive away business, to sully his reputation within the trail community, to minimize his cash flow, to shorten the latency to bankruptcy.

And then I add a post script telling him I truly wish him well and that I hope his behavior wasn't the side-effect of some personal tragedy like a terminal illness or a recent death in his family.

∞

Weeks later I arrive in another trail town, Duncannon, Pennsylvania, at the end of another long day. I've pushed hard to get here, doing 30+ miles, the last couple on "painment." But when I arrive at the perfectly seedy Doyle Hotel, a bastion for over-the-top hiker friendliness, I couldn't be happier. My trailfriends, Zamboni and Strawberry Shortcake, are the only hikers there when I arrive. It's 9 PM and the deep fryer is still on, so I'm just in time to order mounds of fried food. Zamboni and Strawberry join me by ordering their second dinner.

The bartender charges me $3 – that's right, three US dollar bills – to sleep on the floor in Zamboni and Strawberry's room. Off we go, up the creaky stairs, down the creaky hallway, to our creaky room. As we enter the room, I laugh out loud at the sight of Zamboni's bed. It's buried by the contents of his grocery bags. The scene reminds me of those massive hauls we admired as kids upon returning from trick-or-treating forays. He's intuitive. He knows why I'm amused: he's fueling his thru-hike on a monotonous and mountainous diet of candy. A little probing reveals that his girlfriend, a nutritionist, has already scolded him. She's analyzed his diet and discovered potentially toxic levels of magnesium thanks to his gastronomical chocolate intake. Further probing reveals that Zamboni's hike has also been compromised by "anal leakage," the byproduct of overindulging on a certain brand of low-fat potato chips.

In the morning, I announce my spur-of the-moment plan to zero. Zamboni's disappointed that I won't be hiking with him. He tries to shame me into changing my mind. He calls me weak and lame and otherwise casts nasturtiums on my character. I tell him I love him too and I hug him, which he pretends to hate.

Then I seek out Vickey and Pat, the legendary couple who own and run The Doyle. Vickey exudes love, caring, openness, and tolerance. She *loves* hikers and hikers love her. She makes you feel like you're home. She can do this with just her smile. And then she hugs you and tells stories about hikers you know and just plain loves you up. It's a thrill to meet her.

When I congratulate her husband, Pat, for his excellent spousal choice, he doesn't respond in that woe-is-me way you might expect. Instead, he says, "We got married sixteen days after we first met, 37 years ago."

"Sixteen days?! What took you so long? I guess you were commitment phobic?"

"Not me. Vickey didn't even want to go out with me at first, but she caved after a week. Then the wedding got delayed."

"Delayed? I thought you said you got married sixteen days after meeting."

"I did. But we wanted to get married even sooner. We didn't want to wait, but I couldn't get a marriage license right away. In those days, I was such a nomadic countercultural drop-out that I didn't have an official ID, so we couldn't get a marriage license until I could prove my identity."

"So you squandered a whole week of conjugal bliss?"

"Yeah, but we've been making up for it ever since," says Pat.

CHAPTER 10

Hitch-hiker's Guide to the Trailaxy☺☺☺[R]

two miles to trail town
how can I go to and fro?
opposable thumb

I divorced my first car in 1978. I gave it away. I got back freedom, adventure, magic, and I lived a more ethical, mindful, and green lifestyle. I hitch-hiked everywhere I went for the next decade or so. I divorced my last car – never to get remarried – about a decade ago. I gave it to charity and got back all those things I'd been missing. I've lived on a bicycle ever since. As I started hiking, I realized I was on the verge of hitch-hiking again, for the first time in decades.

I didn't divorce my car for freedom, adventure, and magic. Those were bonuses. I divorced it to be ethical, mindful, and green. I divorced it so I would no longer live unsustainably. I could no longer pretend, like the average American, that six planet Earths exist to meet my consumptive demands, or that I didn't see the connection between global warming and the extinction crisis, or that I lived in a country that waged war over fossil fuels. I opted out, as the only right thing to do.

You too can divorce your car. It's the easiest thing in the world. You'll be greener. Your lifestyle may even become sustainable. No longer will you consume fossil fuels like a war-mongering addict who doesn't give a rat about the natural world or the fact that half of all fellow Earthlings have less than three dollars per day.

∞

How can hitch-hiking make your thru-hike greener? If it's so egregious to drive an automobile, why is it OK to sit a few feet away while someone else sits at the controls? Well, it's a making-the-best-of-a-bad-job approach, that's for sure. It's forgivable in the limited sense that when you hitch-hike, you're arguably not increasing the demand for gasoline. If you arrive at a road crossing and phone for a shuttle to pick you up, you're triggering someone to turn the ignition key and so you're causing an increase in gasoline consumption. You're the problem. But if you hitch, you're just tagging along. The driver is already going your way (usually). You're simply participating in a subtle form of car-pooling. There's no appreciable increase in carbon footprint. You're an eco-friendly stowaway.

But it's better than being a stowaway because you're not in hiding. The moment the car pulls over, you become an actor in an experiential play. The implicit social contract between you and your driver demands that you play a co-starring role.

∞

As I hiked solo through the 100-mile Wilderness, I reminisced about my hitch-hiking adventures. And I looked forward to reaching the first paved road, partly because it would be the first hitch-hiking opportunity of my thru-hike. I looked forward to "thumbing" again, after all those years. I was glad to be a thru-hiker because that status legitimizes this otherwise disreputable, obsolete mode of travel. I looked forward to the adventure and freedom and inevitable random acts of trail magic and even the abundant humor hitch-hiking offers.

∞

Day 7, Mile 114.5, southern edge of the 100-mile Wilderness. I arrive mid-day at Route 15. I cross the road and start walking east toward Monson, ready to hitch if a car comes along. I'm mildly pessimistic. I mean, who hitches these days and who would be reckless enough to pick up a hairy stranger in the middle of nowhere? I figure I'll end up walking into town, which is fine by me. But within a minute, I hear a car coming. I turn and display my opposable thumb. It works. Damned if the driver doesn't yank her Subaru wagon right off the pavement. I run to the car, which is now parked precariously with its rear end sticking out for logging trucks to swipe. She's ditched her car on a curve in the road and, wouldn't you know it, here comes a logging truck. It thunders by, clearing the Subaru by inches. I climb into the back seat. It's an elderly couple. We exchange pleasantries. I thank them profusely for stopping. Then the driver, Ethel, says flirtatiously, "I *never* pick up hitch-hikers, but I got one look at that beard and your smile and I said to Frank, 'I'm giving that handsome young hiker a ride.'"

Her husband scolds, "Ethel, behave yourself!"

Then he turns toward me and says, "You see what I've had to put up with for the last 63 years?"

"Sixty-three years! That's amazing!" I say because that's what you're supposed to say. You're not supposed to say, "you poor man, you're lucky to have lived so long."

"And she's a liar to boot," says Frank. "She flirts with *every* man in the State of Maine *and* she picks up *every* hiker she sees on the road."

"That last part's true," says Ethel, "I do pick up every hiker. Last year I picked up a guy right at that very spot where I picked up you, and then a week later I was driving on Route 4 going to visit my sister in Rangeley and I saw a hitch-hiker so I slowed down to pick him up. I recognized him right away. It was the same young man. He was even cuter the second time."

"Ethel!" pleads Frank.

"Anyway, he didn't recognize me right away, but as we were driving along I could see his face in the rear view mirror and he looked a little scared. To calm him down, I said, 'Oh, it's you again. I didn't recognize you at first. Don't worry. I haven't been waiting for you at the road crossing all week. I'm not even, how you kids say it these days, stalking you.'"

She delivered this punch line just as she was dropping me off in "downtown" Monson at the Lakeshore House Inn. I thanked her for the ride and the story and said, "See you next week on Route 4."

She would be a no-show.

∞

A few weeks later, I arrive at US 20 and decide to hitch into Lee, Massachusetts, to resupply. It takes a while to get a ride. Too many cars, so each driver feels that reduced sense of personal responsibility. Just as you're more likely to get quickly rescued from drowning if there's a single onlooker versus, say, 10 onlookers, your chances of getting a quick ride diminish with increasing traffic. In Maine, where there are precious few cars, one of the first few cars usually stopped. But here it helps to be patient. Finally, I summon my reserve telekinetic powers and will a car to stop. It does. The driver's from New York. He's "up for the weekend" visiting his in-laws at their cottage on a nearby lake. At the moment, he's on an important mission. He's been sent solo to the grocery store. He's glad for the reprieve from all the scrutiny. He's glad not to be fielding questions about his reproductive shortcomings. And he's glad to have been excused from hours of tedious antiquing with his in-laws. But he's nervous about his mission. He's feeling the pressure. His assignment is to fetch ingredients and then return to the cottage to make "award-winning pizza" for a dinner party of twelve and have it piping hot and ready for them the moment they come through the door. This isn't exactly his forte, he admits.

We arrive at the grocery store in Lee and go our separate ways. But we keep bumping into each other in aisle after aisle. He looks a bit panicky and I notice that his cart remains empty. I ask, "How are you making out, Scott?"

"Ledge, I should have just gone antiquing. I'm lost. I have no idea how to make lousy pizza, never mind award-winning pizza. Do you know anything about cooking? Can you give me any tips? I don't even know what ingredients to buy."

"Sure, I'd be glad to help."

I stash my pack and trekking poles in his cart and say, "Guard my stuff and I'll see what I can find?"

"Go Ledge!" he shouts.

I start dashing around the store and, in a series of forays, I manage to deliver a great bounty to his cart: capers, fresh basil and oregano and parsley, garlic, green onions, fresh mozzarella, goat cheese, feta, parmesan, artichoke hearts, sundried tomatoes, grape tomatoes, broccolini, asparagus, red bell peppers, balsamic vinegar, olive oil, portabella mushrooms, pine nuts, gorgonzola, dried cherries, Kalamata olives, whole grain flour, and yeast. And then I fetch an arm-load of bottles: zinfandel, cabernet sauvignon, and pinot noir. He looks relieved.

I dictate a few instructions on what to do with the yeast and how to make the dough and which toppings go together and so on. I give him my cell phone number so he can call for coaching if he gets panicky later on.

He thanks me profusely and claims repeatedly that I've single-handedly saved his marriage. I suspect they'll stay together for at least 63 years – and he may even come to enjoy antiquing.

∞

Mile 804.0 from Katahdin, somewhere in New York. I've just passed through the Lemon Squeezer rock formation and I arrive at NY 17. This busy road with cars roaring past on their way to or from New York City seems like a poor place for hitching. But I give it a try. Eventually an SUV pulls over. Score! As I'm loading my pack and poles in back, the driver says, "You look like a thru-hiker?"

"Yeah, thanks, I guess. My trailname's Ledge. Thanks so much for stopping!"

"No worries, where you headed, Legs?"

"Just down to the deli. It's a little less than two miles, I think."

"Sure, I know that place. I drive past it every day. And it's a perfectly fine deli, but you don't really want to go to a deli, do you? It's Friday and that means all-you-can-eat home-made pizza at my house. I live just a little farther down the road in Tuxedo Village, where I happen to have an unlimited supply of beer. And my wife of thirty-seven years will pretend to be annoyed if I bring home another stray. That'll be fun. And you can get a shower and stay in our guestroom."

And then as if to seal the deal, he says, "I'll show you where Whoopie Goldberg used to live. Whaddya say, Legs?"

"I'm in. That's so generous, thanks so much."

"Excellent. Now, there's just one condition: you must agree to be our entertainment for the evening."

"Deal," I say.

∞

The next day I'm about to try hitching to another deli when I get hiker-napped at the trailhead by a couple of day-hiking women. They're out from the city, where they work together in the cutthroat world of high fashion. They take me to a vineyard for gourmet pizza and live music and then show me where Derek Jeter's grandmother lives. As in Connecticut, folks here in the exurbs of New York City feel compelled to let you know which famous people live nearby.

∞

Weeks later I'm hiking along the trail in Virginia and I rendezvous with my trailfriend, Zamboni. He has no filter, so he blurts out, "Ledge, wow, that's terrible. You reek. Why do you smell like rotten eggs?"

"I was hitching back to the trail the other day and I got shamanized."

"You got whatanized?"

"Shamanized. I got shamanized."

"What're you talking about?"

"I'm serious. I got hugged by a shaman."

"That's gibberish, Ledge. Are you being cryptic just to piss me off?"

"But it's the truth, Ruth. Google it when you get to the next trail town."

"What would I Google? 'Why does Ledge smell like rotten eggs and claim he was hugged by a shaman?'"

"Yeah, Google that exact sentence and see if you can figure it out."

"OK, I will."

"You do that."

"Don't worry, I will."

162

Weeks later, I run into Zamboni and he says, "Wow, you still reek. I think it's even worse now. Are you OK? Have you been to a doctor yet?"

"I'm fine. I was hugged by a shaman, that's all. Have you figured it out yet?"

"No, dammit, I Googled that sentence and found a script from the old TV show *Buffy the Vampire Slayer* and all kinds of other weird stuff that had nothing to do with you or your stench or your weird behavior. So, I still don't get it."

"OK, I'll explain. Here's what happened. I was hitching back to the trail from Buchannon. A car pulls over and I'm about to hop in, but the driver warns me that her car smells a little like sulfur. I got in anyway and said, 'That's OK, I smell a little like *hiker*.'"

"I still don't get it. What does that have to do with getting hugged by a shaman?"

"Well, *she's* the shaman. And she was covered from head to toe with sulfur powder. It was all over her clothing. It was in her hair. Apparently, she'd been trying to purge evil spirits from her own soul, but the shamanistic ritual she'd wanted to do required mineral springs and there were no mineral springs nearby so she did the next best thing, I guess."

"She just rolled around in sulfur powder?"

"Right, apparently."

"OK, that explains the rotten-egg odor, but what about the hugging?"

"Well, when we got to the trailhead up on the Blue Ridge Parkway, we talked for awhile. Then she hiked with me for a bit. She said some spooky stuff about my energy. She got pretty upset. She cried a lot. I guess she thought I could help her, even though *she's* the shaman. Anyway, she hugged me. She didn't go into a trance or anything dramatic like that. She just kept crying and hugging me. I didn't know whether she was trying to banish evil spirits from me or herself or what. I really didn't know what was happening, but I just held on and tried to help her in my own non-shamanic way."

"And you've smelled like a billion rotten eggs ever since," concluded Zamboni.

"Yes, but I've never been healthier."

"Or a bigger smartass," adds Zamboni.

"True, thanks for noticing."

∞

Weeks later, Helen, Georgia, 50 measly trail miles from Springer. A trailfriend, Jelly Belly, and I are in hilarious Helen. We walk to the edge of town and begin hitching. We're headed to Unicoi Gap, back to the trailhead. As soon as we induce a driver to stop, we'll be speeding up a series of switchbacks to the gap. We'll be retracing the first few miles of the Trail of Tears, in this most callous way.

As the cars whiz by, I rave about hitch-hiking. Jelly Belly hasn't hitched a lick along her SOBO thru-hike. She doesn't seem to think she's missed out. I suggest she doesn't know what she's been missing. I tell her hitch-hiking has been one the best aspects of the thru-hiking experience. I share micro-versions of some of my hitching tales. And I boldly predict we're about to have a mini-adventure, that something magical is about to take place, that the spontaneous implicit social contract with our soon-to-be driver will open some door, that there will be a scintillating conversation, that it'll be a totally unpredictable surprise. I predict we'll get out at the trailhead and look at each other and say, "OMG, did that just happen?!"

"I won't say the OMG part," says Jelly Belly.

"No, of course not."

Just then, a monstrosity of a king-cab pickup truck pulls over and I call "shotgun." I climb into the passenger seat, into the shotgun position, and glance into the back seat, where Jelly Belly has sidled up to an arsenal of actual shotguns.

"Shotgun," she whispers pointing furtively to her left.

I start chatting up our driver. After the pleasantries are out of the way, I ask him, "What do you get to do today?"

"Solve a murder case up on the trail. If you're lucky, that is."

"What? You're some kind of detective?"

"Yep, I'm with the Sheriff's Office," he says.

"And you're really working on a case on the trail?"

"Several, actually."

He goes on to regale us with tale after tale, all of them gruesome and brutal, mostly involving manhunts for putative serial killers. According to this fellow, hikers like to tell each other that the trail is really a safe place, despite the few well-publicized gruesome murders. He implies that the trail is way more dangerous than we could ever imagine and that only people like him are privy to all the unsolved cases that never get publicized. Plus, he knows where some of the most wanted suspects are hiding out, where they're camping, when they last came into town for supplies, what they've served prison sentences for in the past, and so on. He tells us one gory detail after another, about beatings and a lynching and missing body parts. I glance back at Jelly Belly. She is not amused.

Meanwhile, I'm thinking this guy's just bullshitting us. He's pulling our leg, or as my Latino friends would say, he's pulling our hair. And if he's not just messing with us, even if all he says is true, maybe he's like the proverbial surgeon who sees virtually every medical ailment as a potential surgery (and a boat payment). This guy sees virtually every hiker and backwoods renegade as a potential serial killer. And so he's obsessing about cases he's worked. But this doesn't mean the trail has suddenly become a dangerous place. I mean, if he were to describe in detail one fatal lightning strike after another, would we stay off the trail for fear of getting hit in the head by a rogue lightning bolt?

Another glance confirms that JB is still wearing her best poker face.

We arrive at the trailhead at Unicoi Gap. He pulls over. We thank him and wave as he drives off, looking for his man.

Jelly Belly and I look at each other and say, "O—M—G!!! Did that just happen?!"

CHAPTER 11

Our National Social Trail☺☺☺[B]

Laughter is the shortest distance between two people.
— Victor Borge

The trail is a remarkably social place, so much so that it's been called the National *Social* Trail, a word play on its designation as a National *Scenic* Trail. Not every hiker is highly sociable, of course. At one end of the spectrum are the loners, curmudgeons, troglodytes, even fellows on the lam. At the other end of the spectrum are the super-gregarious types, who tend to be extremely well-connected within the trail community. They crave social contact. Contemporary trail legends like Baltimore Jack and Stumpknocker might rival him, but for my money the most socially connected of all is a wondrous gent who deserves to go by his formal sobriquet complete with honorific title. His trailname is Sir Woodchuck.

I met this sir of the rodent variety on my 50th birthday, July 4th, at the Mizpah Hut, just below treeline in The Whites. I had spent the day going up and over Mt. Washington, bent at the waist trudging against the ferocious winds, which topped out at 97 miles per hour. Two and a quarter inches of rain fell that day. That's the equivalent of 27 inches of snow. And it did snow some, with sleet and hail and freezing rain mixed in. It was a perfect day. But I was shivering as I entered the hut.

I got a chilly reception.

The hut master, before I asked for anything, told me there was no room for me, that I couldn't do a work-for-stay, that I was basically shit outta luck. I said nothing. He then grudgingly conceded that maybe it would be OK if I hung around and warmed up before getting back on the trail. I still hadn't said a word. Then he said I couldn't eat because I wouldn't be doing a work-for-stay, but if I gave him three dollars, he would let me sleep on the floor.

"Thanks, that'd be ideal," I say through chattering teeth.

I turned to survey the cast of characters at the designated thru-hiker table, situated as always near a wall. There were four of them. I went over and introduced myself. They welcomed me in that casual hiker way, accepting and warm but not overly expressive. Wizard was a tall twenty-something NOBO with an untamed thru-beard and a manskirt and a honking big wizard's-eye amulet hanging on his chest, hence his trailname. He was all cool and confident. And who wouldn't be, what with all that protection against evil-doers?

The Boston Boys were a father-son duo out for a summer of serious bonding while hiking the New England portion of the trail. They were so tight that they didn't even have individual trailnames, so I started calling them Boston Lad and Boston Dad. The lad was 17, a stellar cross-country runner, and he and dad were best friends, believe it or not.

And, last but not least, there was Sir Woodchuck. He's regal and not just because of his trailname. He's tall and powerfully built, beautiful, kind, patient, intensely curious and generous, ageless. He's also peerless, in my mind. He's the first African American long-distance hiker I've met on the trail. When I mention this, he says he's the first African American long-distance hiker almost everyone has met on the trail.

Weeks later, I would meet a young NOBO called 4x4 who is thrilled to hear about Sir Woodchuck. He pumps his fists overhead and yells, "I am not alone!" Then, in his ongoing effort to go ultra-light, he gives me his bandana. I accept, despite the fact it weighs nearly an eighth of an ounce.

But for the moment, back at the Mizpah Hut, I'm captivated by Sir Woodchuck's trailname. I kid him a little and then announce that I'm knighting myself and from now on I shall be known as Sir Ledge. I touch my shoulders ceremoniously with a trekking pole. To this day, Sir Woodchuck calls me Sir Ledge. Everyone else just calls me Ledge.

So, we're all gathered together and getting to know each other at our communal thru-hiker table, where no one else dare sit, presumably for fear of absorbing our stench. I ask the Boston Boys where they're from. They both say, "Boston." And I say, "Yes, but you're not really from Boston proper, right?"

"That's right," says the dad.

"OK, then, let me guess? I'd bet a tidy sum that you're not from Roxbury, Cambridge, Summerville, Arlington, or Winchester. Right?"

"Right," they both say.

"Are you ready for my official guess?" I ask.

"Sure, go ahead," they say.

"OK, drum roll please, my official guess is: Lexington."

"How could you possibly know that? Who told you?" They ask incredulously.

"Just a lucky educated guess, or maybe I'm some sort of geographical savant," I say. "Or a clairvoyant." I'm more surprised than they are, but I don't let on.

"Seriously, who told you?" the father asks.

"I can't reveal the source of my powers," I say.

I glance over and notice Sir Woodchuck frantically jotting down dialogue. He's apparently so impressed by my magical cognitive powers that he's dug out his journal and he's writing all of this down.

"That was weird," says Wizard. "Do me next. Where do you think *I'm* from?"

"OK, I'll try. I'll tell you which state you're from, but only if you answer one question first. You *are* from one of the trail states, right?"

"Yes," says Wizard, "I was born and raised in one of the trail states."

Phew, I think. "Wait, it's coming to me," I say. I gaze at the ceiling for about 10 seconds, trying to appear enraptured. They all stare at me. Then I look straight at Wizard and declare, "You were raised in Connecticut."

"Holy shit!" he says. "There are only 14 trail states, so that could've been a lucky guess. But, seriously, how'd you do it? Did I say something earlier that gave it away? Like 'grinder'?"

"I read your mind, Wizard, that's all. And it wasn't really that hard."

"Come on, Ledge, tell us your secret. How'd you do it?" insists Wizard.

"OK, I'll tell you. Your speech gave you away, but not because you have a distinctive regional accent. It's the fact that you're devoid of accent. I first eliminated the southern trail states. There's just no way you're from Georgia, North Carolina, Tennessee, Virginia, or West Virginia. You don't have even a trace of a southern accent. I thought I could eliminate Maryland and Pennsylvania too. I've spent lots of time in those states and you just don't sound like you're from either place. The cues are too subtle for me to describe, but I was pretty sure."

"And then I eliminated the northern New England states. You don't have even a trace of that regional accent either. No way you're from Maine, New Hampshire, or Vermont. And I was pretty sure you aren't from Massachusetts either. My family is from there and you just don't match the template. So that left Connecticut, New York, and New Jersey as the remaining possibilities. Those three states are all bunched together, of course, so you'd think it would be tricky to distinguish among them. But I've spent a lot of time with people from those states and I just couldn't detect any telltale sign that you were from either New York or New Jersey. So, by process of elimination, I guessed Connecticut. By default, you sound like you're from Connecticut, no offense."

"That's impressive," said Wizard. "You could use that as a parlor trick and win lots of money."

"How do you think I'm financing my hike?" I say.

At this point, I notice Sir Woodchuck's still scribbling away in his journal. So I deflect everyone's focus to him. I feign annoyance by telling him I don't recall commissioning my biography. He's instantly apologetic.

Then I get serious and ask him about his hike. He begins by telling us all about his history of volunteer trail-building as a member of ALDHA. He then tells us about how he started section-hiking the trail in 1991. He plans to finish the trail in another year or two. He plans to make it well into Maine this summer. Tomorrow, he's going up and over Mt. Washington.

"Hope you have rain gear," I say, knowing that many thru-hikers carry none, especially in the south.

"I don't, Sir Ledge. I never carry rain gear. Do you really think I need it?"

"Well," I say, "if tomorrow's anything like today, a good rain jacket would be great to have. It won't keep you dry, of course, 'cause it'll just trap all your sweat. But it'll help you avoid hypothermia, just by shielding your upper body from the wind."

"What am I going to do?" says Sir Woodchuck.

"Well, you could buy a rain jacket here at this hut. Look, they have several for sale, complete with the snazzy Mizpah Hut logo."

"I saw those before you got here, Sir Ledge, but they're expensive. They're fifty-five dollars."

"That's a bargain," I suggest, "under the circumstances."

"Not to me. When I come out on the trail for a few weeks each summer, my wife, Chamay, gives me a weekly allowance of twenty dollars. *And I'm not allowed to phone home asking for goodies!*"

"But Sir Woodchuck," I protest, "This isn't a goody. This is an essential piece of equipment above treeline in The Whites. Your survival could depend on it."

"Chamay wouldn't see it that way."

"OK, give me Chamay's phone number right now. I'll give that woman a ring and splain a thing or two to her."

"No, Sir Ledge, I can't let you do that. I'm going to give you our phone number so we can stay in touch, so we can make arrangements to hike together when you get down south, so you can contact us when you get to Georgia, so I can let you know where to find trail magic I'll be leaving for you in North Carolina. But you can't call her now."

"No, of course not," I say. "But what to do, OK, I've got it. Here's Plan B. I'm a SOBO, so I'll be below treeline for the next few days. I won't need a rain jacket, so you can take mine. You can keep it. I'll get a new one in a few days. Or you could just use it till you get through The Whites and then send it to me General Delivery somewhere down the trail. Whaddya say?"

"That's very thoughtful, Ledge, but I wouldn't feel comfortable taking your rain jacket. What if *you* need it?"

"OK, Plan C then. When you're not looking, I'll buy one of the rain jackets for sale here and hide it in your pack. Tomorrow, when your core temperature is falling dangerously, put it on, OK?"

"Sir Ledge, don't worry, I'll use garbage bags. I'll be OK."

"In one-hundred-mile-per-hour winds?" I counter. "Please let me buy one of those jackets. You can pay me back – with interest, if that'll make you happy. I won't even mention it to Chamay."

Sir Woodchuck is stubborn. He won't accept any of my offers. So, Wizard and the Boston Boys reassure me they'll make sure he has adequate gear before he summits tomorrow. And I drop it.

Sir Woodchuck, at our prompting, then tells us stories about his many trailfriends. His intense gregariousness and the fact that he's been hiking every summer for the last two decades combine to make him extremely well-connected. He knows everyone, it seems. He knows all the various trail legends. And when I quiz him about my trailfriends, he's met nearly all of them. He recounts meeting them by describing his conversations with each of them, in detail.

I'm impressed. I get hyperbolic and make the tongue-in-cheek claim that Sir Woodchuck is the single most socially prominent A.T. hiker of all time.

He rejects this claim, but seems pleased at the same time.

I suggest his connectivity within the trail community is so extreme that, by comparison, it seems like Kevin Bacon has yet to act in a movie with any other actor.

Wizard chimes in, "Hey, we could calculate everyone's Sir Woodchuck number, like the Kevin Bacon number, and that way we could see whether Sir Woodchuck really is at the center of a small world, whether he really is as socially prominent as you suggest. Hell, let's do it."

"Let's do what?" says Sir Woodchuck. "What's the Kevin Bacon number?"

"The Kevin Bacon number," I explain, "is a pop culture variant of something called the Erdös number, which was invented to pay tribute to a famous Hungarian mathematician. This guy was extremely prolific and itinerant. He would travel from colleague to colleague, collaborating on journal articles. The Erdös number is a measure of collaborative distance. Most mathematicians know their own Erdös number, even if they won't admit it. It's like a guilty pleasure to go online and compute it. So, what is it? It's simply the degrees of separation between you and Erdös. If you've co-authored with Erdös, then your number is one. If you've co-authored with someone who has coauthored with Erdös, then your number is two, and so on. Mine's four.

"I have a story about the Erdös number. A couple of years ago, I was hosting a party for students and colleagues. It was a potlatch, a tradition among Tlinkits and other native peoples of the Pacific Northwest. It involves hierarchical gifting. I was the host, so I did the gifting. I gave each person a used book, which I had unearthed from stacks around my house. This regifting was more thoughtful than it sounds. I'd carefully chosen each book with a particular person in mind. One of the books was a biography about Paul Erdös, called *The Man Who Loved Only Numbers*. I had chosen this book for one of my colleagues, a guy named Andrew who uses math to gain insights about complex ecological systems. So, I say to Andrew, 'Before I give you this book, it's only fair that you reveal your Erdös number.'

"Looking sheepish, Andrew says, 'I'm sorry to say I haven't published any of my dissertation work yet. Because I have no coauthors, it's impossible for me to calculate my Erdös number. In mathspeak, it's undefined.'

"And then Andrew says, '*I am proud to say, though, that I did sit on the man's lap once!*'

"It turns out Andrew's father, also a mathematician, took a sabbatical in Budapest, where Andrew, then an infant, spent an afternoon bouncing on the knee of Paul Erdös. How's that for a small-world phenomenon?" I say to my new cronies in the Mizpah Hut. They're impressed.

"One more Erdös number story?" I offer.

I get the go-ahead. I tell about stopping off to hear live music one evening on my bike trip to Millinocket. Lucy Kaplansky, a famous singer-songwriter from New York, is playing at a little venue in Maine. During her show, she tells several stories about her father, who was a famous mathematician. After the show, I ask whether she knows her dad's Erdös number. She doesn't, but she's keen to find out. The next day I go online and compute her dad's number, which happens to be one. Turns out, these two titans coauthored a paper way back in the 1940s. I send Lucy an e-mail message to let her know. I also tell her that my Erdös number is four and so my Kaplansky number is five. She's delighted that a member of her audience could be so closely connected to her dear deceased dad.

"Enough about Erdös numbers," I say as a way on interrupting my own monologue.

"But wait, I just remembered one more. Sir Woodchuck, you're from Atlanta, so you might appreciate this: Henry Aaron's Erdös number is one!"

"What?" says Sir Woodchuck, "Henry Aaron broke Babe Ruth's homerun record. He wasn't a mathematician."

"Exactly," I say, "Aaron was no more a mathematician than Erdös was a baseball player, but the two of them did coauthor something one time. They were both awarded honorary degrees by Emery University. After the ceremony, they autographed the same baseball."

"Boo-hiss," says Wizard.

"OK, let me tell you about the Kevin Bacon number. He's been in lots of movies, right? So some geeks thought it would be a hoot to calculate all actors' Kevin Bacon number. Analogous to the Erdös number, your Kevin Bacon number equals one if you've been in a movie with Kevin Bacon, two if you've been in a movie with someone who has been in a movie with Kevin Bacon, and so on."

Wizard chimes in, "Well, I'm not a mathematician, so my Erdös number is undefined. And I've never been in a movie, so my *conventional* Kevin Bacon number is also undefined. But check this out: my Kevin-Bacon-on-the-Appalachian-Trail number is one!"

We're all anxious for clarification.

"It's true," says Wizard. "Ledge already guessed that I'm from Connecticut, right? Well, I'm from Kent, which is right next to the trail. And Kevin Bacon lives nearby in Sharon. He likes to hike on the A.T. near his home, which is where I saw him ... on the trail, with his dogs."

"But not with his wife, Sandwich Face?" I ask.

"Sandwich Face?" asks Wizard.

"Rumor has it that's Kevin Bacon's pet name for his wife, Kyra Sedgwick. Or maybe it's her trailname. Anyway, did you see her too?"

"Naw, it was just Kevin and his dogs," says Wizard. "I didn't see Sandwich Face."

We all enjoy Wizard's mental leap and quirky redefining of the Kevin Bacon number. And then Boston Lad makes an extra leap and says, "If Wizard's Kevin-Bacon-on-the-A.T. number is one, then mine is two because I've encountered Wizard on the A.T., right?"

"Zakly," I say.

"And we all have a Sir Woodchuck number of one, right?" says Boston Dad.

"Right, everyone except Sir Woodchuck," I say. "His Sir Woodchuck number is uniquely zero because he's the only person on Earth who has encountered himself on the A.T."

"Weird," says Wizard.

"Back to my original point," I say. "Isn't it hard to imagine anyone on the trail who has a Sir Woodchuck number bigger than two? I mean, if you haven't met him, then you almost surely know someone else on the trail who *has* met him, right?"

Even Sir Woodchuck concedes this point.

"In principle," I say, "we could just survey fellow hikers and find out who knows whom. Then we could compute any hiker's Sir Woodchuck number, Wizard number, Ledge number, and so on. We could calculate the average for each of these numbers and then we could rank them from smallest to biggest. I bet the average Sir Woodchuck number would top the list. I bet it's about 1.4. And everyone else at this table would be down in the three-to-five range. No offense.

"And we could develop an online Sir Woodchuck number calculator," I add. "Then anyone could compute their Sir Woodchuck number in a fraction of a second. A linear programming algorithm would be ideal for this. It would find the shortest path or fewest links between any two hikers. Who has a pen? Let's jot down a few lines of pseudo-code, whaddya say? We could get this up and running at the next trail town."

Nobody's laughing now.

"Screw that, I'm going to bed," says Wizard.

And then he adds, "Hey, do you realize what this means? My Sharing-a-bunkroom-with-Sir-Woodchuck number is about to be equal to one!"

"Same here," I say.

As we wander off to bed, I refrain from mentioning that I currently hold the world record for lowest combined Erdös-Bacon-Woodchuck number. My EBW number is a miniscule seven, because I've coauthored with a coauthor of a coauthor of Paul Erdös (my E# = 4), and I've met Wizard who has seen Kevin Bacon on the A.T. (B# = 2), and I've met Sir Woodchuck (W# = 1). In this one bizarre way, I'm more socially prominent than the great Sir Woodchuck.

I decide to save this little bomb for breakfast, which of course I won't be allowed to eat.

∞

While we're on the subject of numbers, it seems apropos to share a few numerical factoids.

6.022×10^{23}	Avogadro's constant = number of moose droppings & black flies in Maine, pointy rocks in Pennsylvania, comedic moments on the trail
4,666,321	Number of steps to hike the whole damn trail
4,666,320	Number of key strokes to write a book about hiker humor
38,886	Average number of footsteps per day
29,003	Number of moose in Maine
666	Human population of that most excellent trail town, The Monson, Maine
98.3	Percentage of newbie thru-hikers who believe they're "well above average"
97.2	Percentage of newbie thru-hikers who believe they'll complete their hike
96.7	Percentage of successful thru-hikers who admit to having underestimated how long it would take to complete the thru-hike
79.3	Percentage of thru-hikers who took self-portrait at McAfee Knob
37	Number of pounds lost by typical middle-aged thru-man
35	Number of trail towns I visited

6	Number of Earths needed to support 6 billion thru-hikers & number of pairs of boots I wore
5.4	Percentage of hikers who successfully complete a legitimate thru-hike (past every white blaze)
5	Number of toenail clippers Beagle started his thru-hike with
4	Number of copies of *The Bible* toted by The Sibs, a quartet of smurf-hiking siblings
3	Number of bird species identified by typical thru-hiker
2	Number of times Zamboni climbed Bear Mt. & number of tree types identifiable by typical thru-hiker (those with broad leaves vs. needles)
1	My Sir Woodchuck number & number of times Goose got busted for possession
0.001	Percentage of thru-hikers with realistic self-perceptions about their prospects, abilities, timeline, and budget

CHAPTER 12

Delusions of Awesomeness☺☺☺[R]

what were you thinking?
you're cocky and about to
appalachian fail

Thru-hikers are supremely confident as these factoids reveal. We're overconfident about our prospects for completing the hike and doing so "on time" and "under budget." And that's just for starters. Like all humans, we're prone to a whole suite of cognitive biases. Beyond walking the trail with vastly inflated self-impressions, we make chronically irrationally decisions and we conveniently excuse our own failures as being inevitable consequences of circumstances beyond our control. Meanwhile, we're quick to condemn others for being intrinsically defective. We're irrational thru and thru.

We tend to hike mindlessly. We rely on automated thought processes. We prefer the status quo. We rely on conventional wisdom and expert opinion. We make habitually bad choices and hold distorted opinions of ourselves and others. We stereotype. We keep our minds closed. We fail to update. We don't think straight and we don't realize it. We think we're perfectly rational, but that's our brains on autopilot. We're obliviously irrational – and that's funny.

EVERYONE'S A ROCK STAR

Let's consider what I'll call the awesomeness bias. I began to collect evidence for this bias the night before I started the hike. By the time I'd made it to Monson, I had loads of evidence. And the evidence piled up from there, like scree in a rockslide.

I would simply ask any SOBO I met, "When are *you* getting off the trail?" The answers ran along these lines:

- "Never. Are you serious? I'm not getting off. Not me, no fuckin' way, NFW. I'm living the dream, man. There's no way I'd quit."
- "I might go off the trail to visit my girlfriend for a week, but I won't quit, that's for sure. Dude, I'm walking to Georgia. Why, when are *you* getting off?"
- "Never. I couldn't. There's no way. I bragged myself up for a whole year. There's no way I'm going home until I've walked by every white blaze. I'd never hear the end of it if I quit. I'd have to move and get new friends and a new fiancée."

Or if I felt like being politic, I would ask, "How confident are you that you'll complete your thru-hike?" The answers ran along these lines:

- "Extremely confident. I didn't come out here to fail. I'm going all the way to Georgia, no doubt about it."
- "I've never been more sure of anything."
- "Ninety-nine percent."
- "At least 95%. No, wait, that's too low. At least 98%."
- "I dunno, but at least 95%. I guess I'd have to quit if I took a bad fall and broke my femur."
- "All the way, dude, every white blaze, no doubt."
- "I'm having serious trouble with my feet. Plantar fasciitis, I think. But I'm really determined to stay on. I thought it was like 99% when I started, but now realistically it's probably down to 95%."

- "I guess I'd have to say 98%. I hate to think there's a 2% chance I won't make it, but maybe that's realistic."

These answers reflect a clear and pervasive probability illusion: *Virtually every thru-hiker I met thought she or he had a better than 90% chance of completing the thru-hike, despite the fact that the true underlying probability is less than 10%.*

That's an extreme bias, a big heap of cockiness. It's not surprising that some individual hikers would be extremely confident, but how could nearly everyone be *so* confident, in the face of all that contrary evidence? How could virtually everyone believe that she or he would almost surely be one of the elite few to complete the thru-hike? How could everyone be truly exceptional and yet, magically, year after year the vast majority of hikers fail? How do we account for this extreme mismatch between perception and reality?

To explore this for my own edification, I would probe a bit deeper whenever I encountered a willing "data source." My trail acquaintance would tell me he was "pretty damn sure" he'd finish. And I'd say, "But you're not saying you're 100% sure, are you? I mean, all kinds of acts of god could intervene to get you off the trail. You could get hurt or sick. A family member could die. *You* could die. You could get hit by a train or have an aneurism. Obama could summon you to head up a special top-secret task force. Clearly, it doesn't make sense to be 100% sure, right?"

"Yeah, of course. Realistically, it's not quite 100%."

"But would you say you're at least 90% sure you'll complete the whole trail?"

"Oh, god, yes, absolutely," he says. "That's too low. It's a better than 90% chance, for sure."

"OK if I ask you a few questions to see if you really should be so confident?"

"Sure, go for it," he says.

"OK, what's the probability of successfully completing the Maine segment? Think of it this way: if you were to attempt it 100 times, how many times do you think you'd succeed?" I ask as I get ready to enter the first elicited datum into my cell-phone calculator.

"Well, Maine's supposedly the hardest state. And I'm just getting in shape. I could tear something, like an Achilles tendon, and have to get off the trail. A friend of mine broke his ankle last year and she still can't walk right. And it's been so wet. I've had some bad falls, especially on those bog bridges. And I was off the trail with *Giardia* for a week. Thought I was gonna die. I dunno, maybe 93 successes in 100 tries?"

"OK, how 'bout New Hampshire?"

"Well, New Hampshire's supposed to be tough too. My brother went off the trail in The Whites when he attempted a thru-hike last year. I'll say about the same as Maine, 93%."

"How 'bout Vermont, Massachusetts, and Connecticut?"

"Vermont should be a bit higher cuz the trail gets easier. I'll say 94%. And Massachusetts is even easier, so I'll say 95%."

"And Connecticut?"

"That's a short segment and it's supposed to be easy, but hikers start getting Lyme disease there. I dunno, let's say 96%."

"New York?"

"That should be a little lower. It's a longer segment. I'll say 95% for New York ... and the same for New Jersey."

"OK, Pennsylvania's next."

"Hmmm, everybody talks about the pointy rocks. I'll say 93%."

"And Maryland?"

"Maryland's supposed to be short and easy, so it should be higher. 97%."

"And then the trail enters West Virginia for a whopping 2.4 miles. Think you'll be able to hack that?"

"Yeah, I'm 99.99% sure I can make it through West Virginia."

"OK, but then comes Virginia. That segment's over 540 miles long. What do you think?"

"Yeah, that's a long stretch. But the trail's supposed to be easy. And I'll be in great shape. I dunno, let's say 94%."

"OK, that leaves Tennessee, North Carolina, and Georgia. What do you think?"

"I hear the topography gets a little more challenging. I'll say 94% for Tennessee and North Carolina, and something higher for Georgia. If I make it to the Georgia line, I'll crawl on hands and knees if I have to. I'll say 98% for Georgia."

"Great, thanks for answering those questions," I say as I enter these last three numbers. "Now tell me, are you still more than 90% sure you'll complete the thru-hike now that you've thought about the individual segments?"

"Yeah, I stand by that. I still think my chances of doing the whole trail are better than 90%, maybe just a little better, but definitely not below 90%."

And then I'd drop the bomb, "Well, brace yourself: your probability of completion is nowhere near as high as you think it is. Based on your own guesstimates for the individual states, you have a 49% chance of completing the trail. Even though you were really confident about completing each state's segment, always at least 93%, you have to multiply those individual probabilities to compute the probability of completing the whole trail."

"Why did you multiply them?"

"Think of your chances of getting two consecutive heads if you flip a coin twice. There are four possible outcomes. You could get heads on both tosses, or tails on both, or you could get a heads and then a tails, or a tails and then a heads. So, there's a one in four chance of getting two consecutive heads. You could compute this simply by multiplying the probability of getting a heads on the first toss, 50%, by the probability of getting a heads on the second toss, also 50%. The product is 25%."

"OK, I see that."

"You didn't realize it, obviously, but if you somehow accurately guesstimated the probability of completing each state, your chances of making it to Springer are no better than your chances of getting a heads on a single flip of a coin," I say as I balance an ultra-light dime on my cocked thumb, ready to flip.

"Hell, no, don't flip that coin. I don't want to know my fate."

∞

This fellow was minding his own bidness, hiking his own hike under delusions of awesomeness, like virtually every thru-hiker. And then I revealed his extreme probability bias. Even after reasoning through his chances for each state, he remained overconfident. And when I revealed his chances for completing the whole trail were no better than the outcome of a coin toss, he expressed superstition bias. He thought just maybe I could cause him to fail by flipping a dime.

Maybe this helps explain another curious aspect of thru-hiker behavior. We tend to wear the same clothes day after day, for months. Why? Because carrying even a modest wardrobe is incompatible with going ultra-light. But maybe it's partly explained by superstition. Just like an athlete who wears the same pair of lucky socks for an entire season, thru-hikers wear their lucky socks and shorts and shirt until their luck runs out or they reach the other end of the trail, whichever comes first.

The truth is some thru-hikers have trouble upon re-entry into mainstream society. They're slow to readjust. They sleep on the floor. They play video games in their mom's basement. They stash their trekking poles, but refuse to diversify their wardrobe. They refuse to change out of their lucky thru-shorts.

∞

I would then challenge my trail acquaintance to come to terms with his fatheadedness. I'd ask something like, "So, you started out thinking your chances of finishing the thru-hike were close to 100%. Then, based on your own guesstimates, you agreed that your true chances are closer to 50%, right?"

"Yeah, I guess," he'd say.

"So, in the last few minutes you've gone from thinking Springer's a foregone conclusion to thinking it's a coin flip."

"Don't rub it in."

"This still represents overconfidence, considering the overall rate of completion is less than 10%. So, here's my next question: you must consider yourself to be an above-average hiker?"

"Yeah, of course, I might not be the best hiker on the whole trail, but I'm damn good. I'm better than average, that's for sure. I'm faster. I have better endurance. I'm a better camper. I would've stayed home if I'd thought I was below average."

"That's what I thought you'd say. I've asked one thru-hiker after another for weeks now and it's almost impossible to find anyone who admits to being below average. Some hikers have been a little too shy to brag, but they virtually always agree they're at least above average."

"I see what you mean, how can everyone be above average?"

"Right, that's why this illusion-of-superiority bias is sometimes called the Lake Wobegon Effect."

"The what effect?"

"The Lake Wobegon Effect. Do you know the radio show *A Prairie Home Companion*?"

"Sure, I've heard that show a few times. Plus, it's a movie now too."

"Well, you might recall the part where Garrison Keillor reports the news from his fictional hometown, Lake Wobegon. He tells amusing tales about Norwegian bachelor farmers and ice fishing and church suppers. And at the end he signs off by saying, 'That's the news from Lake Wobegon, where all the men are good looking, all the women are strong, and all the kids are *above average*.' The audience has laughed at that for decades because, I suppose, everyone recognizes that even in a fairytale place like Lake Wobegon, roughly half the kids would be below average."

"And half the thru-hikers are below average too," he says.

"Of course, but either everyone's delusional or nobody wants to admit his or her own ordinariness. What do you think?"

"I dunno. All I know is I'm truly superior. It doesn't matter whether other hikers are self-delusional or lying," he concludes.

"That's raises an interesting question," I say.

"I'll be the judge of whether it's interesting," he says.

"Sure, you do that. I'm just not sure I can trust your judgment. After all, we've already exposed you as a master of distorted logic. You're prone to extreme probability illusions."

"Just ask your fascinating question, Ledge."

"OK, here it is: why do you think well over 90% of thru-hikers fail to complete a legitimate thru-hike? Why don't they walk by every white blaze? Why do they quit or cheat, by yellow-blazing or taking blue-blaze short-cuts? Why do they fail?"

"Well, not to be too blunt, but I think the vast majority of them are lame. They shouldn't be on the trail in the first place. They've never even hiked before. Or they're really unathletic. And they don't have the right kind of makeup. They get homesick. They're not emotionally mature enough for this. They can't hack it. They hate the rain and the pain. They're inferior. What can I say? They fake an injury and go home."

"I see. And what about you, what would put you off the trail?"

"That's easy. It's an extremely short list. I would leave the trail only if I suddenly keeled over or if my femur snapped or if someone in my family died."

"Priceless," I say. "That's what I was hoping you'd say."

"Why? What now, Ledge?"

"Well, you've just expressed yet another cognitive bias, this time a social bias called the actor-observer bias. And in your case it's extreme."

"Go on," he says with that I'm-so-annoyed tone.

"You see, you haven't even failed yet. You haven't quit and gone off the trail. But you already have an extremely biased, self-serving way of rationalizing it if and when you do quit. You have a ready-made excuse."

"Go on," he says, rolling his eyes.

"When other people fail or cheat, you attribute it to their intrinsic shortcomings, their weakness of character, athletic inferiority, personality defects, and overall lameness. But if you were to fail, it would be for reasons beyond your control, like divine intervention. You certainly wouldn't go off the trail because you couldn't hack the pain or the boredom or the homesickness?"

"No, of course not."

"That's fascinating because virtually everyone I talk to has the same actor-observer bias. When *we* fail at something, we tend to blame it on external circumstances. When *others* fail in the same context, we tend to blame it on their lameness."

"But I *am* awesome," he says.

"Of course you are! But if you imagine a continuum with totally awesome people like you on end and totally lame people on the other, how can virtually everyone walk along the trail thinking they're in the awesome tail of the distribution?"

"I dunno, Ledge. I can't answer your riddles *for* you. That's something you're gonna have to do for yourself. But before you explore my superiority any further, let *me* ask *you* a question."

"Shoot."

"How confident are *you*, Ledge? Do you really believe you have only a 5 or 10% chance of finishing a legit thru-hike? Or do you yourself in fact have an overinflated opinion of your own bad self? What's *your* probability of finishing?"

"That's easy. I'd say about 100%."

"And you obviously think of yourself as being way above average?"

"Of course."

"And if you don't make it to Springer, it'll be due to a freak accident, something completely beyond your control, right?"

"Right," I say.

"Thought so. How do *you* reconcile the enormous mismatch between your overinflated self-image and your run-of-the-mill abilities?"

"I don't," I say.

"Gotcha.

"OK, you got me, but let me ask *you* another question?" I say.

"No, it's still my turn, Ledge. You seem to have none of the answers, but I'm going to ask this anyway: why do *you* think the attrition rate is so high?"

"Glad you asked. But I'm going to offer just a partial answer and I'm going to do so by asking you a question, OK?"

"Fine, ask it."

"OK," I say, "this isn't a new question. You've been asked this question many times. You were asked it by your friends and family members before you even got on the trail. You were asked this question by fellow passengers on the bus on your way to Millinocket. You were asked this question by every SOBO you got to know starting in Millinocket."

"Sounds like another fascinating question."

"It is, because it reveals another bias. The question is: how long will it take you to do the thru-hike? Or when do you plan to finish? My hunch is your answer's been changing, right?"

"Yeah, it's true. Before I started, I told everyone it would take three and a half months, four at the max. By the time I got to Monson and kissed that road, I'd been humbled by the 100-mile Wilderness and I started telling everyone it would take about four and half months. Now I see it'll take about five and a half months."

"Parfait, that's what I was hoping you'd say."

"Glad I keep you entertained."

"Me too. Anyway, you may be pleased to know you've just provided data supporting Ledge's Law."

"Ledge's Law? This should be good."

"Yeah, Ledge's Law states 'it always takes longer,' where 'it' refers to a thru-hike. Your initial estimate of completion time was a bit off, wouldn't you say? Turns out it was a gross *under*estimate. You were off by two months, 12 weeks, about 60 days. Let's see, 60 multiplied by 24, that's 1440 hours. Hope you phoned home to let everyone know you're going to be late."

"They know. Believe me, they know. My girlfriend tells me how far behind schedule I am every time we talk."

"OK, this might help. She's in grad school now, right?"

"Right."

"Well, I know, and now you do too, there's no conceivable way she's actually going to finish her thesis on time. She's going to commit the same sort of planning fallacy you committed. She just doesn't know it yet. But it's inevitable. It's a law."

"I bet you're right."

"Of course I'm right. In fact, Ledge's Law is a direct restatement, a blatant rip-off of something called Pilson's Law, which also states 'it always takes longer.' But Henry Pilson wasn't a thru-hiker. He was an oceanography professor at the University of Rhode Island. He was frustrated by his graduate students' glacial progress, so he coined Pilson's Law, where 'it' refers to thesis preparation."

"That's cool. It does make me feel better knowing everyone will take longer than expected to finish their hike. And it really makes me feel better to know my girlfriend's going to commit the same kind planning fallacy."

"Glad I could help," I say.

"I just wish you had a law that would get my parents off my back. They're not upset that it's taking me so long to finish the hike. They're upset because I keep asking them for money so I can stay on the trail."

"Oh, but I do have a law for that. Tell your parents not to feel bad. They've committed the same planning fallacy every parent commits when she or he decides to help finance a grown offspring's hike. They've supported a corollary of Ledge's Law, which states 'because it always takes longer, it always costs more,' where 'it' again refers to an A.T. thru-hike. They might find some consolation in knowing they're like other parents and that they've obeyed a law."

"Fantastic. Can I give 'em your phone number? You know, just in case they think I'm bullshitting."

"Sure. Glad to help. Just tell 'em Ledge says 'to err is human'."

"And to hike is divine."

"Good one."

"But, Ledge, *why* does your law hold? Why does it *always* take *longer*?"

"That's easy. Ledge's Law holds because, like the bumper sticker says: scat happens. Think of it this way, there's really nothing that can happen to magically speed you along the trail. But an infinite number of interventions, some of them imponderable, could impede your progress. On any given day, you could tweak your knee and so cover only 13 miles rather than the planned 23. Or you could become sick with *Giardia* and spend lots of time with your shorts to your ankles, which again could adversely affect your mileage. Or you could rendezvous with a trailfriend, succumb to peer pressure and take an unplanned double zero. Or you could spend an unanticipated day off the trail because your girlfriend breaks up with you and it takes a full day to win her back. Or you could spend an extra day in a trail town because the outfitter didn't have size 12 and you just can't squeeze into a size 11 anymore."

"Or you could be like Lost Cause and waste most of a day walking the wrong direction on the trail."

"Right, good one," I say. "And if you're like most hikers, you often overestimate how far you'll travel on any given day. You'll justify your choice to stop short, by thinking about how nice it would be to stay here alone in this shelter, how you've already gone 16 miles and isn't that enough, how it'll be dark soon, and how that last lightning bolt was only two-tenths from your head. You won't have the option of stopping on the far side of your planned destination – because you haven't got there yet. The inevitable bias is to undershoot."

"OK, Ledge, now for the moment of truth: have you provided support for your own law?"

"Of course, it's a *law*. I started out bragging about how I'd finish in about three and a half months. It took me almost that long to reach the midway point.

"And one last bragging point for Ledge's Law and its corollary: they help account for the high attrition rate, for why so many hikers disappear off the trail even months into their hike and only hundreds of miles from the terminus. Their 'failure' is illusory. They're due in Ashville or Boulder on Tuesday to begin their new career doing the work of angels, working with autistic kids or running a therapeutic backpacking program. Many of these folks, thanks to the universal planning fallacy, simply run out of time or money or both. And of course many hikers who run short on time and money 'skip ahead' and pretend they finished a legitimate thru-hike."

∞

"But, Ledge, don't you think these delusions are helpful? Don't you think overconfidence helps thru-hikers finish?"

"Yeah, that seems plausible. Evolutionary ecologists believe cognitive biases are adaptive under prevailing natural conditions. And migrating on foot is an evolutionarily relevant behavior, something we humans did quite naturally for almost our entire history. Some people remain nomadic to this day. And we're all facultatively nomadic. We're still human. So, it's easy to imagine overconfidence has long been an adaptive trait when you're traveling thousands of miles by foot."

"Maybe thru-hiking isn't such a bizarre thing to do after all?" he says.

"Right, plus overconfidence gets people out on the trail in the first place. Thru-hikers are like explorers, prospectors, and pioneers. Those people who historically traveled, often solo, into extremely remote places must have been really cocky. And let's face it, even something as tame as a thru-hike in 2009 is still a pretty cocky thing to do."

"Sure is," he says.

"You're more likely to try a thru-hike if you're 'sure' you'll finish and be better than other hikers and stay within your budget. And if you maintain a rosy outlook, even after you've been sick and injured and delayed and financially burdensome, you just may finish."

Then you'll walk away from the thru-hike brimming with a newfound level of overconfidence. You may attribute your success to your stellar makeup, sterling character, and intrinsic superiority. And you may not recognize just how truly lucky you were, not because you're lucky to be so darn special – God's gift to all of us – but because you're lucky you didn't get befallen by one of those beyond-your-own-control contingencies that put so many of your cohort off the trail. Or so they say.

WE RULE, YOU DROOL

I arrived at Katahdin Stream in Percival's Park, at the foot of Katahdin, with loads of preconceived notions about cognitive biases. I figured thru-hikers would be extremely confident. We'd be overconfident about our prospects for completion, our native and hard-earned abilities, our stick-to-itiveness, our timetable, and our budget. I wasn't agnostic. I anticipated much of this self-perceived awesomeness.

But I didn't anticipate all of the myriad ways in which thru-hikers would express *social* biases. We should call the A.T. "Our National Social *Bias* Trail." Early on, I observed outgroup-homogeneity bias, the tendency to see members of an outside group as being less diverse than they really are. While still in Maine, we SOBOs started to encounter NOBOs. For some, an instant animosity arose. These hypercompetitive SOBOs hammed it up, but the rivalry was real. They stereotyped NOBOs as being cocky, stuck-up, scrawny wipers of SOBOs' bottoms, who mostly just deserved to be hit in the head. They were sheeple. They were clones. They weren't even worth greeting on the trail, except to say "baaaaaahh" as each clone passed.

In sharp contrast, fellow SOBOs comprised a diverse array of unique individuals who happened to be humble, strong, cool, interesting, multi-talented, friendly, generous, open, kind, tolerant, accomplished, athletic, thoughtful, clever, fascinating, well-traveled, well-read, multi-lingual, burly, altruistic, insightful, skilled, witty god-like hiking machines.

SOBOs were floating face down in a pool of illusory superiority.

I tried to appeal to reason. I argued for parsimony. I challenged the assumption that our modest little SOBO gaggle was somehow magically more diverse than the NOBO multitude. That group, I argued, must include hikers who would self-identify as GLBTQ or African American or Native American or Japanese or Oregonian or Wiccan. That group may include sculptors, Hindi-speakers, K2 climbers, Triple Crowners, Buddhists, shamans, published poets, male prostitutes, and horse whisperers. Our group mostly contained angst-ridden rich kids and verbose retirees. My pontifications fell on wax-clogged ears.

NOBOs, of course, were hardly immune to outgroup-homogeneity bias. Reciprocating with their own brand of us-versus-themism, they pigeonholed SOBOs as cocky newbies. They called us "little beards" and claimed we hadn't accomplished anything yet. When they really got to trash-talking, they'd say we hadn't even earned the right to call ourselves "hikers," never mind "thru-hikers." That really hurt.

Some of this SOBO-directed hostility stemmed from yet another cognitive bias. We SOBOs were prone to what I'll call the recency effect. Whenever we deigned to exchange a few words with NOBO sheeple, we'd rave about how easy the trail would be for them for the next few days. If we'd been rational cognizers, we would've given an unbiased appraisal of the trail conditions. But we were strongly swayed by our recent experience. How could we be objective? We'd just made it through Maine and The Whites. That was our frame of reference. Then we got blown away by how easy the trail became south of Moosilauke. So, we shared our overly optimistic impressions with NOBOs.

NOBO reality would not match SOBO perception. The trail ahead for NOBOs would be hard. It had seemed like a cake walk for us, but it would seem particularly hard for them, partly because we'd tricked them. They'd resent us. They'd think we'd deceived them on purpose, out of malice, or that we were such newbies that we still naively thought everything was easy. They'd think our perceptions were illusory, but they wouldn't realize why. In any case, as self-appointed spokesperson for SOBOs, I say, "we're sorry." We told what we believed to be the truth, so help us Grandma Gatewood.

Speaking of GG, it goes without saying that she was a *NOBO*, on all three of her legendary thru-hikes. In her day, there were precious few thru-hikers and they were all NOBOs. These days, more than 90% of thru-hikers choose to go north, year after year. In a typical year over the last couple of decades, roughly 1000 hikers have headed northbound while only 100 or so have headed southbound. The probability of such an extreme disparity by chance alone is a miniscule 6.7×10^{-162}. That's no accident. Clearly, thru-hikers show an extreme disinclination to go south, but why? Surely, an extreme bias like that must have a good explanation. Is there an impeccable rationale for this directional bias? Or is it yet another byproduct of cognitive bias among thru-hikers?

To explore this bias, I asked many NOBOs why they chose to go north. The vast majority of them claimed they chose to start in Georgia because NOBOs experience better weather. They "knew" this, of course, based on rumor and innuendo, not based on careful analysis of detailed climate data collected at official NOAA weather stations situated along the trail. They "knew" it because their buddy, Goon Unit, had said so. And he'd heard it from another reliable source, Lip Canker. Or they'd read it on the web. It was conventional wisdom. Just for the record, NOBOs often start in the snow and end in the snow. SOBOs rarely hike in snow because they wait till at least mid-May to start, long after spring has sprung in Maine, and they finish up in October or November, when it's usually autumnal in Georgia. Without thinking it through, NOBOs were following the herd, trusting implicitly in the wisdom of the crowd. (This kind of "conspecific attraction" is often adaptive, especially when you're naive.) These copy cats had jumped on the bandwagon. They were perpetuating the NOBO fad.

But I think there's something more at play here. I would often turn the question around and ask, "Why didn't you want to walk south?" This reframing of the question would often reveal a homing bias. Turns out, many thru-hikers are from the overpopulated northeastern states. They were walking toward family and friends. They were walking home. Some of them went by trailnames like Walking Home, Mrs. Going Home, Homer, and Home Girrrrrl. It's a powerful force, that homing instinct.

If I've really uncovered another bias that rules the curious minds of thru-hikers, how do I account for my own choice to go SOBO, despite the fact that I grew up in Maine? Well, because I did a yo-yo, a SOBO thru-bike followed by a return NOBO thru-bike, I did get to follow my homing instinct. As soon as I rounded second base (Springer), I was headed for home (Millinocket).

But I hiked southbound also because that's what anyone with my degree of reactance bias would "choose" to do. People advised me to go NOBO, so I really had no choice. My reaction to advice is to say to myself, "Don't try to constrain my freedom to choose, it will backfire." My cognitive bias simply wouldn't let me follow the northbound herd.

TRAIL-CRED MATTERS

After the wave of NOBOs had passed, the focus of trail chatter switched from those unsavory NOBOs to a problematic SOBO. You see, one of our own had distinguished himself. He'd been busy as a giant aquatic rodent, ruining his own hike. He'd alienated himself from other hikers. Hostel keepers knew his reputation long before he hitched into town. He used trailnames like aliases. He'd destroyed his own trail-cred. It was not going well.

He seemed to think he could do whatever he pleased because he was just hiking his own hike, he wasn't hurting anyone, and he didn't care what anyone thought. Unfortunately, he'd corrupted the hike-your-own hike principle; he was hurting everyone, which he eventually came to acknowledge; and he should have cared what other people thought. Reputation is everything and he was hell-bent on sabotaging his own. He was hiking like he was invisible, but the rest of us could see the turd on his head.

He was operating under delusions of respectability. He seemed to think he could bluff and steal with impunity. He seemed to think he could behave disreputably and yet somehow win the respect of fellow hikers. That didn't exactly pan out.

I tried to intervene. I tried to convince him it was OK for the rest of us to hike our own hike, but not for *him* to hike *his* own hike. He should start hiking someone else's hike tout suite. He should ask himself how Jesus, Thoreau, Grandma Gatewood, or any of his halfway decent trail acquaintances would hike.

But he chose his own path. He did as he pleased. He conned his way down the trail. He amassed an impressive list of crimes and misdemeanors and peccadilloes. The rest of us compiled a list of ways to rob yourself of trail-cred, damage the reputations of hikers in general, wear sanctimony on your sleeve, and become persona non grata. A few examples suffice:

o Shoplift chronically from stores in trail towns
o Skip out on hostels without paying
o Con pastors out of large wads of cash and then misconstrue it as "trail magic"
o Defecate in plastic bags
o Pose as legitimate thru-hiker
o Leave fake mud-turds in shelters
o Draw self-portrait as masturbating Cyclops

What's a fellow thru-hiker to do? I encouraged him to go home or to make amends by apologizing, repaying everyone, and turning the rest of his hike into one of integrity. That didn't work.

So when a direct approach fails, what's a hiker to do? Gossip, of course. Lots of hikers decry gossip, without recognizing its legitimacy. They believe the conventional wisdom that gossip is just plain bad and surely has no place on the trail. To overcome this expedient notion, it helps to think in terms of an actor-observer bias I'll call gossip bias. This is the notion that when someone else gossips it's petty, vindictive, and small-minded. The gossiper is lower than squid scat and obviously harbors a grudge. End of story. But when *you* gossip it's a legitimate indispensible form of social policing and *altruistic* punishment. From this perspective, to refrain from gossiping is selfish. By refusing to pay a cost, you become a social parasite on those who do the right thing. The act of gossip is altruistic because you alone pay the cost. You alone accept the risks of retaliation and of being labeled spiteful; meanwhile, everyone else benefits from your act. Of course, it's not truly self-sacrificial if you benefit in the end by elevating your own reputation as a trail saint.

So, go ahead and gossip to your heart's content, as long as you're truly deliberative and you're doing the right thing and not being petty or spiteful. Just don't gossip about me. And keep in mind that the cause is just, that you're safeguarding the reputation of hikers in general and helping to ensure there won't be fake turds in the shelters. If you gossip judiciously, you'll deserve a reward, like a special commendation from the ATC. You may even get your name engraved on a plaque in Harpers Ferry honoring the Official A.T. Snitch of the Year.

PACK WEIGHTY MATTERS

While we're on the topic of reputation and irrational social behavior, some of my favorite examples involve bizarre cases of showing off by adopting a pack-weight "handicap."

Decades ago, we called it "backpacking," never "hiking" or "walking." Hiking was something suburbanites did while wearing a bookbag and staying within earshot of a road. Walking was something people did on the way to or from their car. *We* were backpackers. We were hardcore. We saved up and bought the biggest external frame backpack available. The bigger the better, we thought. We filled our backpacks with as much stuff as we could jam into all those compartments and pockets. We lashed extra stuff to the outside. And we bragged about how much our pack weighed. That was a reliable way to signal physical superiority. You had to be pretty fit to outshine your peers by carrying the heaviest pack. The handicap of all that extraneous weight on your back was an honest indicator of toughness. You couldn't fake it in the long run. You earned yourself prestige points by adopting an unfakeable handicap.

But that was then and this is now. The pendulum has swung. Carrying an ultra-heavy pack is no longer an effective way to advertise superiority. It's now considered just plain foolish to carry an 80-pound pack, as Gonad did through the 100-mile Wilderness in 2009. Among hardcore long-distance hikers these days, going ultra-light is all the rage. And the best way to advertize your superiority is to carry the lightest pack. Thru-hikers no longer show off by advertising brute strength. Now they're more inclined to signal minimalism as a form of hiking prowess.

Going super-ultra-light says to fellow hikers, "Look at me, look how cool I am. I'm cooler than Ray Jardine. I can walk the entire A.T. with a tiny fraction of what you're carrying. I'm so clever and skilled and experienced that I couldn't be bothered fussing with all that extra gear. I'm better than you. I don't need rain gear or a tent or a hammock. I just carry a sheet of Tyvek to use as an emergency tarp. I can hike through any weather, covering great distances you wouldn't even attempt. I can keep going till I reach the next shelter or town. I can sleep in a hollow log, if I even want to sleep. I certainly don't need to carry a sleeping bag; a liner and an ultra-light bivy sack are all I need. I'm a furnace. I don't get cold. And I don't need to carry a stove or water filter. I have a couple Esbit® tablets and a few Aquamira® drops, just for fun. And I hardly ever carry more than a couple of days' worth of food. I cover so much ground, so effortlessly, that I can resupply any time I get hungry. And I rehydrate opportunistically rather than carry liters of water on my back. You're carrying all that equipment, clothing, shelter, food, and water because you're a cozy comfy camper. I'm an elite long-distance hiker."

I encountered this kind of extreme signaling just moments after arriving at the Appalachian Trail Lodge in Millinocket, the night before beginning my thru-hike. The first incipient thru-hiker I met was a twenty-something fellow who found it necessary to signal his superiority the moment we met. The first thing he said to me was, "Wanna feel how light my pack is?"

And so the first thing I said to him was, "Wanna feel how hard my fist is?"

I was joking, of course. I wouldn't hit the guy. I'm a pacifist. Besides, I could've broken a metacarpal and then I would've hiked for weeks with one trekking pole. I wasn't about to accept that handicap, even if it might have signaled my hiking superiority.

203

By the time this ultra-light showboat had made it to Harpers Ferry, he'd managed to offend everyone in his path. He had no trailfriends, so he had to give himself a trailname. As if to signal that the rest of us were low-quality dog excrement, he called himself "*The* SOBO HOBO." This usage of the definite article pissed off *everyone*. What's more, he didn't seem to realize that SOBO is a play on HOBO, and so the term SOBO HOBO is redundant. And he obviously didn't know the etymology of HOBO, which is short for homeward bound. He's not from the Southeast and so he was not homeward bound. Semantic quibbling aside, it must be lonely at the top. I guess that's the price you pay for world-class greatness.

He was not merely great. He was vastly superior to every lame SOBO he'd left in his wake. He eventually signaled this undeniable superiority by getting rid of his ultra-light pack. He carried nothing more than a Camelbak®. But attached to it, he proudly displayed an adopted handicap, an extraneous item – a canoe paddle. At first glance this seemed like a double-handicap, a way to signal world-class greatness in *two* ways. It was like saying, "Look at me, I'm cool beyond belief. I'm so vastly superior that I don't even need to carry a pack. On top of that, I can even carry extra weight! Virtually no gear *and* a paddle, you try that. No, don't bother, you couldn't pull it off, you poor mediocre mortal."

But closer inspection revealed a fatal flaw in his signaling strategy. The paddle was one of those miniature toys ordinarily used as a tacky decoration. It couldn't have weighed much more than a Snickers bar. That's the flaw: a handicap must have a tangible cost. It's not an honest indicator of anything, other than tackiness, if its weight is negligible. If only he'd attached, say, 50 full-size paddles to his Camelbak ... *that* would have been an impressive double-handicap display.

Alternatively, he could have attached to his Camelbak something substantial – like an 8-lb brass dildo. Don't laugh, that's exactly what's making its way up the trail right now, for at least the third consecutive year. I saw it proudly displayed on the kitchen table at Rob Bird's hostel in Dalton, Massachusetts. I touched it, of course. I picked it up to feel its heft, to satisfy my curiosity as to whether this seemingly useless inanimate object was heavy enough to qualify as a handicap. (Until then, I'd tacitly assumed all dildos on the trail were ultra-light models.) But this one really did weigh as much a gallon of Gatorade. I checked the bottom to make sure it didn't have a secret compartment. I suspected the hikers who carried it might have been bluffing. I thought maybe they were carrying a hollow, ultra-light sex toy each day and then filling it with sand each evening before putting it on display. But, no, the bottom was solid. This status symbol was a single unit of solid brass. So, I asked myself, "Is carrying this object all the way to Katahdin an honest display of hiker quality?" I answered in the affirmative, with the proviso that the object isn't being used for its original purpose. And then I washed my hands with Dr. Bronner's All-One-God-Faith soap, just in case.

∞

If super-ultra-light is the way to go, why doesn't everyone jump on the bandwagon? The main reason, I think, is it's unfakeable. Not everyone can thrive or even survive without a sleeping bag or rain jacket. Some hikers would go hypothermic trying to make it to the next shelter, where they would shiver through a miserable night without a sleeping bag. Not every wannabe minimalist could cope. For some, going super-ultra-light would be imprudent, even death-defying.

Even so, most thru-hikers could carry considerably less than they do. Their packs are too heavy. They resort to slack-packing, rather than back-packing. They travel more highway miles than trail miles. They're ashamed of their growing carbon footprint and their "cheating." And yet when they finish their latest slack-packing stint, they proceed to put on their still-too-heavy pack.

One fellow SOBO refused to lighten his load, expressing several simultaneous cognitive biases in the process. He slack-packed religiously. He hated his own pack. But he wouldn't admit its contents were too heavy. He thought the pack itself was to blame. Along the way, he replaced his pack *four* times. Some thru-hikers don't bath that many times. He bought new packs like most thru-hikers buy new shoes. I replaced my shoes five times, each time hoping for a miracle, hoping *this* would be the make-model-size-orthotic combo that would magically make the foot pain vanish. That didn't work. Meanwhile, my SOBO trailfriend replaced pack after pack, hoping each time the pain in his shoulders and hips would vanish. That didn't happen. Why not? Maybe it had something to do with the fact that each pack he bought was more deluxe and so heavier than the last one. It seems he compensated for excessive pack weight by increasing his pack weight. Ouch.

For whatever "reason," *many* fellow thru-hikers insisted on trudging under a needlessly heavy load. We could attribute this hiker-headedness to a whole suite of cognitive biases, including reactance, status quo, post-purchase rationalization, endowment effect, loss aversion, and so on. Let's just chalk it up to an all-encompassing hiker trait: stubbornness.

But why do thru-hikers start with such a heavy pack in the first place? Why do they get off the bus in Georgia or Maine with a pack full of nonessential stuff, unless of course they're signaling their true heritable stubbornness? I think it's partly attributable to a widespread planning fallacy I'll call the incremental packing trap. Luckily, I offer a preventive way to avoid this pitfall. Here's the foolproof escape. Imagine it's shakedown time. You're getting on the bus tomorrow, heading for the starting terminus. I assume you'd like to avoid Beagle's blunder of arriving in Millinocket with five toenail clippers? If so, and you'd like your pack to be comfy and light, just follow this simple recipe:

1) Dump contents of pack on floor.
2) Create two piles.
   a. Place each *essential* item in Pile A. Note: essential items do not include underpants, binoculars, razor, soap, coffee mug, Frisbee, GPS unit, or *The Laughalachian Trail*.
   b. Place remaining items in Pile B.
3) Put contents of Pile A back into pack.
4) Put contents of Pile B into garbage bag.
   a. Get rid of this bag. Hide it in a closet. Bury it in a time capsule. Give it away. Forget it ever existed.

If you hate step 4a, then follow this alternative step. Lift the garbage bag containing all of that Pile B junk. Hold it with one hand at eye level. Straighten your arm. Hold it steady for one hour. Be forewarned: this will hurt. At one-minute intervals, ask yourself, "Do I really want to carry all this nonessential junk?" Allow yourself to say "No Sirree, Robert." Allow yourself to opt for 4a.

This approach provides an escape from the trap incipient thru-hikers routinely set. They do this by gazing longingly at Pile

B, at all of those goodies. And they ask, "Should I take this tiny container of Doctor Bronner's all-purpose peppermint soap?" And they answer, "Of course, I'm going to bath daily and this stuff's biodegradable and it weighs next to nothing." And then they ask, "Should I bring my harmonica?" They answer, "Why not, I'll entertain everyone with my awesome blues harp playing." "Should I bring my binoculars?" "Yep, I chose this feather-weight model specifically for *hiking*." "And my spare tube of blister salve?" "Yeah, I'll probably need that after a couple weeks." In a matter of minutes, pack weight has skyrocketed. And yet, each of those individual decisions seemed rational.

But there's a pronounced hidden bias here. You're likely to say "yes" repeatedly when each such reply increases pack weight incrementally. But if you were to ask yourself to say "yes" just once when the question is whether to include the same pile o' junk in one lump sum, you'd probably say, "No!"

Do yourself a favor. Don't set the incremental packing trap for yourself. Use my recipe for avoiding this mistake. You'll thank me later, unless of course you're reactant like me. In that case, I apologize because my recommendations will backfire and you'll probably end up carrying a pack filled with toe-nail clippers and AA batteries and a beach towel – until that quiescent disc in your lower back bulges and you go off the trail with debilitating sciatica. Sorry, I tried to warn you.

∞

While I'm on a pack-weight roll, I should describe the curious case of "The Sibs." This smurf-hiking quartet shared everything, or so I thought. They shared their trailname. They shared a water filter and a stove. They shared meals. They shared a family-specific body odor. They shared a positive outlook. They shared a cutoff mesh tank top – hubba hubba. They shared a cooking pot. I suspect they even shared a toothbrush. But they didn't share a *Bible*! Instead, each of them carried a full-size Bible, like those ultra-heavy monsters hidden in the bedside table in motel rooms. In aggregate, they carried about a dozen pounds of Bibles. Why? Were they signaling their superior devoutness by toting redundant copies of the Bible?

Faced with such puzzlements, I usually resort to that trendy question, "What would Jesus do?" Would he share a Bible with his siblings? My vote is "yah," for two reasons. First, Jesus was by all accounts a super-ultra-light hiker. He didn't even need to carry food. Second, Jesus was an only child, but let's assume that any hypothetical sibs would have been haploid, meaning produced from an unfertilized egg like their brother. If so, Jesus would have been 50% more closely related to his siblings than The Sibs are to each other. Accordingly, Jesus and *his* sibs probably would have been really cohesive and extremely cooperative. I can only imagine they would have shared a Bible. And it probably would have been an ultra-light condensed version, *sans* New Testament of course. He certainly wouldn't have signaled superiority by carrying extraneous heavy copies. After all, we have no reason to suspect Jesus of showing off.

∞

Speaking of biblical parables, one of our fellow SOBOs, Sphincter, reminded me of the little dude with the bent frame. You know, the guy Jesus straightened by laying on hands? Sphincter looked like that dude, not because his frame was bent but because his poles were bent. They were so badly bent that he had to bend deeply at the waist to use them, which he did even though he couldn't put any appreciable weight on them. They were no longer utilitarian. They were now just decorative. He might as well have used two of those miniature canoe paddles.

Why was he so stubborn? He held onto those bent poles like he had something to prove. This wasn't rational. It was a byproduct of a cognitive bias called loss-aversion bias (aka, sunk costs or endowment effect). The notion is that we tend to value a thing more highly if we already possess it than if we're given the opportunity to acquire it.

To explore whether Sphincter's hiker-head might have been ruled by loss aversion, I begin by asking him, "How much you want for those bent poles?"

"What?! You shittin' me, Ledge? You wanna buy 'em?"

"Yeah, maybe, depends how much you want for 'em."

"Well, I paid about $85 and I know they're bent but I'd like to recoup as much as I can."

"That's understandable," I say. "Would you sell 'em for $30?"

"No, I'd need to get more than that. How 'bout $50?"

"But what if you were to lose that pair?" I ask. "How much would you be willing to pay for a pair just like those, same bend and all?"

"Not much, I wouldn't want to buy bent ones. Maybe $5."

"Let me get this straight, what's the real value of those poles to you? Is it $50 or $5?"

"That depends on whether I'm the seller or the buyer," concludes Sphincter.

"Bingo."

"What bingo? Don't bingo me, Ledge."

"OK, I retract my bingo. But that's clearly not economically rational, right?"

"Duh," says Sphincter, "I guess it is kinda weird that I thought they were 10 times more valuable in one context."

"Can you think of an alternative to your state-of-the-art but severely bent trekking poles?"

"I could, but I'm not too worried about it. I'll get new poles eventually, maybe in Hanover."

"But why not solve the bent-pole problem in the interim, until you do eventually get new ones? How 'bout this: imagine you'd never used trekking poles at all, but you're open to the idea of trying them."

"OK, go on," says Sphincter.

"Imagine I were to present you with a binary choice. Suppose you could choose two wooden sticks I'd just found versus those two bent poles. Which would you prefer?"

"The sticks, I guess," says Sphincter.

"That's interesting because that particular form of tool use must be quite ancient. Proto-humans presumably used walking sticks a couple hundred million years ago. Our ancestors probably invented the stick long before they invented the wheel. And modern humans had been using walking sticks for a quarter of a millions years before Christ went on his walkabout on the present-day 86-mile Jesus Trail in the Galilee region of Israel.

"And even gorillas in the wild are known to use walking sticks, for gauging water depth and for supporting themselves while fording. They've even been observed using walking sticks as makeshift bog bridges. I wouldn't try that with your bent poles."

"Yeah, whatever, I get it, Ledge."

"Where did you say you just finished a degree in mechanical engineering?"

"Georgia Tech."

"Isn't that the third best mechanical engineering program in the country, behind MIT and Cal Tech?"

"Supposedly."

"And you couldn't figure out how to solve this problem? You couldn't figure how to use two sticks?"

"I could've. I just didn't want to."

"I see."

"You suck, Ledge."

"I know, but you love me anyway, right?"

"Wrong."

But I couldn't stop there, so we explored whether Sphincter's mental block might have been an expression of the not-invented-here bias. He was arguably so preoccupied with visions of partial derivatives that he couldn't see the forest for the sticks. He didn't arrive at this most elegant ancient solution on his own. He also apparently failed to notice that some of his fellow hikers, including The Sibs, had solved the elusive "Stick Problem." This quartet shared an octet of wooden sticks. But maybe the ever-reactant Sphincter didn't want to mimic the eons-old hiking practices of folks who also chose to carry redundant copies of the Bible.

IT'S NOT EASY BEING GREEN

Speaking of the ultra-green hiker named Christ, I began my hike intending to analyze thru-hiker behavior for evidence of greenness. I was prepared to see an enormous gap between perception and reality. I figured most thru-hikers would consider themselves to be green but their consumptive choices – their addiction to gasoline and cheeseburgers – would make them brown. I figured this greenness bias would be just another facet of their awesomeness bias. I would not be disappointed.

It took less than a minute upon arriving at the A.T. Lodge in Millinocket to identify my first case study. In the bunkroom, I was immediately accosted by a fellow SOBO-to-be. He bragged about how green he was, how he lived an extremely low-impact lifestyle, how he had spent the last year and a half living in a tent. He was a voluntary peasant, an eco-saint of the nth degree. His ecological footprint must be miniscule, I thought. This guy could be the exception that proves the rule. He could be the one and only person I'd meet who was doing a truly sustainable thru-hike. But then he bragged without the slightest hint of self-recrimination that he'd just flown from Australia to Maine, with five stopovers along the way. His hike would not be sustainable, not by a long shot.

His carbon footprint was monstrous. He'd just commuted 20,000+ miles by jet plane. That's a carbon footprint of 4.6 hectares (ha). In other words, we'd have to set aside about nine football fields' worth of ecologically productive land to sequester his share of the carbon emissions for those flights. There are 15.7 ha available per person globally to meet our annual needs. Prorated for a 4-month thru-hike, his Global Fair Earthshare was 5.2 ha. In just a few hours of puddle-jumping, he'd used 4.6 ha, or 88%, of his allotment. His carbon footprint all by itself, just for getting to Maine, had made his hike teeter on the brink of unsustainability. And he hadn't even set foot on the trail or reached into his food bag yet.

The next day he started fueling his furnace, eating his way down the trail. How big would his thru-hike footprint become? Would his appetite make his hike unsustainable? Yes, by a very wide margin. His *food* footprint would grow to 13.6 ha, assuming a typical thru-hiker diet. I assume he ate omnivorously, scarfing down three large meals and several substantial snacks per day; got most of his food from supermarkets, convenience stores, and restaurants; and rarely ate certified organic or sustainably produced food. Under these plausible assumptions, his food footprint (13.6 ha) to move his body down the trail combined with his carbon footprint (4.6 ha) just to get to his body to the northern terminus was a whopping 18.2 ha. We can safely say this self-professed greenhead hiked an unsustainable hike. He surpassed the sustainability threshold (5.2 ha) while still in Maine.

We would need 3.5 planet Earths if everyone behaved like this thru-hiker. And we haven't even accounted for his housing footprint (including stays at hostels and motels), his goods-and-services footprint (including hiking gear), and other components of his carbon footprint (including shuttles along the trail and flying home after the hike).

His food footprint (13.6 ha) all by itself exceeded his Global Fair Earthshare (5.2 ha). So, if everyone on Earth ate like this thru-hiker, we'd need 2.6 Earths just to produce the food. And then we'd need to set aside additional nonexistent Earths to compensate for the carbon, housing, and goods-and-services footprints.

I started this diatribe by condemning his carbon footprint. But a quick look at his food footprint suggests every thru-hiker will be full of green guilt, regardless of how she or he arrives at the trail terminus. Hiker hunger is insatiable *and* unsustainable. Or is it?

Can we find a loophole, a way of minimizing our food footprint and hiking a genuinely sustainable hike? Well, back home in the other world, it's feasible to shrink your food footprint to a tidy 2.7 ha per year, well below the annual Global Fair

Earthshare of 15.7 ha. All you have to do is: a) eat a vegan diet; b) buy locally from farmers markets and cooperatives that sell certified organic and sustainably produced food; c) grow most of your own vegetables and herbs; and d) keep your metabolism low enough to maintain the appetite of a non-hiking mouse, eating just one large meal and two small snacks per day.

I've tried to live this way ever since 1976, when as a teenager I unilaterally decided to minimize my footprint by going vegetarian. (The fact that this lifestyle choice pissed off my parents I considered a bonus.) But the moment you step on the trail, there's a real temptation to fall off the veggie wagon, to turn into a top-of-the-food-chain carnivore, to become a junk food junkie. It's tempting to be expedient and just eat omnivorously without worrying too much about where the food came from, what it's made of, whether it's highly processed, whether it's traveled more miles than you will hike, and so on. All you know is you're hungry and you need calories and protein and fat, and you're a long way from your favorite co-op. Power bars from convenience stores will do just fine.

But getting sloppy about how you fuel your furnace will make your food footprint astronomically unsustainable. It will skyrocket to 55 ha if you put yourself at the top of the food chain, rely on grocery and convenience stores and restaurants, eat three large meals and several substantial snacks each day, and almost never buy certified organic, sustainably produced food. Pro-rated for a 5-month thru-hike, that's 22.9 ha – just for your biscuits! If everyone ate like that, we'd need 3.5 Earths just to produce the food. We'd be as guilty as our fellow SOBO who flew from Australia, even if we'd ridden a bicycle to begin our hike.

Don't get me wrong. I'm not saying thru-hikers are single-footedly destroying Earth through their ferocious appetites for oil, flesh, and junk food. Just think, Donald Trump's footprint probably trumps the aggregate lifetime footprints of all the thru-hikers who've ever lived. And contemporary thru-hiker appetites would have been sustainable back when the A.T. was created – when there were only about 2 billion Earthlings and global warming was an imponderable prospect. Even so, if *you* prefer to live in a just and sustainable way on today's shrunken Earth, you'll be alarmed by your own yeti-sized food footprint.

Here comes the positive spin. It's *possible* to maintain a sustainably tiny food footprint during a thru-hike, while eating a robust diet of three big meals and several substantial snacks per day. All you need to do is eat a vegan (2.1 ha for 5 months) or vegetarian (4.2 ha) diet of locally grown food bought at farmers markets and cooperatives that sell certified organic and sustainably produced food. The only real drawback to this plan: unlike convenience stores, organic farmers markets and food co-ops tend not to be distributed conveniently along the trail. Truth be told, they're few and far between. Hope you like hitching.

But seriously, there are several obvious and not-so-obvious ways to shrink your food footprint and so hike a greener hike:

o Go vegan or veggie. Take advantage of local farmers markets and co-ops. Eat locally grown foods. Minimize items in your diet that came from 2179+ miles away. Otherwise, we'll need to set aside enormous areas to sequester the carbon emissions from transporting your food. Minimize the McFood component of your diet. If you eat at the top of the food chain, your footprint will be ginormous. We'll need to set aside enormous areas to grow the grain to feed the domestic animals you like to consume. This is terribly inefficient. You could just eat your food's food. Remember, thanks to your raging hiker hunger, you're eating for three: 1) to meet your elevated basal metabolic demands, 2) to cover the expenditure for the ~10 miles of AM hiking, and 3) to cover the expenditures for the ~10 miles of PM hiking. Just be glad you're not pregnant.

o Rethink the old-fashioned approach of using mail drops. Each box could contain light loads of sustainably produced, organic food. You could make your own hiker foods, including dehydrated fruits and veggies and even power bars. Of course, an honest accounting of this approach must incorporate the embedded carbon-emissions cost of using USPS to deliver your food. But anything would be better than the current approach used by most thru-hikers, which is about as green as having each cheeseburger air-dropped by personal helicopter.

o Consider adopting an organic-farm refueling strategy. Step 1: Hitch to nearby organic farm and do work-for-stay. Step 2: Fill food bag with organic food. Step 3: Hitch back to the trail. Repeat steps 1-3 as necessary. Ideally, trail guides will soon list organic farms offering this sort of arrangement. And ALDHA could encourage hostel keepers to emulate Elmer at Sunnybrook Inn (Hot Springs, NC), where hikers feast on veggies and herbs grown by hikers on the premises.

o Garden remotely while you're on the trail. Rather than letting your garden lay fallow, ask a surrogate to tend it while you're off hiking. That kind soul and others could consume the food. Alternatively, donate your CSA share to someone less privileged than yourself. You'll indirectly shrink your food footprint and grease the skids for getting into eco-heaven.

o Forage for wild edibles along the trail. Shrink your footprint by consuming a tiny fraction of nature's surplus. Do as Grandma Gatewood did. Sautee puffballs and ramps. Put berries on your goatmeal. Munch on wild cucumber. Make sarsaparilla tea.

Scrump "wild" apples from abandoned orchards. Feast on fiddleheads.

To corrupt Bill Clinton's note-to-self during his successful 1992 campaign for the presidency ("It's the economy, stupid!"), if you really want to plan an ultra-low-impact thru-hike, keep in mind, "it's the food footprint, genius!" Fortunately, strict adherence to the above advice will accomplish just that.

But even after you've figured out the greenest way to refuel your scrawny thru-body, you'll still want to minimize the impacts of your other activities, especially transportation. Here are a few easy steps to shrink your carbon footprint:

o Don't fly or drive to and from the trail termini. Don't commit the but-the-plane-was-going-there-anyway fallacy. Don't fall for that bogus but-it's-a-hybrid ploy. Driving a hybrid car to the trail is on par with flying in a jet. Their carbon footprints are about 4.7 times bigger than a bus ride and about 7.5 times bigger than a train ride. If you're really cool, you'll travel to and from the trail by pedal power.

o Hitch-hike to and from trail towns. Your carbon footprint will remain tiny as long as you don't ask shuttle drivers to chauffeur your privileged thru-bum to and fro.

o Don't let your mom and dad, paramour, college roommate, or AA sponsor visit you on the trail. The footprint spike would go on *your* ledger. Besides, you'll be home soon enough.

o Don't slackpack. It's now stigmatized. The only thing more unsustainable than slackpacking would be to hire separate helicopters to shuttle you and your pack to and from the trailheads. Go light or stay home. If you don't hate your pack for its heftiness, you won't be tempted to slack off.

While you're getting all green on your bad self, you might as well obey a few more footprint-minimizing tips. First, to reduce your housing footprint, you could start by minimizing the number of times you rent a room. If you were to stay in motels as often as I did, your TV-shower-AC footprint could exceed your pizza footprint. Second, to reduce your goods-and-services footprint, you could resist the urge to buy new gear every time you feel like a shopaholic. Don't trade in your cosmetically blemished pack just because the company's policy is to replace it. Duct-tape it. Buy your next manskirt at a thrift store. Get your "new" socks from a hiker box. Store-bought socks would be putrified in a few miles anyway. See if you can reduce your consumption and waste production as dramatically as the trail reduces your waist line and stress level.

To keep it simple, you could just sweat the big stuff. Stay off planes and out of cars. Find another way to and from the trail. And when you get there, don't eat like you're at the apex of the food chain. Eat veggie, local, organic. Eat food rather than food products. The food footprint police will thank you. You may even find yourself nominated for A.T. Green-hiker of the Year.

CHAPTER 13

Laughing Matters☺☺☺[R]

Man, when you lose your laugh, you lose your footing.
— Ken Kesey

LIFE'LL KILL YA

Does it matter whether you hike with humor? I think so, especially if you've been recently diagnosed with an untreatable disease of the ultimately terminal variety. You see, I hiked and biked in the "early" stages of Huntington's, a degenerative neurological disease caused by a genetic mutation. I got my copy of the defective gene, like my passions for baseball and brook trout, from my dad. He went sideways after his diagnosis. To put it euphemistically, he died from self-inflected ventilation of the cranium with lead projectiles ordinarily used for dispatching the likes of Bambi. I went sideways after my diagnosis too. I considered copying his choice of exit strategy. But I chose a different path for myself. I chose the path of most resistance, a therapeutic thru-hike on the A.T.

I put myself on this 2179-mile treadway. I hoped all that LSD (long slow distance) would help me stave off suicidal depression and even cognitive deficit, as it apparently does for laboratory animals running daily ultra-marathons on treadmills for food pellets. I hoped the thru-hiking experience, with all that walking and laughing, would be neuroprotective – like megadoses of fish oil, creatine, blueberries, crossword puzzles, and Sudoku.

I thrived on the trail thanks to my propensity for taking a mindfully humorous approach to all aspects of life. From the moment I set foot on the trail, I saw the humor in all things, including my own health status.

But what's so funny about hiking with Huntington's, you're probably wondering? Well, for one thing, Huntington's makes you wobble. But unlike Weebles®, which wobble but don't fall down, I did fall down. I fell numerous times a day, especially in Maine. I usually fell while I was alone, but sometimes I fell in front of fellow hikers. One day in Maine, I fell in front of a former thru-hiker, Hostel Witness, who was out for a day hike. We had just met. We exchanged life stories and chatted about mutual trailfriends. We were lost in the moment. I made the mistake of setting down my trekking poles. Almost immediately, I lost my balance. I lurched and reeled and performed a quasi-pirouette. It wasn't graceful like the pirouette former Canadian Prime Minister Pierre Elliot Trudeau once performed in Buckingham Palace, as he trailed in Queen Elizabeth's footsteps. His pirouette was apparently a planned act of disdain for aristocracy. It was caught on camera. Trudeau's performance ended as gracefully as it had begun. He didn't miss a stride. My crude facsimile was a spontaneous byproduct of Huntington's. It was performed in front of an audience of one. As I came out of the spin, I staggered down a slope, bounced off a tree, and crashed facedown. Splat.

Hostel Witness reacted in a surprisingly generous way. He didn't laugh at my impromptu pratfall. That was surprising because it defied comedic logic. To corrupt an old joke by Mel Brooks, tragedy is when *I* get a little blister on my toe while hiking, and comedy is when *you* fall facedown into a pile of moose droppings – and suffocate. But rather than split a gut laughing at me, Hostel Witness hurried over and said in an empathic tone, "Ledge, are you OK?"

"Yeah, I think so."

"What was *that*?!"

"I fell."

"Yeah, I noticed, but why? What happened? Did you faint?"

"Not exactly."

"Well, how do think you're going to walk all the way to Georgia if you can't even stand up?"

"Trekking poles, it's all about the trekking poles," I said, as if he could intuit the rest.

∞

More dramatic than all the other times I fell in private or in the presence of other hikers was the time I fell *into* another hiker. It was in a bunkroom in one of the huts in The Whites. I had stashed my trekking poles. I walked toward my bunk, ready to hit the hay. But I lost my balance and stumbled and staggered through the dark, falling against something – or someone. I quickly realized that, by some miracle, I'd broken my fall when my right hand cupped the rock-hard buttock of a fellow hiker. I had a vice grip on it. I let go as soon as I realized what it was. He said nothing. I said nothing.

I know it's a long-overdue apology, but I do want to say, "I'm sorry, Sir Woodchuck. It was an accident. You're a beautiful man, but if I'd wanted to make a pass at you, I would've just made lingering eye contact."

∞

Solitary crashes kept me amused too. I'd usually feel the wheels coming off and then I'd go ass over teakettle and splat packside down. I'd lay there like an overturned turtle for a few seconds while mentally replaying scenes of Ingmar, the little Swedish boy in the movie *My Life as a Dog*, who did back-splats on the beach to cheer up his morose mother.

∞

I know how to laugh at myself, including when I fall. But I also knew the next splat could be my last. It could put me off the trail, literally by ending my thru-hike and figuratively by ending my thru-life. So I used my trekking poles like canes, especially on boulder scrambles and steep sections. And I developed a technique for monitoring and practicing my balance. (Not interested in just gracefully accepting my Huntington's fate, I'm trying to turn back the hands of time, to enjoy improved health over time.) I used yoga-like poses where I stood on one leg, with arms outstretched. One of these poses soon took on a secondary purpose. In addition to using it as a way to check my balance throughout the day, I co-opted it as a signal as soon as I detected other hikers mimicking it.

This pose has three names. Some hikers called it "The Tricky Part" or "The Big Fig Newton," but most hikers called it "Ledge's Aloha Pose."

Here's the backstory: I stole this signature move from a Fig Newton® TV commercial circa 1972, in which a portly middle-aged actor in a leotard and bulbous fig-body outfit does a little song-and-dance number. He sings the praises of this fruit-filled cookie. Toward the end, he looks into the camera and says, apropos of nothing, "Here comes the tricky part." He then stands on one leg, with knees slightly bent and with arms outstretched, and croons, "The ... Big ... Fig ... Newwtonnnnnnnnnn."

I used it as a long-distance aloha. I used it to say ciao, so long, fare thee well, hello, see you soon, I miss you already, or it's so great to see you again, depending on the context. Much to my delight, the receiver always reciprocated, always with laughter. It was like a long-distance hug, a high five, a fist bump. It was a semaphore-like maneuver. It was performed as if choreographed and yet it always felt like spontaneous and playful.

And like any good fad, it spread like wildfire. Hikers I'd never met before would use it in my presence. One trailfriend even incorporated a stick-figure drawing of the pose into his signature at the end of each of his hundreds of register entries.

You have my blessing to use it too. If it's disappeared from the thru-hiker repertoire, you can take a gander at the original TV commercial, which is available as a You Tube video. Or just give me a holler and I'll send you a photo via cell phone. Aloha.

∞

Between tricky-part alohas, I spent hours and hours hiking alone each day. I'd be gliding along, hitting my stride and feeling fine, when I'd suddenly realize that once again I was listening to the jukebox in my mind. I'd catch myself singing silently while hiking in a mindfully meditative way. At that moment of self-awareness, I'd switch to an old Free Hot Lunch song: *I talk to myself / But I don't listen to what I say / I get along pretty well with myself / Although I'm with me every day.* And then, sometimes, I'd entertain myself and laugh in the face of Huntington's by singing a few songs written by the late great Warren Zevon after he'd received his diagnosis. I'd sing,

> *I went to the doctor*
> *I was feeling kinda rough*
> *I said 'give it to me straight'*
> *He said, 'your shit's fucked up.'*

And I'd usually finish with my favorite,

> *Some get the awful, awful diseases*
> *Some get the knife*

Some get the gun
Some get to die in their sleep
At the age of a hundred and one

But life'll kill ya
And then you'll be dead
Life'll find ya wherever you go
Requiescat en pace
That's all she wrote

That *always* made me smile, regardless of pain or rain.

MEDICINAL HUMOR

Does hiking-with-humor improve your chances of completing a thru-hike? Can't you leave your atrophied sense of humor at home, put your head down, and trudge on autopilot all the way to Katahdin or Springer? You could, of course, but you could also attempt a thru-hike with no Snickers or ibuprofen in your satchel.

And does having a keen sense of humor really lead to better health? Does it really reduce your risk of heart disease, suicide, hemorrhoids, halitosis, and incontinence? Is laughter really the best medicine, or is that just an ole husbands' tale? That proverbial notion could be yet another example of mindless reliance on conventional wisdom, but I'm not taking any chances. I'll take placebo-laughs over pharmacologically active pills any day of the week and thrice on Sunday, except of course when the foot pain gets to be too much or when I've been hit by a runaway truck – as happened while writing this book, but that's another story. In those contexts, ibuprofen kicks humor's ass. No contest.

From a blithely Darwinian perspective, a keen sense of humor may be a semi-reliable indicator of mental fitness or general intelligence. And presumably individuals that are highly intelligent tend to fit in other ways, perhaps especially in their ability to resist disease. So, expressing a keen sense of humor could be an indirect way of honestly advertising general fitness including your stellar immune system.

From this perspective, any association between humor and health could be spurious. In other words, just because individuals with a better sense of humor tend to be healthier doesn't imply that good humor *causes* good health. Instead, humor may signal mental fitness and so indirectly signal overall Darwinian fitness, including a good immune system. From this view, you could no more reasonably expect to refine your sense of humor and get healthier than you could expect to have a growth spurt in your 40s and become a basketball star.

But I don't really believe my own caveat. Instead, I'd like to think we all have an enormous capacity to improve our sense of humor. And doing so will yield all sorts of imponderable benefits.

But is it even possible to reach our full comedic potential and reap these benefits? I think so. Think of it this way: I believe I could become a halfway decent pianist or cellist or oboist, if I really put my mind to it. Likewise, I think we could realize some of our untapped humor potential, if we really put our mind to it. Our sense of humor might become hypertrophied, keen, supple, sophisticated, even nuanced. And by hiking mindfully, we should enjoy an enhanced appreciation for trail humor.

But what does it mean to thru-hike in a mindful way? At the risk of misappropriating Ellen Langer's ideas, the first step is to turn our brain's autopilot to the off position. That way, we'll be better at noticing novelties that arise along the trail. We'll be more attuned to ourselves and other wacky apes we encounter. We'll be attuned to features of the natural environment that we otherwise might have filtered out. We'll soon discover that the more we notice, the more humor we see. We'll appreciate the humor in bizarre juxtapositions, rampant delusions, herd behavior and so much more. Then we'll become more inclined to generate our own humor. And we may find ourselves shedding some of our status quo views. Suspicions, stereotypes, and delusions of superiority may fall by the wayside. This transformation, like that of our shrinking backside, will make us happier. We'll be healthier and more likely to complete a legit thru-hike. And we'll probably live longer to boot.

To recap, by hiking mindfully you'll hone your sense of trail humor and so you'll be a happier healthier hiker. You'll have more fun. You'll improve your chances of doing the whole dang trail. You'll have more adventures along the way. You'll have magical moments and beautiful days and you'll make wonderful friends. You'll be happier about your own kinder and gentler worldview. You'll add years to your life.

I call this Ledge's Grand Unified Theory on How even Half-hearted Heathens can Hike with Hearty Humor and Holistic Health, or, for convenience, H9 hiking. Don't scoff, I think I'm really onto something more far-reaching than suggested by the corny alliteration. I speculate that mindful hikers will maximize their smileage, measured as smiles per mile, and this enhanced smileage will improve longevity.

And let's not overlook the added benefit of LSD. All that long-slow-distance hiking should increase life expectancy. And here's the beauty part: Ellen Langer's work on the connection between mindfulness and health suggests you might not even have to set foot on the trail to live longer. She and her colleagues have shown that: 1) elderly men lived longer after spending a week at a retreat pretending it was 1959, and 2) hotel chamber-cleaners lost weight after being told their on-the-job activities satisfied the

Surgeon General's recommendation for an active lifestyle. With these tantalizing, if controversial, results in mind, doesn't it seem obvious that you the reader will live longer for having read this book?

Here's my bold pledge: the vicarious experience of reading this book will add several *years* to your life, thanks to the powerfully synergistic mind-over-matter benefits from its emphasis on humor, mindfulness, and thru-hiking. How you choose to squander those bonus years is entirely up to you. But why not take a hike?

HUMOR DEFICIT DISORDER

Call me presumptuous, but I assume you're buying what I'm selling. If so, you may be wondering how you might enhance your sense of trail-humor. Well, the first step towards remediating any deficiency is to establish a baseline. We need to know where you fall on the sense-of-trail-humor spectrum at the outset. Perhaps you're homozygous for trail-humorlessness and there's simply no conceivable way of rescuing you from the abyss. Or perhaps you're at the other end of the spectrum and would actually benefit by toning it down a bit. But most of you will fall somewhere along the continuum. And you just might be able to slide yourself toward happier healthier hiking.

Lucky for you, I've developed a quick-and-easy method for quantifying trail-humor, assuming you have one. It's called Ledge's Appalachian Unified Grand Humor Scale, or LAUGHS. Whether it's valid I can't say. This will require careful study. In the meantime, go ahead and imagine yourself on the trail as you complete the survey. For each scenario, circle the numeral next to the least implausible response.

Scenario #1 — You and your trailfriends pause for a food fix. You make an open-face sandwich by besmearing King-size Snickers bars with wads of peanut butter, honey, and Nutella. It's a 2000-calorie bomb. You're just about to start cramming the gooey masterpiece down your gullet, when you drop it into a pile of soggy moose droppings. How would you respond?

1. I'd fly into a rage and stomp on the ruined food and maybe cry a little, especially on the inside.
2. I'd drop an F-bomb, put my pack on, and start walking.
3. I'd smile and then have something else to eat.
4. I'd make a joke about how this is a special exception to the 5-second rule, have a good chuckle, and then eat a power bar.
5. I'd laugh my scrawny thru-ass off. I'd scoop up whatever I could salvage and then I'd savor every molecule, whether Nutella or sloughed mucosal cells from the GI tract of the massive twig-eating herbivore. I'd joke about how the "moose juice" makes it taste a little like Spam®.

Scenario #2 — Your trailfriend drops his hi-cal Snickers sandwich in a pile of moose droppings. What would you do?

1. I'd shake my head in disgust because he's a real screw-up and I lost my patience with him the first day on the trail.
2. I'd look away and whistle while waiting for him to resume walking.
3. I'd smile a sublime Mona Lisa smile and take his photograph.
4. I'd laugh out loud and offer him a handful of dried mangoes.
5. I'd laugh my underfed ass off. Gatorade might dribble out my nostrils. I'd give him a new trailname right on the spot. I'd say, "By the powers invested in me, I hereby pronounce you shall be known from this moment on as 'Moose Juice.'"

Scenario #3 — You're resupplying with a trailfriend. When you're not looking, she slips a romance novel into your grocery cart. You don't notice it until the cashier swipes the book across the barcode scanner. How would you respond?

1. I'd give my trailfriend a condescending look and call her a "juvenile delinquent." I'd ask the cashier to purge the charge for the book. Then I'd hitch solo back to the trailhead.
2. I'd nonchalantly ask the cashier not to charge me for the book. I'd hitch back to the trail with my friend, but I wouldn't give her the satisfaction of mentioning her little prank.
3. I'd smile at my friend, congratulate her for her mildly amusing practical joke by saying "cute," and then I'd ask the cashier to expunge the charge.
4. I'd laugh out loud, complete with involuntary snort. I'd pay for the book. Later that day I'd sneak it into my friend's pack, stashing it at the bottom where it might go unnoticed all the way to Springer.
5. I'd laugh my thru-bum off. I'd pay for the book. Over the next few days, I'd write synopses in the registers. Each installment would chronicle the growing sexual tension between the two main characters. These models of Victorian prudishness would eventually make direct eye contact across a moor, in Chapter 9. The tension would build. The anticlimactic act would finally happen on page 331. They'd do it, like a couple of NOBOs overdosing on aphrodisiacs.

Scenario #4 — You arrive at the Lakeshore House Inn in Monson, Maine. While you're in the shower, Rebekah, the owner, chooses an outfit for you from the loaner-clothes box. It's a gender-bending ensemble, a stretchy top that *might* fit a kindergarten kid and a matching pink mini-skirt. She expects you to sashay around town in this get-up. How would you respond?

1. I'd tell her I wouldn't be caught dead in those clothes. Then I'd put my filthy trail clothes back on.
2. I'd pass off her offer as a joke and then choose some boring loaner clothes.
3. I'd smile and politely decline her kind offer to dress me in her daughter's hand-me-downs.
4. I'd laugh out loud and wear her hand-picked outfit around the hostel but not around town.
5. I'd laugh myself silly. Then I'd retreat to the bathroom to get gussied up. I'd even paint my nails and tie my hiker hair with a pink ribbon. I'd borrow a matching purse. And I'd hike all the way to Dalton, before trading Rebekah's outfit for a manskirt and wicking T-shirt.

Scenario #5 — You hitch back to the trailhead along Skyline Drive. You get dropped off at night in the rain. You turn on your headlamp and begin hiking. Just after first light you spot some hikers coming toward you. You recognize them. At that moment, you realize you've spent the whole night walking in the wrong direction! How would you respond?

1. I'd curse and mope for the rest of the day. I'd beat myself up for making such a stupid mistake, even if it was in the dark and rain and at a trailhead where the trail ran east-west.
2. I'd bluff. I'd try to save face. I'd tell 'em I'd lost my wallet and was retracing my steps to look for it.
3. I'd smile. I'd wait for the laughing-at-my-expense to stop and then I'd hike with my friends.
4. I'd laugh. I'd turn it into a joke by claiming I'd backtracked because I missed them so much.

5. I'd laugh my busted thru-bum off and ask them to share *their* most embarrassing trail-gaffe stories.

Scenario #6 — You spot a trail acquaintance at the outfitter in Hanover, New Hampshire. You haven't seen her in weeks. She hasn't spotted you yet. How would you respond?

1. I'd probably act like I hadn't seen her and sneak out.
2. I'd go over and chat for a minute or two.
3. I'd wave and smile. We'd have a good chat, catching up on mutual trailfriends with special emphasis on their foibles.
4. I'd walk over and give her a hug. We'd laugh about how her mom joined her for a month of hiking, but discovered by the end of Day 1 that she simply "didn't enjoy walking."
5. I'd run over, give her a huge hug, and share a laughfest over all the news we have for each other. Then we'd wander through town reminiscing about the first time we met, when we were plump trail newbies and her legs were shaven.

Scenario #7 — You fall and break a bone in your wrist. You check into a sleaze motel in the next trail town to heal for a few days. How would you respond?

1. I'd spend most of the time feeling sorry for myself, hiding out in my room, watching TV.
2. I'd bide my time, trying not to get too depressed about the prospect of ending my hike.
3. I'd smile now and then, especially while re-reading my journal and thinking about getting back on the trail.
4. I'd laugh a few times a day, especially while chatting with friends and family members on the phone.
5. I'd laugh my injured butt off, especially while getting to know some of the local folks and quizzing them about their love for lawn ornaments, including those sparkly orbs.

Scenario #8 — You meet a fellow thru-hiker who tells you he's a Vietnam Vet and that he still *misses it.* How would you respond?
1. I'd resume walking immediately.
2. I'd look for a graceful way to extricate myself from the conversation and vow to avoid this hiker in the future.
3. I'd smile. I'd ask about other thrill-seeking aspects of his personal history.
4. I'd laugh nervously. And then I'd spend an hour or so listening to his stories.
5. I'd laugh a good hearty laugh. I'd ask one question after another. I'd give my best performance yet in the role of amateur trail therapist. We'd become great trailfriends.

Scenario #9 — You're a few hundred miles into your SOBO thru-hike when you encounter a NOBO who immediately puts you down by claiming you're such a newbie that you can't justifiably call yourself a thru-hiker. How would you respond?
1. I'd give him the evil eye and mutter something under my breath like, "Don't make me hit you in the head."
2. I'd do my best to ignore the insult and just keep walking.
3. I'd smile and ask when I'd be reaching the threshold of legitimacy.
4. I'd laugh and ask him jokingly whether he treats all SOBOs like that or whether he'd singled me out for some reason.
5. I'd laugh my insulted ass off. I'd ask him whether he'd been offended by SOBOs and when he'd started stereotyping us. I'd chat him up for a few minutes and wish him well and tell him how lucky he was to be approaching the best trail state: Maine. We'd be pals, for a few minutes at least.

Scenario #10 — You wake in a lean-to in Maine. It's raining. It's been raining for the 19 consecutive days. One of your fellow hikers starts whining about the rain. How would you respond?
1. I'd commiserate with Negative Ned and complain about how everything I own is waterlogged.
2. I'd gunk down a handful of soggy trail mix and start wading.
3. I'd smile and say something about how I don't mind the rain.
4. I'd laugh and show off my prune-feet and say "that's what happens when you thru-hike on the Appalachian Stream."
5. I'd laugh my "splash" off. I'd rave about the rain. Bonus #1: It makes the footing soft and spongy, which makes for pain-free hiking. Bonus #2: It makes the blackflies and mosquitoes take cover. Bonus #3: It replenishes the springs and streams. Bonus #4: It increases the incidence of pratfalls. Bonus #5: It eliminates the need for taking baths or doing laundry. I'd argue against the negativity bias, where nearly every thru-hiker pisses and moans ad nauseam about the weather on rainy days but fails to mention the weather during stretches of sunny days. And then, for everyone's comedic betterment, I'd set off splashing down the trail barefoot in a downpour.

And now, for the moment of truth! Add up your circled answers. If your total score is less than 20, the prognosis is bleak. Let's not sugar-coat it: you don't have the sense of trail-humor that god gave geese. No offense, but you're a sourpuss. Do yourself a favor and stay home. Your negligible sense of trail-humor probably wouldn't carry you very far. If your total score exceeds 20, there's hope for you, especially if you follow my handy dandy advice below. If your total score exceeds 47, you're bound for glory. You should thrive. My prognosis: you'll finish your humor-filled hike in style and ultimately croak at a very advanced age while still in near-pristine condition. Just try not to act too giddy in public.

GENTLE TIPS FOR MINDFUL HIKING

Assuming your sense of trail humor isn't fixed at either the floor or ceiling, here are a few tips for mindfully humorous healthy hiking. These tips won't replace conventional advice like, "keep your sleeping bag dry," "take care of your feet," keep your pack light," and "make sure you actually enjoy walking before attempting a thru-hike." But these tips will enrich your thru-hike and thru-life.

I offer these tips even though it may seem like any thru-hike attempt will be mindful, almost by definition. You'll be *hiking* after all, through the *forest*. Aren't those ideal conditions for mindfulness? Yeah, sure, but it's also easy to put your brain on autopilot as you trudge all the way to Springer or Katahdin. It's easy not to be present. It's easy to be detached, inflexible, impatient, unkind, competitive, and obsessed with "finishing." So, here are some DOs and DON'Ts for staying in the present, for staying healthy and happy.

- **Do** love every day on the trail like it could be your last. **Don't** obsess over "finishing." Remind yourself daily, "It's the journey, genius!" The destination is just one arbitrary infinitesimal point in the time-space continuum. And according to Ledge's Law, there's no conceivable way you'll arrive on schedule anyway. So enjoy each day to the fullest. Don't treat it as a box to ex-out on the calendar. Don't hike robotically. Don't rob yourself of adventure and learning by obsessing over what may prove to be an anticlimactic photo op at the cairn. Evaluate your progress in smileage rather than mileage. Just keep on smiling and you'll eventually run out of trail. You'll finish and then you'll wish you hadn't.

- **Do** radiate lovingkindness. Be open, expansive, nonjudgmental. When you meet a fellow hiker, **don't** make unwarranted assumptions based on travel direction or scrawniness. (I mean, are NOBOs really so bad?) Eschew social biases that pollute the mind. Put yourself in his/her shoes, no matter how smelly or wide. Be as kind as Rebekah, The Mayor, and Elmer. You may find yourself sending lovely telepathic thoughts to strangers, including those motorists who scoff in your general direction when you're trying to hitch into Buena Vista, VA.
- **Do** get rid of that mental stopwatch. **Don't** look for an escape from chats. Don't replicate your town habit of truncating conversations by acting harried and saying, "well, gotta go now." Enjoy each encounter, like I did with fellow hikers (including Blazy, Carolina, Poison Sumac, Sir Woodchuck, Déjà Vu, Sad Hands, Chin Music, and Jukebox) and town angels (including Elmer, Rebekah, Ole Man and Navigator, Vickey and Pat, Sue, The Mayor, Bob Peoples, and Leigh and Josh). Don't squander your finite allotment of precious moments.
- **Do** be a Positive Pedro. **Don't** be a Negative Ned. Don't get demoralized by stuff that's beyond your control, like the rain in Maine. Try this little coping device: each time you catch yourself pissing and moaning about something beyond your control, turn right around and say 14 positive things. This will prove to be exhaustive and pretty soon you'll just stop with all that negativity.
- **Do** hike in a meditative way. **Don't** always chase away painful thoughts. Sit with them. You went to the trail after getting out of a bad situation – prison, college, marriage, rehab, or war. And you went with a firm expectation that the thru-hike would

be therapeutic. So do the work. It's better to resolve your issues on the trail, to forgive yourself and others, rather than carry all that baggage back to the other world (where you'll have to dip into your hiking fund to pay someone to exorcise your demons).

- **Do** let yourself be bombarded by natural stimuli. **Don't** routinely distract yourself with toys. You've turned off your cell phone and kicked your internet habit. Now take out those ear buds. Turn off your iPod. Listen to the natural world. You'll have plenty of time to distract yourself from the tedium and stress of that other life when you get back to Jersey and shit. (Disclosure: I allowed myself the guilty pleasure of listening to *Fresh Air* throughout New England, where the trail goes through one college town after another and so NPR came in loud and clear.)
- **Do** ease up on the accelerator. **Don't** hike so competitively. It's hard to hike mindfully when you're trying to keep up with The Joneses. Besides, the last I heard The Joneses were off the trail with stress fractures. A thru-hike isn't like football tryouts. Nobody's going to tell you to "suck it up, Princess" or ridicule you if you pause to put duct tape on your hotspots. (But if you show up in Monson with blisters on every toe and both heals, Sad Hands will say, "of course, you're all so injured that you can't even put on your shoes – *you're boys!*") And it's not like you're going to receive special commendation at Trail Days.
- **Do** listen to your body. Learn its limits. Push it a bit. **Don't** put yourself off the trail in a vain attempt to keep up with those teens and 20-somethings. They have unfair advantages like intact patellar tendons.
- **Do** walk solo at least some of the time. **Don't** get subsumed by someone else's hike. It's very hard to be mindful when you're

hiking with El Grupo or with a smurf-hiking shadow. Just when you're on the verge of a mindful moment, your hiking partner will ask how you're doing, which is about as distracting as a bee sting on the eyelid.

- **Do** allow yourself to revel. **Don't** be bored and boring. Howl with the coyotes. Hoot with the barred owls. Yodel with the loons. Sleep under the stars. Rename the constellations. Cook your food in those giant catalpa leaves. Scan the skies for "kettles" of migrating raptors. Put a millipede in your mouth. Watch a salamander for one hour. Put your face into the sphagnum moss and see what happens. Chew wintergreen leaves and the inner bark of yellow birch twigs. Watch the water striders. Take a nap in a rhododendron thicket.
- **Do** walk slowly at times. **Don't** treat the whole hike like a workout session on a treadmill. Pause for one minute each hour, not just to cram cookies down your gullet, but also to listen. Or pause long enough to identify 10 bird species, 5 tree species, and 10 vascular plant species, before resuming your kickass march. If you're lucky, you may discover the woodcock's spectacular aerial courtship display, always performed at hiker midnight. Be forewarned: this discovery could earn you a trailname, Woodcock, or one of the woodcock's alternative handles, Timberdoodle or Bogsucker.
- **Do** treat your hike like a freeform experiential play, where you're a co-star and everyone you meet instantaneously joins the cast without even auditioning. **Don't** treat your thru-hike like a J-O-B. Be flexible, spontaneous, and adventurous. Use your itinerary as TP. If you overplan, you'll limit your opportunities for magic, surprise, adventure. Be forewarned, this approach could add years to your life, in which case you might as well attempt another thru-hike.

- **Do** take an occasional zero *on the trail*. **Don't** spend all your "down time" hunkered in a motel. Spend on-the-trail zeroes connecting with the natural world. Sit in one spot and look, listen, smell, feel, taste. Before you know it, woodland jumping mice will be sproinging all around you, a garter snake will bask on a nearby rock, a red squirrel will scold you from within arm's reach, a ruby-crowned kinglet will sing overhead, and a beaver will scare the scat out of you when it slaps its tail to warn of your menacing stench.
- **Do** experiment with walking with your eyes closed. **Don't** walk too fast this way. Allow your feet to feel the trail. Imagine what it would be like to do a sightless thru-hike, like Bill Erwin did.
- **Do** notice the rhythm of your body. **Don't** lumber all the way to Katahdin or Springer. Learn your own biomechanics. Retrain your brain and body to walk with symmetry, balance, grace, beauty. Use your trekking poles like you're an Olympic cross-country skier, not as decorative leaf collectors. Rewire your brain so your body moves with optimal efficiency. Trekking poles should be used gracefully, not haphazardly. You wouldn't run the Boston Marathon with a hand on your hip or canoe the Yukon River with one leg dangling over the gunwale. There's no virtue in being herky-jerky and inefficient in your movements. Of course, all bets are off when you're making your way through Mahoosuc Notch or stumbling over the roots and rocks of Maine.
- **Do** share your humor. **Don't** be stingy. We know how funny you are. Tell us your stories. Use the trail registers as a comedic outlet. Leave us your daily affirmations, caustic one-liners, Shakespearean corruptions, Hannah Montana hiking tips, hallucinogenic claims that your food bag's been stolen yet

again, this time by a capybara or wombat or dingo. And while you're at it, you might as well go ahead and rate the privies.

- **Do** pay homage to the sacred ground. **Don't** forget every peak and river and stream once had a Native American name. Imagine what it was like to live without cars or ridgerunners or power bars or Spam® singles.
- **Do** live in the moment. **Don't** dwell on the past. What's done is done. Ignore the future. Don't fret about what may never happen. Don't overlook the present. Be open, accepting, nonjudgmental, observant, adventurous, and flexible.

If you follow these tips, I pledge you'll be a happier healthier hiker, on and off the trail. You'll have a better chance of completing a thru-hike. And you'll end up living longer. If not, speak to my attorney.

And one last bit of advice: don't take any brass dildos, unless of course you're compelled to show off your true hiking superiority.

CHAPTER 14

Traveling at the Speed of Bike☺☺☺[B]

It's the first day of the last month of the penultimate year of the first decade of the 21st century. I've arrived at the southern terminus. I've done it. I've completed the first leg of my yo-yo. It doesn't feel anti-climactic to finish up as a SOBO thru-hiker because I'm now a NOBO thru-biker. Well, not quite. I still need to walk the 7-mile approach trail from Springer Mt. down to Amicalola Falls and then hitch-hike to Leigh and Josh's luxurious Hiker Hostel in Dahlonega, where my bike awaits in a cardboard box.

Thru-hikers like to ask each other that one most obvious question, "Why are you doing a thru-hike?" Most thru-hikers offer up a one-liner about how they just got out of prison or rehab or Afghanistan or Virginia Tech or a bad marriage. I always said, "Well, I mailed by bicycle to Georgia, so now I'm walking down to get it." Mission accomplished. Now I'll make an abrupt transition back to cycling.

Ordinarily, I *live* on my bike. I've pedaled everywhere, every day, year-round, for years. I never miss a day, except when I'm hiking or when my ribcage is so crash-mangled that I'm flat on my back making shadow puppet shows on the ceiling. It's my religion – biking, not amateur puppetry. When the snow gets too deep for my Surly Cross-check, I switch to a winter bike, the Surly Pugsley, which has 4-inch-wide knobby tires. And I keep on pedaling. So, you might think switching from hiking back to biking would be a perfectly natural, seamless transition. It wasn't.

At the hostel, I tear open the bike box like I'm a kid and it's my Christmas present from Aunt Shirley. I pop on the wheels, inflate the tires, reaffix the handlebars, screw in the pedals, and attach the brakes. In minutes, I'm ready to roll. I mount the steel beast for the first time in half a year. It feels high, shaky, fragile. It feels like an accident waiting to happen. And then I take it for a little test spin down the road. I'm scared. Speed kills.

I've spent the past six months creeping across the Earth's surface at 1 or 2 miles per hour, with my feet firmly planted on terra firma. Now I'm suddenly hurtling down this mountain road at breakneck speeds. If I crash – like I did so often on the trail, especially in Maine – I'll shatter my ribcage again. Or worse, I'll be a stain, like those gruesome scenes where a deer got smucked by a truck. But within a few minutes, I've regained confidence in my cycling prowess, at least in my ability to keep the rubber side down. I'm convinced the balance problems that dogged me on the thru-hike won't keep me from doing the thru-bike. At this stage of living with Huntington's disease, it's much easier for me to balance on a bicycle than on uneven footing even while using trekking poles for support. And it's exhilarating to be back gripping handlebars rather than trekking poles. Speed thrills.

It also feels strange to generate my own microclimate again. For six months, I traveled at the pace of a dehydrated snail. And snails, even hydrated ones, don't travel fast enough along their slime trail to generate their own weather. But now, I'm going so fast that I create windchill, especially on the downhill runs. If I were still hiking right now, it would feel like 20°F, the actual air temperature. But flying down these hills at 40 mph, it feels more like -1°F. I'll be going through hot-cold cycles for weeks, sweating profusely on the ups and freezing my stuff off on the downs. Speed chills.

Biking now feels like cheating, especially while coasting. There's no coasting in hiking. If you're not moving your legs, you're not moving. Every inch hiked is an inch earned. And it's not done with panniers suspended on a rack; it's done with a pack on your back. And the downhill sections are the ones that hurt in hiking, hurt your inflamed patella tendons and bulging cervical disc and frayed medial collateral ligament. Biking is easy on the body. Bike-speed means no more pills.

Bike-speed sure doesn't feel like the evolutionarily relevant, natural pace of walking. This makes sense because the bicycle is a new invention. Modern humans have existed for a quarter of a million years or so and bicycles for just the last 120 years. Rescaling modern human history to one day, the bicycle has been around for just the last 40 seconds. It's a modern contrivance. No wonder it feels so unnatural. For 99.95% of human history, bikes didn't exist. Humans walked. Even today, many of the three billion fellow Earthlings who have $2 per day walk to meet their subsistence needs. We are naturally pedestrians. From this perspective, 2 miles per hour seems just about right.

Traveling at bike-speed feels like time travel. I leave Dahlonega at noon and roll into Helen by 3 PM. That's the equivalent of 57 trail miles, from Amicalola Falls to Unicoi Gap, in just three hours. That's three days' worth of hiking in three hours of biking. My travel speed has increased by about nine fold. If I don't put a governor on myself, I'll be in Damascus in a couple days, in Duncannon soon after. I'll be back in Maine in no time. That won't do. So, to compensate for my now-excessive speed, I stop way prematurely for the night in hilarious Helen.

Traveling at bike-speed also feels culturally insensitive. In the morning, I speed out of Helen, the origin of the Trail of Tears. It feels disrespectful to be whizzing along at such high speed while

243

sitting on a padded saddle and just making my legs move. It feels especially disrespectful because I'm *on* the Trail of Tears, following in the footsteps of 13,000 Cherokee and their US Army "escorts." Leaving Helen, I'll be speeding along the Unicoi Turnpike (present-day routes 17/75), up and over Unicoi Gap, and then to Hiawassee and beyond. I won't be on foot. I won't be barefoot. I won't be a victim of quasi-genocide, unlike the 4000 or more Cherokee who died on their way to Oklahoma. I won't be on a death march under a Presidential directive, at a time when one sixth of "Americans" are slaves. I won't be subjected to any of these indignities and atrocities. I'm on holidays.

My speed feels excessive for all of these reasons, but it's anything but constant. While hiking, my speed varied within a narrow range, 1-3 mph. On the bike, it fluctuates wildly. On the climbs starting with Unicoi Gap, I grind away in grampa gear. I travel at hiking speed, inching my way up the switchbacks alongside rhododendron thickets. It feels like I'm still hiking. But then I reach the crest and slalom down the other side in a 40-mph tuck.

As I glide along the Trail of Tears, I imagine a peloton of 13,000 Cherokees traveling the same route. Riding their bikes in single file, the peloton would be about 25 miles long, stretching all the way from Helen to Hiawassee. If only they could have delayed their own "forced removal" for a few decades – until bicycles became available – they could have traveled as I am. They could have sailed all the way to Hiawassee and beyond in just a few hours. They could have made it to Oklahoma in a few weeks. Rather than a death march, it would have been a life ride. Who knows how low the death toll might have been. But, of course, this fantasy presupposes the same US Government that appropriated

Native American homelands would have provided bicycles if only they'd existed.

Our peloton was just two bicycles long. Riding in single file, we stretched only 0.01% of the way between Helen and Hiawassee. We saw no one else on bikes. This held true all the way to Millinocket. We were a community of two for a long stretch. Then I was reduced to a community of one. Thru-hiking has its built-in community, but thru-biking is asocial aside from each evening's opportunity to scandalize townsfolk when they see you in tights and sandals. Unlike the thru-hike experience, where I encountered fellow travelers virtually every day, on my return thru-bike I didn't encounter anyone who was doing what I was doing. It turns out that riding a bicycle from Georgia to Maine, paralleling and crisscrossing the A.T. and doing so *during winter*, isn't very popular. Unlike thru-hiking, thru-biking hasn't exactly caught on ... yet.

In a couple hours, we arrive in Hiawassee, take a right and head up and over, crossing the A.T. and then slaloming into Franklin, North Carolina. It was a tough day. Our hands got so cold we had to bite the power bar wrappers to get at our food rewards. Our feet got so cold that we stopped and put some of those hot-foot insoles filled with unoxidized iron filings in our shoes. And we thought of the Cherokee, all of whom lacked power bars and some of whom lacked shoes. In the evening, we arrived in Franklin and stopped for submarine sandwiches and cookies and lemonade. We thawed our privileged bones by the hand warmer in the bathroom. We were so stuffed and snoozy that we had trouble pedaling over to the Microtel, where we watched the giant flatscreen TV, drank hot cocoa, and gorged on a second dinner of bagels and waffles. We spent the evening wallowing simultaneously in cultural guilt and sheer luxury. At the crack of noon, we'd buy waterproof socks and neoprene biking booties and handfuls of hot-foot insoles. And then we'd speed off, without fellow travelers, in the general direction of Millinocket.

Thru-biking is asocial in another way: it's too fast for proper visitin'. For months I've been looking forward to visiting friends I made on my thru-hike. But these folks – hostel owners, trail angels, trail town characters – are too close together, now that I'm whizzing along at bike-speed. On the hike, they were spaced conveniently at about 20-mile intervals. So, if I'd chosen to hike back up the trail, I could have visited them nightly. But because I'm biking, I could pay visits almost hourly. I do manage to stop for overnight visits in Hot Springs, Damascus, Duncannon, Monson, and Millinocket. But I end up cruising right on through many other inadequately spaced trail towns. Day after day, I overshoot favorite trail towns, only to end up alone in yet another rundown mom-and-pop motel run by yet another lovely three-generation family from Gujarat.

Thru-biking is like time-lapse photography. Traveling at bike-speed compresses the trip at a regional scale. Rolling across the landscapes reveals rapid cultural shifts. Hourly impressions are like snapshots. These images show a rapid transition from The Deep South to The North. It unfolds right before your eyes. Walking is too slow to get the same impressions. It's like trying to watch a flower open with the naked eye. But biking is like seeing snapshots taken at intervals, through the lens of an amateur anthropologist and aspiring cinematographer.

What did I see? Well, starting in Dahlonega, I saw countless unleashed pit bulls along the 83-mile stretch, to Franklin, NC. I saw them up close as I sprinted past frothy mouth after frothy mouth. I also saw many other southern markers: 26 Baptist churches, 18 barbeques, and six boiled peanut stands. Days later,

I would pedal a 51-mile stretch along US 7 in Massachusetts. There I couldn't find pit bull one. I didn't see any unleashed dog of any kind. Dogs throughout the Berkshires strut on leashes held by humans who inexplicably carry transparent bags of feces. And I saw just six Baptist churches, one per town, two barbeques, and zero boiled peanut stands. But what Massachusetts lacks in these southernisms, it makes up for with a profusion of antique shoppes (47), coffee houses (10), and bookstores specializing in rare, used, out-of-print titles (10). It seems the well-caffeinated Yankees are so busy buying each other's old stuff and keeping up the appearance of being well read that they don't have time to breed pit bulls or boil peanuts.

But I didn't always travel at such high speeds as 6 Baptist churches per hour. Sometimes I didn't travel at all. I got waylaid for five days in Lynchburg, Virginia, when it got buried by a record-setting 16 inches of snow, which the local folks didn't know what to do with. Folks all over town said, "Sorry it had to be Lynchburg." But I didn't mind. I hung out at the lone coffee house and devoured its library of books about Stonewall Jackson. And later I got waylaid by a storm in Poughkeepsie, New York, where folks said, "Sorry it had to be Poughkeepsie." But I didn't mind. I hung out at Vassar College, which my cousin attended briefly, in 1969 – the first year it accepted applicants with spindly y-chromosomes (aka men). He chose newly coeducational Vassar for two reasons. First, he thought he'd have his choice of spouse what with the extraordinarily favorable 300-to-1 female-to-male sex ratio. That didn't work out. He might have married a certain classmate by the name of Meryl Streep, but she was not impressed. Second, he thought he'd star on the varsity baseball team. But with only six men in that first co-ed class, that didn't work out either. Vassar didn't begin their varsity baseball program until 1992. (They've struggled ever since with just one winning season in their first 19 and an abysmal overall win-loss record of 172-390.) Tail between his legs, he left Poughkeepsie almost as quickly as I did. He left for points unknown. Forty years later, I left for Millinocket.

I made it to Millinocket, finally, on February 6th. I hadn't walked back up the trail – barefoot – like those famous sisters, but it still felt like a small win to complete my yo-yo. I sprinted into this hardscrabble end-of-the-trail town in tights and sandals (covered with neoprene booties), with a thoroughly frozen thru-beard. I knocked on the door at the Appalachian Trail Lodge. Jamie opened the door, hugged me and said, "Ledge, it's great to see you! I was just thinking about you yesterday."

And Paul chimed in, "Yeah, we thought you were dead. We figured you got hit by a logging truck. What took you so long?"

"What took me so long?!" I said as if righteously offended. "I just left Monson at noon. That's the equivalent of doing the 100-mile Wilderness in four and a half hours. It took me a week to walk to Monson back in June, but it took just a few hours to bike the return leg this afternoon. And you ask what took me so long?!"

"That's impressive, Ledge, but you were supposed to spend Christmas with us, remember?" said Paul.

"Well, I took the scenic route."

🚲

Glossary☺☺☺[R]

ALDHA
1. Appalachian Long-distance Hikers Association.
2. Nonprofit organization that will soon promote green-hiking practices. *ALDHA's gonna promote the idea of an organic garden at every hostel.*

Anal leakage
1. Uncontrollable flow of fluid from rectum through anus.
2. Common experience among A.T. thru-hikers who overindulge on certain kinds of potato chips. *Dude, did you hear about Zamboni's anal leakage? He ate four bags of those chips. Serves him right. The warning's right on the label. Plus, we warned him. Guess he had to find out for himself.*

Appalachia
1. Region where this word is pronounced /apple-at-cha/, as in "Git outta my field or I'll throw this here apple atcha."

Appalachian Trail
1. 2179-mile-long continuous footpath put in place back in the 1930s so people would have an easy way of walking from Maine to Georgia without using map and compass.
2. Booty call in Argentina.
3. Euphemism for subterfuge designed to hide an extramarital affair. *I told my husband I was out hiking on the Appalachian Trail. What a dope. I think he bought it.*
4. The most popular therapeutic hiking escape following a mid-life crisis and/or release from prison.

Aquamira®
1. Commercially available drops used to treat drinking water.
2. Usually the third or fourth heaviest item in a hardcore ultra-light hiker's little toy pack.

A.T. symbol
1. Logo superimposing a capital A and capital T, such that the horizontal segments of the two letters are one and the same.

2. Not a symbol for tent or mountain or shelter or roof, despite what Jelly Belly thought through much of Maine.

ATC
1. Appalachian Trail Conservancy.
2. Appalling trail conditions.

Avogadro's number
1. Number of atoms or molecules in one mole, 6.022×10^{23}.
2. Number of times Ledge laughed out loud or laughed his thru-ass off while hiking the Laughalachian Trail.
3. Number of pointy rocks in Rocksylvania.

AYCE
1. All you can eat.
2. All you can excrete.

Bear cables
1. What thru-hikers should use to hang their bear bags so they don't become bear food.
2. More realistically, what thru-hikers should use so they don't unintentionally reward local bears with food, which often leads to their extermination.

Benton MacKaye
1. Sire of the Appalachian Trail.

Bike-speed
1. Varies between 1 mph when climbing switchbacks in grampa gear and 40 mph when coasting down other side.
2. Roughly nine times faster than hiking speed.

Bill Irwin
1. Trail legend who in 1990, at age 50, became the first sightless person to complete a thru-hike.
2. Author of *Blind Courage*.
3. Recipient of 1990 Presidential Sports Award, presented by Prez Dubya (aka Shrub).
4. Former thru-hiker who, like so many others, settled near the trail. Resides in Sebec, Maine, about midway between Monson and Millinocket.

Bivy sack
1. Bivouac bag used by minimalists.
2. Ultra-light waterproof shelter used as a sleeping-bag cover in place of a tent or hammock.
3. An overpriced plastic bag that some super-ultra-lighters use instead of a sleeping bag (see **hypothermia**).

Black flies
1. Little black gnats that slurp up your blood after slashing the skin, often behind your ear.
2. A scourge to hikers in Maine. Avogadro's number emerges each spring, during what Mainers semi-officially call, "Black Fly Season." Luckily, only females bite. Assuming a 1:1 sex ratio, that's just 3.011×10^{23} potential biters.
3. Official Bird of the State of Maine.
4. Number one reason for SOBOs getting off the trail, followed closely by number two reason: hiking sucks. *Dude, I totally thought I'd love hikin'. I didn't realize it would be so much freakin' walkin' and black flies and shit.*

Blister
1. Pocket of fluid skin on feet, caused by hiking-related friction, especially in the 100-Mile Wilderness.
2. Common complaint among boy hikers who refuse to put duct tape on their hotspots until the surrounding tissue becomes necrotic and they become septic.
3. Convenient excuse for lollygagging at the Lakeshore House Inn in Monson for an extra day or two or three.

Blue blazer
1. Illegitimate thru-hiker who cheats his or her scrawny thru-ass off by taking short cuts on blue-blaze trails.

Bog bridge
1. Slippery boards and logs put in place by trail-maintenance crews to elevate the risk of humorous pratfalls.
2. See **puncheon**.

Boot size
1. Synonym for shoe size.

2. A proxy for distance hiked, which increases by one
   increment per 1000 trail miles.

Bounce box
1. Cardboard box thru-hikers send to themselves repeatedly
   c/o General Delivery.
2. Cardboard box containing stuff thru-hikers never should
   have had in their pack in the first place, including tent, extra
   socks, underpants, GPS unit, waterlogged copy of *The
   Laughalachian* Trail, and **brain**.

Brain
1. Detachable top section of backpack usually filled with about
   4 pounds of nonessential odds and ends.
2. Section of pack often sent to oneself in bounce box so as to
   constrain one's ability to carry extraneous crap.
3. Complex organ of the central nervous system with autopilot
   switch often set to "on" position, especially in Rocksylvania.

Breakfast
1. The most important of the 6-9 daily thru-hiker meals.
2. Meal consumed at first light, usually consisting of five or
   more power bars (weed optional).
3. See **hiker breakfast**.

Caloric shortfall
1. Net effect of expending 6,666 calories in one day, while
   consuming just 4,444 calories.
2. Chronic condition for thru-hikers leading to significant
   shrinkage of adipose cells and *gluteus maximus*.

Carbon footprint
1. Amount of ecologically productive land required to
   sequester a hiker's carbon emissions due to addictive use of
   fossil fuels for travel to and from trail termini and towns.

Challenge
1. A hard-to-achieve voluntary task involving self-abuse and
   stimulation used by competitive thru-hikers to stave off
   boredom and bond with peers.

2. Opportunity to gorge, overindulge, and risk self-inflicted injury, disguised as a friendly competition.
3. Voluntary activity pursued by thru-hikers to show off their expanded gut capacity or world-class fitness or heightened sense of play.
4. Common tasks include four-state, ice-cream, burger, and Pennsylvania pizza challenges. *Dude, I totally hornked on the sidewalk after about 12 scoops. I never should've done the lunch buffet right before attempting the ice-cream challenge.*

Change of clothes
1. Extra garments that many thru-hikers wouldn't dream of carrying in their pack. *Dude, I'll sleep when I'm dead and I'll change clothes when I get home.*

Chinese buffet
1. Thru-hikers flock like sheep to these AYCE opportunities, like moose to a salt lick.
2. Gathering site for MSG-depleted thru-hikers.

Cigarettes
1. What many thru-hikers smoke and hence the expression, "a fire on one end, a thru-hiking fool on the other."

Cowboy/cowgirl camping
1. Camping under the stars without tent or hammock or tarp.

Cold food
1. What some ultra-lighters eat exclusively after jettisoning their stove and fuel and pot.
2. Not to be confused with **Knorr-Lipton Sides**.

Crocs
1. Lightweight plastic footwear that thru-hikers dangle from their pack for decorative purposes.

Damascus
1. The trail town that put "friendly" in the phrase "hiker-friendly."
2. Host to Trail Days.

Day hiker
1. Tame upright ape that smells like strawberry-kiwi shampoo and sports a plaid Jansport daypack.
2. Easily confused with **weekender**.

DEET
1. Teratogenic chemical compound, commercially available in liquid form.
2. Used to attract mosquitoes and other biting insects.

Dehydrated water
1. Powder form of H_2O.
2. A key innovation in super-ultra-light hiking, but not yet commercially available.

Double zero
1. See **zero** and then multiply by two.
2. Rebekah of Monson's honorary trailname.

Duct tape
1. The one and only item in some thru-hikers' first aid kits. *Dude, I got a gangrenous blister on my heel and I've run outta duct tape. You got any extra?*

Easy hitch
1. Any trail town in Maine.
2. Not to be confused with a recklessly impulsive wedding at one of Gatlinburg's wedding chapels, where the fee for annulment is included.

Ecological footprint
1. Amount of land and water needed to meet a thru-hiker's demands for jet travel and slack-packing and animal flesh and junk food. *Dude, Ledge says my ecological footprint is way bigger than the Global Fair Earthshare. He's such a greenhead. He's all greener than thou. I hate him.*

First aid kit
1. See **duct tape**.

Flip flop
1. An alternative to the conventional thru-hike where the entire trail is hiked in one hiking season but in two segments (for

example, from Harpers Ferry to Katahdin and then from Harpers Ferry to Springer).
2. That panicky state induced by waking to the realization that you're trapped upside down in your hammock.

Food footprint
1. The enormous land area effectively dedicated to producing the obscene food demands of a thru-hiker.
2. An area of ecologically productive land several times larger than the area available per person worldwide. *Dude, if I ate like that all the time, I'd need to have a garden as big as 100 football fields.*

Food products
1. What most thru-hikers eat instead of food.

Ford
1. What thru-hikers pretentiously call wading across a stream in Maine.

Four-state Challenge
1. Hike beginning in Virginia, passing through West Virginia and Maryland, and ending the same day in Pennsylvania (or vice versa for SOBOs).
2. Ideal excuse for taking a triple zero.

GA-ME
1. Abbreviation designating a thru-hiker's travel direction, from Georgia to Maine.
2. Not to be confused with "game," as in "that dude's got game."

Gatorade®
1. Commercially available electrolyte replacement beverage.
2. Alternative to water, apparently preferred by hikers who wish to produce expensive urine.

Giardia
1. Flagellated protozoan parasites that thrive in intestines of thru-hikers who once thought they were magically immune to these water-borne unfriendlies.
2. Alternative weight-loss program involving cataclysmic diarrhea.

3. Excellent antidote to constipation. *Dude, think I'm gonna have to get off the trail for a while. I've got the* Giardia *and can't stop peeing out my butt.*

Grandma Gatewood

1. Trail legend extraordinaire. The first woman to complete a thru-hike, which she did solo at age 67 in 1955. She did a second thru-hike at age 72, and completed a third hike in sections at age 75.
2. Ultra-light hiker long before it became fashionable.
3. Grandmother who wore Keds® sneakers and just threw a handmade bag over one shoulder and used a single wooden walking stick.
4. Not to be confused with Benton MacKaye's mother.

Green thru-hiking

1. Hypothetical mode of hiking that achieves genuine ecological sustainability.
2. Car-free, plane-free, meat-free thru-hiking.
3. Not to be confused with the near-universal alternative style, brown thru-hiking.

Hammock

1. Portable shelter that many thru-hikers mail home or send to themselves repeatedly in a **bounce box**.
2. Sometimes called a "bear bag."

Head lamp

1. What thru-hikers turn on just before hiker midnight, with the intention of reading their Bible or writing in their journal.

Hiker box

1. Grab-box of jettisoned hiker gear and supplies that's free for the taking. Found routinely in hostels.
2. Often contains Ziploc bags filled with off-white mystery powder or flakes, not to mention machetes, flashlights, stray marshmallows, used Chapstick, and unread Bibles.

Hiker breakfast
1. Morning meal designated as such at diners and home-style restaurants in trail towns.
2. Usually consists of three of more eggs, a stack of Frisbee-sized pancakes, several pieces of fried pig flesh, mounds of home fries, grits, toast, biscuits and gravy, orange juice, and a bottomless pot of translucent tepid water with a faint hint of coffee flavor.

Hiker carbon footprint
1. Enormous amount of land hypothetically set aside to sequester a hiker's share of carbon spewed into the atmosphere as the hiker travels to or from trail termini and trail towns.

Hiker food footprint
1. Amount of ecologically productive land hypothetically set aside to produce enough food to meet a hiker's obscene requirements.
2. An area of land typically several times larger than the per capita land area available worldwide.

Hiker friendly
1. Any eatery, hostel, or town that loves up thru-hikers and celebrates them like the conquering heroes they are.
2. Not to be confused with hostel called Hiker Friendly Hostel, where fiercely unfriendly neighbor blares National Public Radio broadcasts, including *All Things Considered*, as an act of psychological warfare.

Hiker hunger
1. Intense craving for pizza induced by voluntary deprivation including extreme overexertion and inadequate nutrition.
2. Oral craving caused by voluntary mining of one's own tissues to finance excessive walking.

Hiker loaner clothes
1. Retro garments provided at hostels so thru-hikers can walk around town looking even goofier than usual.

Hiker midnight
1. One half hour after sunset, when sonic boom-like baritone snoring begins in earnest in lean-to.
2. Coincides with daily end of legal bear-killing hours.

Hiker portions
1. Mounds of food roughly 2.7 times larger than town portions.
2. One serving is roughly the size of your own head.

Hiker sexy
1. That attractive quality of thru-hikers that can only be explained by extra-potent pheromonal cues thanks to infrequent bathing, laundering, and shaving.
2. Mythical quality of thru-hikers that ensures protracted celibacy.

Hiker wallet
1. Small Ziploc® bag containing cash (no coins), mom's credit card, and marijuana (optional).

Hotel
1. A roof overhead and a fourth wall.
2. A luxurious kind of town shelter where most thru-hikers cannot afford to stay.

Hut
1. One of a network of alpine manses in The Whites where thru-hikers pause momentarily to scarf blueberry cake or overnight to sleep on the floor.

Hypothermia
1. Humbling state of depressed core body temperature leading to stumbling, fumbling, bumbling, mumbling, tumbling, and grumbling.
2. Physiological state leading to disappearance off the trail or the purchasing of a better sleeping bag, whichever comes first.

Ice-cream
1. Sweetened, chilled baby food produced by the mammary glands of a nonhuman mammalian species, usually the domestic cow.

2. One of the thru-hiker's major food groups.

Ice-cream challenge

1. An udderly ridiculous opportunity to pay someone for the privilege of distending your stomach, pushing your lactose tolerance to the limit, and eventually vomiting on the sidewalk. *Dude, that ice-cream challenge at the Appalachian Trail Café in Millinocket was badass. It's 14 scoops, plus a King-size Snickers, and a bunch of M&Ms and whipped cream and god only knows what else. I think I could do it if I trained.*

Jerky

1. Staple of thru-hikers who have fallen off the veggie wagon.

Knorr-Lipton Sides

1. Synonymous with dinner for many thru-hikers.
2. Hot dinners made by thru-hikers until they realize these "meals" are – as the name implies – *sides*, and that it's not worth carrying a stove and fuel for low-cal evening rituals.

LASH

1. Long-ass-section hiker.
2. Misnomer: there's no evidence that doing this sort of hike elongates the gluteal muscles appreciably.

Lean-to

1. A free-standing log or plank structure with a curious design flaw: one of the four walls is missing.

Lyme disease

1. Tick-borne bacterial disease commonly inflicting thru-hikers and often leading to string of 10 or more zeroes, while trailfriends continue on without you.
2. Treatable with antibiotics. Preventable by scrutinizing each other's nude body every hour or so.

Mark Sanford

1. Esteemed governor of South Cackolacky.
2. See **Appalachian Trail**.

ME-GA

1. Abbreviation designating a thru-hiker's travel direction, from Maine to Georgia.

2. Not to be confused with "mega," as in "that pack's mega awesome."

Millinocket

1. Trail town 19 miles from northern terminus of A.T., home to the Appalachian Trail Lodge and Café.
2. Out-of-stater's destination in famous Marshall Dodge comedy piece called, "Which way to Millinocket?" Punchline: "You can't get theyah from heyah."
3. Town mentioned in many limericks. *There was a young thru-hiker from Millinocket; he put a power bar in his pocket ....*

Monson

1. Trail town extraordinaire (population 666).
2. Trail town situated at the southern edge of the 100-mile Wilderness.
3. Sometimes affectionately called "The Monson."

Moose

1. Massive twig-eating herbivores that put bears to shame when it comes to defecating in the woods.

Mosquito

1. Bloodthirsty insect that has the decency to drink your blood through a straw (proboscis) after gently piercing your skin and injecting anticoagulant-containing saliva, unlike other biting insects that shall remain nameless (see **black flies**).

Mt. Katahdin

1. Northern terminus of A.T. Panawahpskek word meaning "The Great One."
2. "Borrowed" from Native Americans and, generations later, bequeathed by Governor Percival Baxter to the "people" of Maine, to be protected in natural state in perpetuity.
3. Wake-up call for SOBOs.
4. Photo op for NOBOs.

Mt. Washington

1. Called Agiocochook ("Home of the Great Spirit") prior to "contact." Renamed after wig-wearing, wooden-toothed first

US President, which paved the way for the autoroad, cogway, giftshop, pizza oven, and weather observatory.

2. Record-holder for highest windspeed ever recorded anywhere on Earth with an anemometer – until 2009, when Australia trumped up a bogus record and tried to steal Mt. Washington's thunder.

3. See **hypothermia**.

Naked Hiking Day

1. A day in June for frolicking in Nature as Nature intended.

2. Observed by thru-hikers who insist on collecting insect bites in their nether regions.

Nero

1. A near **zero**. *Dude, I did a nero into Damascus, spent a double zero in town, and then got a late start and did another nero on the way out of town. So, I did about 8 miles in the last 4 days. I'm prolly about 90 miles behind my trailfriends.*

NOBO

1. See **northbounder**.

Northbounder

1. See **NOBO**.

Nutella®

1. Edible concoction of oil and sugar and milk with a hint of hazelnut flavor (100 hazelnuts per 26-ounce jar). Intended as a PB-like spread, but thru-hiker's typically **spork** huge gobs of it directly into their oral cavity.

2. Thru-hiker food with high caloric density: 4000 calories per "serving" (i.e., one 26-ounce jar), or 154 calories per ounce, which beats Snickers bars by 13.5%. (Half of the caloric content comes from fat.)

One Hundred Mile Wilderness

1. Self explanatory.

Pack shakedown

1. Ritual of dumping pack contents, identifying nonessential items, and boxing them up so the USPS or UPS can take them to your destination of choice. *Gonad's pack weighed 78*

pounds in Millinocket, but Fiddler did a shakedown that trimmed about 50 pounds of hatchets and knives and latrine shovels and other crap. Gonad was so happy that he wore his pack around Shaw's all day.

Pennsylvania Pizza Challenge
1. Attempt by thru-hiker to eat pizza everyday while passing through Pennsylvania, even if it means maximizing your food footprint by calling for delivery to shelters and roadsides.
2. The real challenge is in eating day after day the same generic cardboard pizza – sans capers or artichoke hearts or fresh basil or sun-dried tomatoes.

Pink blazer
1. Thru-hiker who pursues other hiker(s) with motive of engaging in mock reproductive activities. *Dude, I've been pink-blazing that guy for a week. I'm doing 30 miles every day trying to catch him. The other night I got so desperate that I cuddled with Gonad in his sleeping bag in a full lean-to.*

Pizza
1. The numero uno town food of thru-hikers, rivaled only by sleazeburgers.

Powerbar
1. Generic term for bars of the energy, protein, granola, and meal-replacement varieties.

Privylessness
1. See **Tennessee**.

PUD
1. Pointless ups and downs.
2. Not to be confused with its antonym, PUS (pointlessly unchallenging section).

Puncheon
1. See **bog bridge**.
2. Word that thru-hikers dare not utter for fear that it could be French and hence unpronounceable.

Purell®
1. Favorite hand-sanitizing gel of germaphobes. *Dude, Ledge, can I borrow your toe-nail clippers? I'll soak 'em in Purell afterwards.*

Purist
1. Thru-hiker who insists on walking by every white blaze, taking no short-cuts and never slack-packing.
2. Used pejoratively by cheaters and other ne'er-do-wells.

Rain
1. Liquid form of precipitation that falls heavily in Maine.
2. Wet stuff from above that chases off all biting insects and makes the footing soft.

Rain pants
1. Waterproof garment that travels along the A.T. in a **bounce box** courtesy of the USPS.

Ramen®
1. Instant noodles with two virtues: they're cheap and light.

Register humor
1. Comedic entries in spiral-bound notebooks in lean-tos and shelters, written with communal pen right after sanitizing it with Purell®.
2. Open access, self-publishing outlet for creative hikers who scrawl quips, zingers, puns, poems (especially quasi-haikus called hikoos), Shakespearean corruptions, Hannah Montana hiking tips, and privy reviews.

Resupply
1. Act of replenishing one's food bag with fat, sugar, and protein.

Roxanne Quimby
1. Co-founder of Bert's Bees in Maine in 1984.
2. Zillionaire who has purchased and set aside many 100s of 1000s of hectares of forestland along the A.T. in Maine.
3. Trail angel of a sort, destined to become a trail legend.

Shuttle
1. Limo service for privileged thru-hikers who insist on maximizing their carbon footprint.

Slackpacking
1. Carbon footprint-maximizing practice of hiring a driver to transport one's pack to and fro along the A.T. so one doesn't have to backpack.

Sleeping bag liner
1. What some gung-ho super-ultra-lighters switch to when they can no longer bear the thought of carrying a sleeping bag that weighs over a pound.
2. See **hypothermia**.

Snoring
1. Noisy nocturnal emission that *others* do.

SOBO
1. See **southbounder**.

Southbounder
1. See **SOBO**.

Spork
1. Hybrid spoon-fork made of brightly colored molded plastic and used for scooping goatmeal, noodles, and rice into your oral cavity. Washed after each meal by licking it clean.
2. Exemplar of the principle that Americans will gladly spork over $8 to be one of the cool kids.

Springer
1. Southern terminus of the A.T.
2. Photo op for SOBOs.

Stealth camping
1. The act of cleverly sleeping out of view of passersby only to discover at first light that – oops – your sleeping bag is plainly visible to hordes of tourists walking and cycling a few feet away on the Creeper Trail.
2. Not to be confused with rogue camping, the practice of flying into a once-pristine lake to stay at a log-mansion and shoot

mother-humping moose out the window of the plane, Palin-style.

3. See **cowboy/cowgirl camping**.

Stove

1. Device sent to oneself in a **bounce box**.

Super-ultra-light backpacking

1. Base pack weight less than 5 pounds.
2. See **hypothermia**.

Switchback

1. See **Virginia**.

Tennessee

1. See **Privylessness**.

Tent

1. Portable shelter that many thru-hikers mail home or send to themselves repeatedly in a **bounce box**.

Thru-ass

1. Scrawny bilateral bits of bum you laugh and hike off, until it looks like two grapes dancing in your **thru-shorts**.

Thru-beard

1. Facial hair that simultaneously looks cool and ensures celibacy.

Thru-bike

1. Analogous to thru-hike but done on roadways without trekking poles.

Thru-hike

1. Continuous 2179-mile trek *on* the A.T. between Springer and Katahdin, with minimal shenanigans along the way.

Thru-shorts

1. Those short-legged pants you will change in Millinocket or Dahlonega.

Titanium

1. Extremely low-density metal, ideal for making super-ultra-light equipment such as feather-light $74 cooking pot (to carry in 7-pound pack).

Town food
1. Pizza, cheeseburgers, and ice cream – not necessarily in that order.
2. Sometimes refers to hiker breakfast, AYCE Chinese buffet, BBQ, or calzones.

Trail angel
1. One who performs one or more acts of **trail magic**.

Trail guide
1. Book that thru-hikers tear pages from as an apparent way of keeping track of progress, analogous to crossing off days on a calendar.

Trail magic
1. Act of generosity toward a hiker, ideally a spontaneous and seemingly random act of kindness from a stranger.
2. Not to be confused with trail catering or scamming.

Trailname
1. Nickname often given to a thru-hiker on day 1 when she or he commits a whopper of a faux pas.

Trail town
1. Place to overindulge on **town food**.

Trekking poles
1. Expensive lightweight sticks used by hikers who wouldn't dream of using freely available wooden sticks or $5 used ski poles.

Twenty
1. A 20-mile day on the A.T.
2. Distance hikers claim to have walked when they actually walked anywhere between 15.1 and 20.4 miles.

Two tenths
1. The specified yet generic distance, in miles, to a nearby shelter or spring or viewpoint. *Dude, it's just two tenths to the shelter. Wanna go see who's signed the register?*
2. Purported distance to landmark where actual distance is between 0.2 and 0.69 miles.

Tyvek®
1. Synthetic material used for hazmat suits, USPS Express Mail envelopes, and "house wrap."
2. Supposedly breathable-yet-waterproof material sometimes used by hikers as a ground cloth, tarpaulin, or makeshift bivy sack.
3. Material used by some ultra-light thru-hikers as a cocoon-like substitute for a proper sleeping bag (see **hypothermia**).
4. Synthetic material used to make two-piece outfits worn by rock band *Devo*.

Ultra-light backpacking
1. Trendy approach to long-distance hiking where base pack weight (without food and water) is less than 10 pounds.
2. See also **light backpacking, super-ultra-light backpacking**, and **hypothermia**.

Vegan
1. A vegetarian who doesn't partake of bee spit (honey), calf food (dairy), or poultry ova (eggs). *Dude, did you see Moose Gut glug that jar of honey? Guess he's not a vegan anymore.*

Vegetarian
1. What many thru-hikers were until the 3rd or 4th day, when they started specializing on Spam® Singles and sleazeburgers.

Vitamin I
1. Ibuprofen. Recommended daily allowance in Maine is 16 tablets.

Yellow blazer
1. One who skips one or more sections of the A.T. by hitch-hiking down a paved road, as if the eye-in-the-sky doesn't exist.
2. See **Lost Cause**.

Yogi
1. The act of looking so emaciated and pathetic that day hikers give you sandwiches from their pickanick basket.

Yo-yo
1. Continuous round-trip between Springer and Katahdin by foot and/or bicycle.

Water filter
1. Equipment mailed home upon switching to Aquamira®.

Weed
1. Marijuana.
2. See **breakfast**.

Weekender
1. Tame upright ape that walks along A.T. for a few days at most. Hard to distinguish reliably from day- and section-hikers without a dichotomous key.

White blazer
1. One who walks along the A.T., passing every white blaze, without taking any shortcuts via blue-blaze trails or roads (see **yellow-blazer**).

Notes and Recommended Resources

A.T. in the News (Chapter 3):
- For an encyclopedic list of late-night television jokes about Gov. Mark Sanford's scandal, as compiled by Daniel Kurtzman, see: http://politicalhumor.about.com/od/sexandpolitics/a/mark-sanford-jokes.htm.

Fuel for the Hiker Furnace (Chapter 6):
- To generate estimates of the caloric value of breakfast and dinner I used a calorie counter: http://caloriecount.about.com/.

All Things Scatological (Chapter 7):
- To generate factoids about privies I used ALDHA's 2010 edition of the *Appalachian Trail Thru-Hikers' Companion*, available as a free download (http://www.aldha.org/comp_pdf.htm).

United State of Appalachian (Chapter 8):
- Throughout this chapter, I obtained many factoids from the 2010 edition of the *Appalachian Trail Thru-Hikers' Companion* (http://www.aldha.org/comp_pdf.htm).
- Maine – A brief biography of Myron Avery can be found at: http://en.wikipedia.org/wiki/Myron_Avery.
- New Hampshire – Details regarding the Mt. Washington autoroad and Josh the Camel's kudos can be found at: http://www.mtwashingtonautoroad.com/.
- Vermont – Insights regarding Vermont's ecological history were inspired by my prior reading of *Reading the Forested Landscape: A Natural History of New England* (Wessels, T. 2005. Countryman Press, 200 pp.).
- Massachusetts – Thoreau's essay *Walking* is available online at: http://thoreau.eserver.org/walking.html. For a goldmine of Thoreauvian resources see The Walden Woods Project (http://www.walden.org/Library). See also:

http://www.library.ucsb.edu/thoreau/writings_journals.html. Marijuana arrest statistics were taken from: http://norml.org/pdf_files/state_arrests_2004/. For the complete list of official symbols of Massachusetts see: http://en.wikipedia.org/wiki/List_of_Massachusetts_state_symb ols. For a glimpse at the Fluffernutter and its contentious status see: http://en.wikipedia.org/wiki/Fluffernutter.

- Connecticut – For speculation regarding Connecticut's nickname, the Nutmeg State, see: http://www.cslib.org/nicknamesCT.htm.
- Pennsylvania – For a primer on the Ridge of Blue Mountain see: http://en.wikipedia.org/wiki/Blue_Mountain_(Pennsylvania). For everything you ever wanted to know about hawks migrating along the A.T. in PA see: http://www.hawkmountain.org/.
- Maryland – For a description of Camp David and its history see: http://en.wikipedia.org/wiki/Camp_David.
- West Virginia – To learn more about the ATC see: http://www.appalachiantrail.org/site/c.mqLTIYOwGlF/b.48058 59/k.BFA3/Home.htm. For a brief look at Harpers Ferry see: http://en.wikipedia.org/wiki/Harpers_Ferry,_West_Virginia.
- Virginia – To compute the sinuosity for each state's segment of trail, I used a great-circle distance calculator (http://www.gpsvisualizer.com/calculators#distance), ATC's interactive map of the Appalachian Trail (http://www.appalachiantrail.org/site/c.mqLTIYOwGlF/b.4850 633/k.9733/Interactive_Map.htm), and a clickable online map for generating latitude and longitude of points (http://www.mapmart.com/scripts/hsrun.exe/Single/MapMart _New/MapXtreme.htx;start=HS_Handle).
- Tennessee – Exalted verbiage about G-burg was found at: http://www.gatlinburg.com/default.asp.

- North Carolina – Background on hound hunting can be found at: http://www.humanesociety.org/issues/bear_hunting/facts/hound_hunting_fact_sheet.html.
- Georgia – A link to Helen's "rich history" can be found at: http://www.helengeorgia.com/.

Trail Towns as Hiker Havens (Chapter 9):

- Benedict Arnold's "expedition" to Quebec is summarized at: http://en.wikipedia.org/wiki/Arnold's_expedition_to_Quebec. For an example of how high-ranking politicians perpetuate the myth that Canada provided a haven for the 9-11 hijackers see: http://www.ctv.ca/servlet/ArticleNews/story/CTVNews/20090424/.

Our National Social Trail (Chapter 11):

- For background on Erdös and Kevin Bacon numbers see: http://en.wikipedia.org/wiki/Erd%C5%91s_number.

Delusions of Awesomeness (Chapter 12):

- For a list of cognitive illusions and biases see: http://en.wikipedia.org/wiki/List_of_cognitive_biases.
- Ecological footprint factoids were generated by using the Center for Sustainable Economy's online calculator (http://www.myfootprint.org/). To evaluate the potential for shrinking one's footprint, I explored the impact of manipulating the variable of interest while holding others constant.
- For an introduction to the theory of honest signaling of heritable quality including immunocompetence see: http://en.wikipedia.org/wiki/Handicap_principle.

Laughing Matters (Chapter 13):

- For information about Huntington's disease consult: http://www.hdsa.org/living-with-huntingtons.html.
- My ideas about mindful hiking and its potential health benefits were inspired by Ellen Langer's (2009) book, *Counterclockwise: Mindful Health and the Power of Possibility* (Balantine Books).

CPSIA information can be obtained at www.ICGtesting.com
Printed in the USA
BVOW031743240212

283758BV00005B/88/P